Spelling

Improvement:

A Program for

Self-instruction

Patricia M. Fergus

University of Minnesota

McGraw-Hill Book Company

New York   San Francisco   Toronto   London

Spelling

Improvement:

A Program for

Self-instruction

SPELLING IMPROVEMENT

Library of Congress Catalog Card Number 64–18897

6 7 8 9 10 11 12 13 14 HD 10 9 8 7

Preface

The problem of poor spelling has been a source of concern to educators and businessmen for some time. The situation in many schools today is crucial. It is this critical need that prompted the writing of *Spelling Improvement: A Program for Self-instruction.*

The text is not a speller in the usual sense of the word. Based on the findings of numerous research studies relating to causes of poor spelling and habits of good spellers and on the general psychological principles of learning, it aims specifically to:

1. Provide the learner with a background of the inherent difficulties of the English language and its written expression
2. Acquaint him with the various reasons for poor spelling
3. Motivate him to a greater appreciation of the necessity to spell correctly
4. Teach him to use the three key sense organs
5. Assist him in developing a basic knowledge of generalizations (commonly called rules) upon which to build a foundation for independent work
6. Make him cognizant of the importance of the meaning of words
7. Help him to learn to spell and use correctly a number of demons

As the title indicates, self-instruction is the keynote of the book. It is this feature that makes it employable in a number of situations. Educationally, it can be used at high school and college levels as an integral part of a regular course, or it can be used for independent study. It can be utilized in business by all employees, from supervisors to those supervised. Finally, any adult who can read and comprehend secondary school textbooks can use *Spelling Improvement* independently to develop his ability to spell correctly.

The words included for illustration, spelling, or criterion purposes have not been extracted from any one list or source. On the contrary, they were selected somewhat subjectively for their general usefulness and versatility from many authoritative textbooks, spelling lists, and research studies.

The author wishes to extend sincere thanks to the many teachers and administrators in colleges and high schools for their encouragement and enthusiasm for this project and to the reviewers of the original manuscript for their valuable assistance.

Patricia M. Fergus

Contents

Preface   v

Introduction   1

1   Syllables   9

2   Doubling the Final Consonant   43

3   Final *e*   63

4   Final *y*   81

5   Plurals   95

6   *ie* and *ei*   119

7   Homonyms and Confused Words   133

8   Demons   169

9   Suffixes   239

10   Ceed, Cede, Sede   319

11   Prefixes   327

12   Hyphen   349

Answers to Tests   367

Index   372

Spelling

Improvement:

A Program for

Self-instruction

Language and Spelling

The English language has had an interesting development. It was introduced in its earliest form about the middle of the fifth century by the
Angles, Saxons, and tribes from the northern part of Germany. These
invaders eventually founded kingdoms of their own and from the language of these Teutonic settlers developed the national tongue. This
Anglo-Saxon period, usually called the Old English period, extended
until about the middle of the eleventh century.

Influences on the language were many. The ancient Britons belonged
to the Celtic race, and through their association with the Angles and
Saxons some Celtic words came into the English language. Among
those of Celtic origin were such words as *basket, cradle,* and *mop.*

The Teutonic settlers also borrowed a few Latin words which the
conquered Britons had retained from the days of the Roman Empire.
Many more Latin words were brought into the language with the introduction of Christianity among the English toward the close of the sixth
century. This undoubtedly accounts for such words relating to the
church as *altar, bishop, church, priest, psalm,* and *temple.* However, of
the above words, three (*bishop, church,* and *priest*) were originally
from the Greek but passed into our language through the Latin tongue.

Other influences during the Old English period included the incur-
sions of the Danes into England and other Northmen into northern
France. The latter, called Normans, settled in France, founded the
duchy of Normandy, and gradually adopted the customs and language
of the French people. In 1066 the Norman soldier, William the Con-
queror, invaded England, and it was this event, with its tremendous
influence on language and customs in England, that brought about the
second period of development of the English language.

After the Norman Conquest the two languages, French and English,
were spoken side by side. French became the official language of the
court and of the highest classes; English was still the language of the
people. Gradually, the Normans and the English became one people,
and the two languages fused into one—English. This admixture brought

1

many Norman French words into English—words which, of course, were derived from Latin as the French language is descended from the Latin tongue.

During the Middle English period, which extended from the middle of the twelfth century until the middle of the fifteenth, the Norman words brought into the language represented the customs of these people. For example, terms relating to feudalism, the chase, law, and warfare became common everyday words. Titles of nobility, including *count, countess, duke, duchess,* and *peer,* were introduced, as were certain articles associated with the art of living, such as *carpet, mirror,* and *parlor.* The old English names for animals (*swine, calf, ox, sheep*), were still used, but the Normans had words to distinguish the flesh of these animals when used as food: *beef, pork, veal,* and *mutton.*

The last stage of the English language development, usually called Modern English, covers the period from approximately the end of the fifteenth century to the present time. During this period many other Latin words, as well as Greek and Italian, came into the language through the revival of classical study, namely, the Renaissance. The fifteenth and sixteenth centuries saw the influence of the printing press. Although the introduction of this device in England in 1476 did not greatly change the language at first, the attempts toward greater regularity of written and oral expression did affect the language, especially when a greater number of people became more proficient in the art of reading.

Trade and commerce in the sixteenth century also had its influence on the language. Words from the Spanish, Italian, French, German, Dutch, Chinese, Russian, Persian, and Arabic languages became part of the English language. To illustrate, the word *potato* came from the Taino (West Indies) *batata* through the Spanish *patata,* the word *balcony* from the Italian *balcone,* the word *kindergarten* directly from the German *kindergarten,* the word *tea* from the pronunciation of the Chinese *ch'a,* and the word *shawl* from the Persian *shāl.*

The English language of today differs greatly from that of the Old English period. The Anglo-Saxon language was one based on inflection; that is, the relation of words to each other was expressed by the endings of the words. After the conquests by the Danes and the Normans many of the inflectional endings disappeared, and today we show the relation of words by their position in the sentence and by various types of words such as prepositions and auxiliary verbs. The character of Modern English also differs from that of Old English. Very few foreign words were found in Anglo-Saxon, whereas Modern English consists of many loan-words from different languages, some of which are in their original native form.

Spelling and Its Difficulties

It was during the Middle English period that the change in spelling conventions was most noticeable. Some changes attributed to the Anglo-Saxon scribes are still in effect today: the *o* for *u* in such words as *some* and *son,* and the *gh* in *night* and *sought.* However, the influence of the French scribes was decidedly greater as they endeavored to represent the sounds they heard more or less phonetically. The *ch* in our word *choose* became fairly well regulated in the twelfth century and later the doubling of the *c* into *cch* became *tch.*

From the last of the fifteenth century the number of spellings for any one word was greatly reduced. Although some words still retained two spellings, the difference in meaning kept the two spellings as separate and distinct words, as *flour* and *flower,* or *metal* and *mettle.*

The sixteenth and seventeenth centuries saw many changes in spelling. It was during this period that the Great Vowel Shift occurred, which created a chaos as the vowels symbols no longer corresponded to the sounds. However, the printing houses endeavored to standardize the spelling of various words, and conventions such as the initial and medial use of *i,* the final use of *y,* and the reduction of double consonants in many words became prevalent.

The spelling of the English language has also derived some of its difficulty from the fact that many foreign loan-words have found their permanent place in the language, with a tendency for some of these words to retain their native spelling.

There has been somewhat of a tendency to retain in written language a phoneme or sound which has been ignored in the pronunciation of a word. For instance, the pronunciation of the initial *k* and *g* disappeared in the last part of the seventeenth century, but the *k* in *knave* and *knight* and the *g* in *gnat* still persist in the written words. The initial *p* in *pneumonia* and *psychology* has long been omitted from the spoken words, but has been preserved graphically.

Sounds in the English language can be generally divided into two general classes, consonants and vowels. There are eighteen vowel types (six front, five back, and seven central) and thirty-two consonant sounds of common occurrence. Vowels differ from other sounds in that there is no stoppage of the oral cavity in their utterance, and they are always more prominently pronounced in the syllables of a word. The letters of the alphabet, which constitute the written representation of these sounds, can be categorized into two main types: vowels (*a, e, i, o, u*) to represent the vowel sounds, and consonants (all letters but *a, e, i, o, u*) to represent the consonant sounds. Of these consonants, four (*h, r, w, y*) are called semivowels because they can be used as either vowels or consonants.

Because the writing system is based on the twenty-six letters of the alphabet, the use of various letters or combinations of letters to represent sounds must be duplicated in some way. To illustrate, take the combination of the letters *ea*. These two letters can be used in words like *cream, break,* and *head*. In *cream,* the *ea* has a long *e* sound, in *break* a long *a* sound, and in *head* a short *e* sound. Not only do various combinations of letters stand for different sounds, but also one sound can be represented by different letters or combinations of letters: The sound of a long *a* appears as *a* in *cave, ai* in *maid, ei* in *weight, ea* in *break, ay* in *decay, ey* in *obey,* and *au* in gauge.

When one considers that there are over forty elementary sounds in the spoken language and only twenty-six letters of the alphabet to represent these sounds in written English, it is no wonder that spelling can present somewhat of a problem. Nevertheless, linguistic research has shown that a greater proportion of the English language is more phonetic than one realizes. In view of this fact, it is *not* impossible to learn to spell, and no one should be deterred from the worthwhile goal of learning to spell better.

Need for Correct Spelling

How many times have we heard such statements as these: "I can't learn to spell," "My father can't spell, so I don't have to either," or "I don't need to spell because my secretary will know how." Yes, many students, and graduates of high schools and colleges for that matter, have made these emphatic assertions.

Such assertions usually imply a lack of understanding of the need for correct spelling and the specific problems involved, together with the solutions to the problems. There *is* a definite need for good spelling. In the first place, spelling is needed in written communication. Words are important in communication, whether it be their selection, use, or spelling. Everyone communicates orally and in writing with someone else. In school we write letters, themes, term papers, and even notes to our fellow students. In a business office employees, from the messenger to the supervisor, have some necessity for writing their thoughts on paper. When an individual applies for a position, he must invariably write a letter of application or complete an application form.

Whether we like to remember this or not, effective written expression *is* important. We may lose a good opportunity, business-wise, because of our inability to spell. We may be considered socially inferior if we cannot produce a presentable piece of written work.

An improvement in spelling will naturally relieve us of much strain and pressure, and the time saved in consulting the dictionary (or the nearest person) for many common words, and in rewriting themes or business communications, can be spent in a better presentation of the ideas and thoughts themselves. In addition to the time factor, we feel better as we will not have to compensate for our poor work by such excuses as "I can't learn to spell," or "My father can't spell, so I don't have to either."

The importance of spelling thus established, the student will undoubtedly pose this question: How can I spell better? One problem involves motivation! Let us address several answers to the questioner: You *do* want to spell better! You *do* have a positive attitude toward learning! You *do* have the patience, diligence, and sustained attention to learn! You *will* take pride in correct spelling! You *are* responsible for your own work!

Reasons for Poor Spelling

Although there are some phonetic inconsistencies in written English, the main reasons for poor spelling are concerned with the individuals themselves.

Foremost, most poor spellers do *not* have a systematic method for learning to spell. Many people spell by letter, trying to memorize each letter without regard to sound, syllables, or meaning of the word.

Another reason is faulty discrimination, visual or auditory. In other words, a person does not see or hear what the word contains. If these faults are due to defective vision or hearing the problem can usually be resolved by the oculist or hearing specialist. But if he does not hear the *pri* in *appropriate* or see the *ai* in *captain,* mistaking the *ain* for *ian,* then he is probably careless in his spelling habits.

Faulty pronunciation also accounts for errors in spelling. Most of us are careless to some degree in our pronunciation of words. For example, many people are guilty of sliding over the word *government,* not pronouncing the *n* distinctly; therefore, these same people will often misspell this word by omitting the *n.* Others will pronounce the word *disastrous* in four syllables instead of three, resulting in the addition of an extra syllable (an *e* before the *r*) in the spelling of this word.

Sometimes a word is misspelled because its meaning is unknown or hazy or because it is confused with another word which is similar in sound. Words that sound alike but differ in meaning and spelling are called homonyms. Examples of homonyms are: *their, there, they're; to, too, two; principle, principal.* Words that are not identical in sound but are similar enough to be confused include *affect* and *effect, accept* and *except, access* and *excess.* If the meaning of each of these words were known to the speller, no misspellings would need to occur.

Other words are just troublemakers. They are difficult for some students in grade school and persist in their difficulty throughout high school and adulthood. But, these words do *not* have to remain demons. They *can* be learned.

Good Spelling Habits

Three of our five senses are involved in spelling: sight, hearing, and touch. We see words with our eyes, we hear words with our ears, and we write words with our hands. In spelling some individuals can rely for the most part on visual imagery (seeing it in the mind), whereas others use a kinesthetic or an audible approach (writing the word, or pronouncing and hearing how the word sounds).

To become a good speller, however, one should combine the three approaches into a single method, as the best way to learn to spell involves the eyes, ears, and hands. This method can be stated very simply:

1. Look and say
   a. See the whole word.
   b. Pronounce the whole word.
2. See and say
   a. See the whole word in your "mind's eye" as you pronounce it.
   b. See the parts or syllables of the word.
   c. Recall the whole word.
3. Write
   a. Write the whole word, spelling in syllables as you write.
   b. Write the word again and again, as often as necessary.
4. Use the word
   a. Use it in sentences.
   b. Use it in letters, themes, and conversation.
   c. Use it in its various meanings.

By learning a systematic method by which to study spelling, a person will formulate a foundation for good spelling habits. In addition, he can increase his production of correctly spelled words by checking his written work, whether it is in the classroom, in the office, or at home. Many errors could be eliminated if the speller would proofread his work and catch his own mistakes.

A student should learn about word structure. Many words contain prefixes and suffixes which have specific meanings and functions. Believe it or not, the dictionary will supply much of this information. The knowledge of the meanings of these affixes will prevent many misspellings.

Word families are usually built by adding prefixes and suffixes to a basic or root word. Two examples will suffice to illustrate this point:

Root word: *appear*

appear	reappear	disappear
appeared	reappeared	disappeared
appearing	reappearing	disappearing
appearance	reappearance	disappearance

Root word: *just*

just	justification
adjust	justifiable
justness	justifiableness
justice	justifiability
justify	justifier

The Purpose of the Book

Primarily, this programmed textbook, with its emphasis on the meaning of words, offers the individual the opportunity to learn how to spell by using a systematic method.

While the student is learning methods of spelling, he is also learning a number of useful words. Words which are used merely to illustrate the generalizations are also treated as useful words to know and use.

A number of units are based on generalizations for spelling. The term *rule* has not been employed because a rule may indicate a hard and fast statement to which there would be no exceptions. Inasmuch as there are some exceptions, the term *generalization* seems more appropriate. Because of a lack of knowledge of such generalizations, many students make a number of spelling errors. For instance, a large percentage of errors can be prevented if the student is familiar with the generalizations about *ie,* dropping the final *e* before adding the suffix, changing the *y* to *i* before adding a suffix, or doubling the final consonant.

Specific Instructions to Students

Inasmuch as the majority of the book is based on syllabication (breaking up of words into parts or syllables), it will be to your advantage to complete the first chapter on syllables before proceeding to any other chapter. In fact, it will be best if you take each chapter in order, proceeding from syllables to hyphens.

Each item (or frame) has been constructed so as to elicit a certain response from the student. Responses are in various forms:

1. Dashes which stand for letters or certain omitted letters in a word
2. Lines which stand for certain parts of a word
3. Lines which call for the entire word
4. Questions which require a "free" response, as in the statement of a generalization
5. Two or more words from which you choose the correct answer

Each item (or frame) is important. Learn the generalization or spelling of words in each frame as the material in later frames is sometimes dependent upon the earlier ones. Review items are interspersed throughout each chapter, so learn your material well. Also, criterion (or test) frames have been built into the last part of each chapter to show you how well you have learned the material in each unit.

The answer to every frame is immediately available. The importance of this device is to keep you informed at all times of the correctness of your responses. Because these answers are available, it is possible for you to cheat. The best way then to study the program is to keep the answers completely covered with a piece of heavy paper or cardboard so that you cannot see the correct answer before you write yours. However, if you do look at the printed answers, you will only cheat yourself. Learning is doing, not copying!

Learn the meanings of the words. This is essential because you want to increase your vocabulary as well as your ability to spell.

The test at the beginning of each chapter is a diagnostic device; that is, it will show how well you know the principles involved and how well you can spell words employing these principles. If results of this test are very good, you can assume correctly that you have no special difficulty with generalizations presented in the chapter. If you make many mistakes on this test, you should study the chapter very carefully so that you will master the spelling principles and the various words included. Should you desire, you may again take the test as a post-test upon completion of the chapter to indicate what progress you made. Always remember that the amount of concentration and effort expended on the programmed material in each chapter will be shown in the results of the post-test.

chapter 1

Syllables

A systematic approach to good spelling is usually based on the whole-word–parts–whole-word method. This chapter gives you a basic knowledge of how to break up a whole word into its parts or syllables, and with this knowledge you will find how much easier it is to spell correctly.

If words like *accommodate, privilege, temperament,* and *necessary* are difficult to spell, you will find that a foundation in syllabication (breaking up words into syllables) will aid you in the spelling of old and familiar words as well as new ones.

Test for Chapter 1

A. Using the symbols for long and short vowels, write the following words, marking the italicized vowel appropriately.

1.	pl*a*tter	_____	6.	r*o*de	_____
2.	n*i*ght	_____	7.	r*u*sty	_____
3.	k*i*tchen	_____	8.	c*e*ntury	_____
4.	m*o*p	_____	9.	L*a*tin	_____
5.	c*u*te	_____	10.	c*u*t	_____

B. Using the slash mark, divide the following words into syllables.

1.	reward	_____	11.	manufacture	_____
2.	silly	_____	12.	dictionary	_____
3.	carpenter	_____	13.	accommodate	_____
4.	diligent	_____	14.	separate	_____
5.	forgotten	_____	15.	influence	_____
6.	appearance	_____	16.	syllable	_____
7.	triple	_____	17.	parable	_____
8.	necessary	_____	18.	achievement	_____
9.	performance	_____	19.	undoubtedly	_____
10.	geology	_____	20.	tribulation	_____

Vapels and Consonants

■ In written English there are five vowels: *a, e, i, o,* and *u*. The letters *a, e, i, o,* and *u* are called _____.

vowels

■ The word *apple* begins with the vowel __.

a

■ The word *every* begins with the vowel __.

e

■ The words *indigo, olive,* and *usual* begin with the vowels __, __, and __.

i o u

■ *A, e, i, o,* and *u* are called _____.

vowels

■ If we subtract 5 from the 26 letters of the alphabet, we have 21. These 21 letters are called consonants. You can summarize this by saying that there are 5 vowels and 21 _____.

consonants

■ Of the 21 consonants, 4 (*h, r, w, y*) are known as semivowels; that is, they can be used as either vowels or consonants. There are four _____ in written English.

semivowels

■ In written English the letters *h, r, w,* and *y* are called semivowels because they can be used as either vowels or _____.

consonants

■ For instance, look at the letter *y*. In the word *yes,* the *y* operates as a consonant. In the word *my,* the *y* operates as a _____.

vowel

■ Some of our generalizations on syllables involve the long and short sounds of the vowels. Let us take up the *long* sounds first. The long sound of a vowel is the same as the name of the letter. For instance, a *long a* sounds like the name of the letter __.

a

■ Look at the letter *e* and say it to yourself. You have just uttered the *long* sound of the vowel __.

e

long

■ Look at the letter *i* and say it to yourself. This sounds the same as the name of the letter *i* and is called the _____ sound of the vowel *i*.

o

■ Look at the letter *o* and say it to yourself. It sounds the same as the name of the letter __.

long

■ The name of the letter *o* sounds the same as the _____ sound of *o*.

u

■ When you name the letter *u*, you also make the long sound of the vowel __.

a e i o u

■ The long sounds of the five vowels have the same sound as the names of the letters __, __, __, __, and __.

is

■ Say the word *able* softly to yourself. The sound of the *a* [is, is not] the same as the name of the letter *a*.

is not

■ Read the following sentence: Mabel and Alice are cousins. The *a* in *Mabel* [is, is not] the same as the *a* in *Alice*.

long

■ The *a* in *Mabel* sounds the same as the name of the letter *a* and is therefore the _____ sound of *a*.

does

■ Now say the word *me* softly to yourself. The *e* in *me* [does, does not] sound the same as the name of letter *e*.

long

■ The *e* in *me* is therefore the _____ sound of *e*.

has

■ Say the word *light* softly to yourself. The *i* [has, has not] the same sound as the name of the letter *i*.

i

■ The *i* in *light* has the long sound of __.

o

■ Say the word *nose*. The *o* is a long *o* because it sounds the same as the name of the letter __.

■ Now say the letter *u* to yourself. This [does, does not] sound the same as the *u* in *music*.

does

■ The word *music* has the _____ sound of *u*.

long

■ Sometimes the sound of a long *i* is represented by one of the semivowels *y*. Say the word *my*. The sound of the *y* in *my* is the same as the sound of ___ in *light*.

i

■ The long sound of the *i* can be represented by the vowel *i* and the semivowel ___.

y

■ The *o* in the word *over* has the long sound of ___.

o

■ Say the word *fate*. The *a* in *fate* sounds the same as the name of the letter ___.

a

■ The sound of *a* in *fate* is the _____ *a* sound.

long

■ Write the word in which the *a* has the long sound: *match, orange, apple, pray*.

pray

■ Say the word *find*. The sound of *i* in *find* is the same as the letter ___.

i

■ The sound of *i* in *find* is the _____ *i* sound.

long

■ Write the word in which the *i* has the long sound: *itch, ivy, rabbit, ink*.

ivy

■ Say the word *key*. The sound of *e* in *key* is the _____ *e* sound.

long

■ Write the word in which the *e* has the long sound: *yellow, garden, knee, dress*.

knee

■ Say the word *hold*. The sound of the *o* in *hold* [is, is not] a long *o* sound.

is

hole

■ Write the word in which the *o* has the long sound: *brook, hole, now, cot.*

u

■ Say the word *use.* The *u* in *use* sounds like the name of the letter ___.

a e i o u

■ The five vowels are ___, ___, ___, ___, and ___.

consonants

■ *B, c, d, f, g, h, j, k, l, m, n, p, q, r, s, t, v, w, x, y,* and *z* are called _____.

four

■ Of the twenty-one consonants, _____ are called semivowels.

vowels

■ *H, r, w,* and *y* are semivowels as they can be either consonants or _____.

long

■ The sounds of the five vowels that are the same as the names of the letters *a, e, i, o,* and *u* are called the _____ sounds.

short

■ The other sounds that we shall take up are the *short* sounds of the vowels. Say the nouns *Mabel* and *Alice.* The *a* in Mabel is a long sound, whereas the *a* in Alice is a _____ sound.

short

■ A little jingle which will help you to recognize the sounds of the short vowels is *pitter, patter, petter, potter, putter.* The first vowel in each word has the _____ sound of the vowel.

vowels

■ Say the jingle again to yourself, stressing the vowel: p*i*tter, p*a*tter, p*e*tter, p*o*tter, p*u*tter. These are the short sounds of the five _____.

does

■ Say the word *pitter,* stressing the vowel *i.* Now say the word *bitter,* stressing the *i.* The *i* in *bitter* [does, does not] have the same sound as the *i* in *pitter.*

short

■ The vowel *i* in the word *bitter* has the _____ sound.

■ Say the word italicized in this sentence: The theme was *written* in green ink. The vowel *i* in *written* [is, is not] the same as the *i* in *bitter*.

is

■ Say the word *picture,* emphasizing the *i.* The sound of this vowel is the [long, short] sound.

short

■ The *i* in *picture* sounds the same as in the word *pitter.* Both these words illustrate the [long, short] sound of *i.*

short

■ Write the word in which the *i* has the short sound: *whip, kind, mine, light.*

whip

■ Let us look at our jingle again: p*i*tter, p*a*tter, p*e*tter, p*o*tter, p*u*tter. The second word contains the short sound of the vowel ___.

a

■ Say the word *patter* softly to yourself, stressing the vowel *a.* This is the short sound of ___.

a

■ Now say the word *sad.* Say the key word *patter* again. The *a* in *sad* [is, is not] the same short sound of *a.*

is

■ Look at the word *apple.* Say the key word *patter.* Now say *apple.* These two words are good examples of the [long, short] sound of *a.*

short

■ Say the word *match,* stressing the vowel *a.* The sound of *a* is the [long, short] sound of *a.*

short

■ Pronounce the word italicized in this sentence: The boys had to remain in the house because they were *bad.* The vowels in *bad* and the key word *patter* [do, do not] have the same sound.

do

■ The words *sap, snack, map,* and *pad* have the [short, long] sound of the vowel *a.*

short

■ Write the word in which the *a* has the short sound: *crane, fall, camp, frame.*

camp

short

■ The third short vowel is *e*. The key word in the jingle is *petter*. The first *e* in *petter* is the _____ sound of *e*.

short

■ Say the word *petter* softly to yourself, stressing the first *e*. This sound is the [long, short] sound of *e*.

short

■ Now say the word *wet*. Compare it with the key word *petter*. The sound of the *e* in *wet* is the [long, short] sound of the vowel.

short

■ The words *pet, met, bed,* have the [long, short] sound of the vowel *e*.

is

■ Say the word *petter* again, stressing the first *e*. Now say the word *send*. The pronunciation of the *e*'s [is, is not] the same.

short

■ The *e* in *send* is the _____ sound of *e*.

short

■ The *e* in *desk* is the _____ sound of the vowel *e*.

yellow

■ Write the word in which the *e* has the short sound: *week, shears, kneel, yellow*.

short

■ Now let us turn to the short sound of the vowel *o*. Say the key word *potter*, stressing the *o*. This is the _____ sound of *o*.

short

■ Now pronounce the word *cotton*, stressing the first *o*. Now say the word *potter*. The *o* in *cotton* is the [long, short] sound of *o*.

short

■ Say the word *potter* again. Now say the word *lot*. The *o* in *lot* has the same sound, so it has the _____ sound of the vowel *o*.

does

■ Say the word *knock*. The *o* in *knock* [does, does not] have the same sound as the *o* in *potter*.

■ The *o* in *knock* is the _____ sound of the vowel *o*.

short

■ The key word for the short sound of *o* is _____.

potter

■ The words *hot, bother, dock,* and *rotten,* are good examples of the _____ sound of the vowel *o*.

short

■ Write the word in which the *o* has the short sound: *colt, chose, overseer, hobby.*

hobby

■ The last vowel is *u,* and the jingle word to show the short sound is *putter.* The word *putter* is the key word for the [long, short] sound of *u.*

short

■ Pronounce the word *putter* softly to yourself, stressing the vowel *u.* This is the short sound of ___.

u

■ Say the word *putter* again. Now say the word *nut.* The *u* in *nut* [is, is not] the same as the *u* in *putter.*

is

■ The *u* in *nut* is the _____ sound of *u.*

short

■ Now say the word *rubber,* stressing the sound of the *u.* This *u* has the [long, short] sound as in *putter.*

short

■ Say the word that is italicized in this sentence: There is too *much* rain this season. The *u* in *much* is the _____ sound of *u.*

short

■ The words *mud, puppy, dump,* and *lucky,* all have the _____ sound of the vowel *u.*

short

■ Write the word in which the *u* has the short sound: *pupils, bubble, duty, cube.*

bubble

■ The key word in our jingle to show the short sound of *i* is _____

pitter

patter

petter

potter

putter

long

short

long

long

short

long

short

short

long

long

■ The key word for the vowel *a* short sound is
_____.

■ The key word for the short sound of the vowel *e*
is _____.

■ The jingle word to show the short sound of *o* is
_____.

■ The short sound of *u* is represented by our jingle
word _____.

■ When you call the vowels by their letter names (*a, e,
i, o,* and *u*) you are sounding the _____ sound of
these vowels.

■ The jingle *pitter, patter, petter, potter, putter* illus-
trates the _____ sound of each vowel.

■ The *a* in the word *lady* is a [long, short] *a.*

■ The first *e* in the nickname *Pete* is a _____ *e.*

■ The *e* in the word *melody* is the [long, short] sound
of *e.*

■ The *a* in the proper noun *Mabel* is the _____
sound of *a.*

■ The *e* in *mend* is the _____ sound of *e.*

■ The *o* in the word *lottery* is the [long, short] sound
of *o.*

■ The *i* in *mile* is the _____ sound of *i.*

■ The word *Moses* has the [long, short] sound of *o.*

short	■ The *u* in *rusty* is the _____ sound of *u*.
short	■ The word *rich* has the [short, long] sound of *i*.
short	■ The *u* in *must* is the _____ sound of *u*.
short	■ The word *platter* has the [long, short] sound of *a*.
short	■ The word *basket* has the _____ sound of *a*.
long	■ The *i* in *night* is the _____ sound of *i*.
long	■ The word *cute* has the [long, short] sound of *u*.
short	■ The *o* in *cock* is the _____ sound of *o*.
long	■ The *o* in *rose* is the _____ sound of *o*.
short	■ The word *kitchen* has the [long, short] sound of *i*.
long	■ The *e* in *be* has the _____ sound of *e*.
long	■ The word *union* has the [long, short] sound of *u*.

Syllables

■ When consonants and vowels are written together in various combinations they form words. A *syllable* is a part of a word consisting of a vowel alone or a vowel with one or more consonants. A part of a word is called a

syllable   _____.

*syl*lable   ■ A part of a word is called a _____*lable*.

syl*la*bles   ■ A word can be divided into *syl___bles*.

sylla*ble*   ■ A part of a word which consists of a vowel alone or a vowel with one or more consonants is a *sylla____*.

one

■ The word *mat* has _____ syllable.

two

■ The word *garden* has _____ syllables.

■ Vowels and consonants can be combined to form written words. A part of a word consisting of a vowel alone or a vowel with one or more consonants is called

syllable

a _____.

■ To form a syllable the vowel alone or in combination with consonants must be pronounced. That is, you must hear its sound. For example, in the word *met* you pro-

e

nounce the vowel ___.

two

■ In the word *meat* there are [one, two] *written* vowels.

■ In the word *meat* there is only _____ *pro-*

one

nounced vowel.

one

■ Therefore, the word *meat* has [one, two] syllables.

■ Whenever you have a pronounced vowel, you will

syl*lable*

undoubtedly have a *syl*___.

■ A syllable will contain a vowel that [is, is not] pro-

is

nounced.

Generalization 1

■ Now let us begin our work in syllabication, or dividing words into syllables, with two-syllable words. When there are *two consonants between two vowels,* divide the word between the consonants. In the noun *doctor,* the two consonants *c* and *t* come between two

o

vowels *o* and ___.

■ In the word *doctor* two consonants *c* and *t* come be-

vowels

tween two _____ *o* and *o*.

■ You divide the word *doctor* into syllables between the

c t

two consonants ___ and ___.

■ When two consonants come between two vowels, you divide the word into syllables between the two _____.

consonants

■ Using a slash mark (/) to show the division into syllables, divide the word *doctor* into two syllables: _____.

doc/tor

■ Now look at the word *rubber*. There are _____ consonants between _____ vowels.

two
two

■ In the word *rubber* there are two consonants *b* and *b* between the vowels __ and __.

u e

■ Just as you divided the word *doctor* between the *c* and *t* because these consonants came between the two *o*'s, you divide the word *rubber* between the consonants __ and __.

b b

■ Using the slash mark (/) as a syllable divider, write the word *rubber* in syllables: _____.

rub/ber

■ In the words *doctor* and *rubber* there are [one, two] syllables.

two

■ Of the twenty-one consonants in written English, four are semivowels; that is, they can be used as either consonants or vowels. The letter *y* is called a _____.

semivowel

■ In the word *my* the *y* is used as a [consonant, vowel].

vowel

■ Now look at the word *hurry* and say it softly to yourself. The *y* at the end of the word acts as a _____.

vowel

■ The letter *u* is a [consonant, vowel].

vowel

■ In the word *hurry u* and *y* are vowels. Both vowels [are, are not] pronounced.

are

u y

■ The two consonants *r* and *r* in *hurry* come between the two vowels ___ and ___.

r r

■ You would therefore divide the word *hurry* between and letters ___ and ___.

hur/ry

■ Using the slash mark, divide the word *hurry* into syllables: _____.

vowels

■ There are two syllables in the word *hurry* because there are two pronounced _____.

■ Look at the word *garden,* and say it softly to yourself. The generalization that if two consonants come between two vowels you divide the word into syllables between the consonants [does, does not] apply to the word

does

garden.

gar/den

■ Using the slash mark, divide the word *garden* into two syllables: _____.

■ Look at the word *sentence* and say it to yourself. The

is not

final *e* (sentenc*e*) [is, is not] pronounced.

■ The final *e* in the word *sentence* is not pronounced, and is therefore known as a silent *e*. The final *e* in *sen-*

silent

tence is _____.

■ Say the word *sentence* again. The other two vowels

are

in the word (s*e*nt*e*nce) [are, are not] pronounced.

■ Inasmuch as there are two pronounced vowels, there

two

are _____ syllables.

■ Look again at the word *sentence.* The two consonants

two

n and *t* come between the _____ vowels *e* and *e*.

■ Because the *n* and *t* in *sentence* come between two *e*'s, you divide the word into syllables between the con-

n t

sonants ___ and ___.

two	■ The word *sentence* contains [one, two] syllables.
does	■ Look at the two-syllable word *powder,* and say it to yourself. Our generalization [does, does not] apply to this word.
two two	■ The word powder has _____ consonants between _____ vowels.
w *d*	■ Because the consonants *w* and *d* in *powder* come between two vowels *o* and *e,* you divide the word into syllables between the letters __ and __.
pow/der	■ Using the slash mark, divide *powder* into syllables: _____.
pronounced	■ There are two syllables in *powder* because there are two [pronounced, unpronounced] vowels.
syllable	■ A part of a word which consists of a vowel alone or a vowel with one or more consonants is called a _____.
alone	■ A syllable is a part of a word consisting of a vowel _____ or a vowel with one or more consonants.
consonants	■ A syllable can be defined as part of a word consisting of a vowel alone or a vowel with one or more _____.
between	■ In syllabication, when there are *two* consonants between the *two* vowels, you divide [between, after] the consonants.
two two	■ In syllabication, you divide between the consonants if there are _____ consonants between _____ vowels.
pup/pet	■ Using the slash mark, divide the word *puppet* into two syllables: _____.
mar/gin	■ Divide the word *margin* into two syllables: ___ ___.

san/dal

■ Divide the word *sandal* into syllables: _____.

When there are two consonants be-tween two vowels, divide between the consonants.

■ Look at the division of the word *shelter* into sylla-bles: shel/ter. State the generalization used for this division.

Accent

■ The word *accent* can be defined as stress or special emphasis. In words we often find an emphasis or stress on certain syllables or parts of a word. The emphasis or stress placed on syllables is properly called _____.

accent

■ *Accent* means stress. If one syllable of a word is stressed more than another, it is _____ed.

accent

■ In the word *basket,* one syllable receives more ac_____ than the other.

*acc*ent

■ Say the word *basket* quickly. The accent comes on the [first, last] part of the word.

first

■ If one or more syllables in a word are stressed more than others, they are _____ed.

*accent*ed

■ Special emphasis or stress of a syllable in a word is called _____.

accent

■ If a syllable is *not* accented, it is called *un*_____.

un*accented*

■ Say the word *basket* quickly. The *unaccented* syllable comes in the [first, last] part of the word.

last

■ There are two main kinds of accent: *primary* and *secondary*. The chief or principal accent in a word is the primary accent and is marked with the symbol ′. The main stress is called the _____ accent.

primary

primary	■ The symbol ′ is used to show the [primary, secondary] accent in a word.
*second*ary	■ Just as the heavy-type symbol ′ indicates the *primary* accent, the lighter-type symbol ′ indicates the _____ary accent.
primary	■ When one syllable of a word receives the main stress, it has the [primary, secondary] accent.
primary	■ The heavy-type symbol ′ indicates the [primary, secondary] accent.
secondary	■ When a word has two accented syllables, one primary and one secondary, the syllable that has the lighter-type symbol ′ is the [primary, secondary] accent.
first	■ Look at the following word which has been properly accented: *car′pen ter*. The accent is on the [first, second, third] syllable.
two	■ Look again at the word *car′pen ter* and say it to yourself. This word has one accented syllable and _____ unaccented syllables.
primary	■ In the word *car′pen ter* the accent is [primary, secondary].
two	■ Now look at the word *pre par′a to′ry*. There are _____ accents.
second	■ Look again at *pre par′a to′ry* and say it to yourself. The primary accent is on the [first, second] syllable.
fourth	■ The secondary accent in the word *pre par′a to′ry* falls on the [third, fourth, fifth] syllable.
primary	■ In pronouncing *pre par′a to′ry* the syllable *par* is given the [primary, secondary] accent.

■ In pronouncing *pre par'a to'ry* the syllable *to* is given the _____ accent.

secondary

■ In the word *pre par'a to'ry* the first, third, and fifth syllables are [accented, unaccented].

unaccented

■ Let us look at one more word: *pres'en ta'tion*. The primary accented syllable *ta* has the [most, least] accent.

most

■ In the word *pres'en ta'tion* the syllable receiving next to the most accent is the syllable [pres en ta tion].

pres

■ The first syllable in *pres'en ta'tion* has the [primary, secondary] accent.

secondary

■ The third syllable in *pres'en ta'tion* has the [primary, secondary] accent.

primary

■ Special stress or emphasis on one or more syllables is called _____.

accent

■ The main or principal accent is the _____ accent.

primary

■ Stress which is not as pronounced as the main accent is called the _____ accent.

secondary

■ Syllables which do not receive accent are called [accented, unaccented] syllables.

unaccented

Symbols for Vowels

■ Just as there are symbols for primary and secondary accents, there are also symbols for long and short vowels. The symbol for the *long* sound of a vowel is a short horizontal mark placed over the vowel ($\bar{a}$). For instance, marking the *a* in *Mābel* would signify that the *a* has a _____ sound.

long

■ The *o* in *Mōses* is a _____ sound of *o*.

long

■ The first *e* in *mēter* signifies that the *e* has a _____ sound.

long

■ The *i* in *mīle* has the [long, short] sound of *i*.

long

■ If you wish to show that the *i* in *light* has the long sound, you put the horizontal mark [over, under] vowel.

over

■ Say the word *local*. The marking of the word *lōcal* [is, is not] correct.

is

■ The symbol for the *short* sound of a vowel is a curved mark over the vowel (ă). For example, the marking in the word *căt* would signify that the *a* has a _____ sound.

short

■ The *i* in *rich* is the short sound of *i*. Write *rich* and mark the *i* correctly.

rĭch

■ Say the word *mop*. Listen to the sound of the *o*. Write *mop* and mark the *o* correctly.

mŏp

■ The *u* in *mud* is the short sound of *u*. Write *mud* and mark the *u* correctly.

mŭd

■ The symbol for the short sound of a vowel is a [horizontal, curved] mark placed over the vowel.

curved

■ The *i* in *slip* is the short sound of *i*. Write *slip* and mark the *i* correctly.

slĭp

■ The symbol which indicates the long sound of a vowel is a [horizontal, curved] mark placed over the vowel.

horizontal

■ The symbol which indicates, the short sound of a vowel is a _____ mark.

curved

■ Say the word *slope*. Listen to the sound of *o*. Write *slope* and mark the *o* correctly.

slōpe

short

■ The marking of the word *nŭt* indicates that the *u* has a [long, short] sound.

short

■ The *a* in *lădder* has the _____ sound of *a*.

long

■ The *a* in *pāle* has the _____ sound of *a*.

long

■ The *u* in *mūsic* has the _____ sound of *u*.

syllable

■ A part of a word which consists of a vowel alone or a vowel with one or more consonants is a _____.

one

■ Now look at the word *stream*. It has only one syllable because it has only _____ pronounced vowel.

one

■ Although there two vowels in the written word *stream, e* and *a*, only _____ is pronounced.

e

■ The sound of the vowel in the one-syllable word *stream* is that of the vowel [e, a].

one

■ The word *stream* has _____ syllable.

between

■ When two consonants come between two vowels, you divide the word into syllables [between, after] the consonants.

cur/tain

■ Using the slash mark, divide the word *curtain* into two syllables: _____.

chim/ney

■ Divide the word *chimney* into syllables: _____.

shel/ter

■ Divide the word *shelter* into syllables: _____.

for/got/ten

■ Divide the three-syllable word *forgotten* into syllables: _____.

accent

■ The stress or special emphasis that is given to one or more syllables in a word is called _____.

■ There are two main kinds of accent: primary and secondary. The syllable that has the *primary* accent is the one that is [most, least] accented.

most

■ The accent which is *second* to the primary accent is called the _____ accent.

secondary

■ The symbol ′ indicates the _____ accent.

primary

■ The symbol ′ indicates the _____ accent.

secondary

Divide between two consonants when these two consonants come between two vowels.

■ The word *compass* is divided into syllables in this manner: com/pass. State the generalization used. _____ _____.

Generalization 2

■ Now we are ready for the second generalization. If a single consonant comes between two vowels (pi*l*ot) and the first vowel is *long* and *accented* (pī′ lot) the consonant will usually go with the *second* vowel. Look at the word *pilot*. The one consonant *l* comes between two vowels __ and __.

i o

■ Say the word *pilot*. The first vowel *i* has the _____ sound of *i*.

long

■ Say the word *pilot*. When you pronounce the word you accent the [first, second] vowel.

first

■ In the word *pilot* you find one consonant between two vowels, the first of which is long and accented. The consonant will go with the [first, second] vowel.

second

one
two

■ Look at the word *lōcal*. You have _____ consonant between _____ vowels.

o a

■ The consonant *c* in the word *local* comes between the vowels __ and __.

long
accented

■ The first vowel in the word *local* is [short, long] and [accented, unaccented].

a

■ When you divide the word *local* into syllables, the consonant *c* would go with the vowel ___.

lo/cal

■ Using the slash mark, divide the word *local* into two syllables: _____.

second

■ When you find a single consonant between two vowels, the first of which is long and accented, the consonant will probably go with the [first, second] vowel.

one
two

■ Now look at the word *nātive*. There is _____ consonant between _____ vowels.

a i

■ In the word *native* the consonant *t* comes between the vowels ___ and ___.

a

■ Say the word *native*. The accent is placed on the vowel [*a*, *i*].

is

■ The marking of *nā'tive* [is, is not] correct.

long

■ The first vowel (*a*) in *native* has the [long, short] sound of *a*.

accented

■ In the word *native,* you find the consonant *t* between the vowels *a* and *i*. The first vowel is long and [accented, unaccented].

second

■ Therefore, in dividing the word *native* into two syllables, place the consonant *t* with the [first, second] vowel.

does

■ Now look at the word *silent* and pronounce it to yourself. The generalization we are now studying [does, does not] apply to this word.

long
accented

■ In the word *silent* you have the consonant *l* between the vowels *i* and *e*. The *i* is _____ and _____.

si/lent

■ Using the slash mark, divide the word *silent* into two syllables: _____.

fī'nal

■ Pronounce the word *final* to yourself. Using the symbols for a *long* vowel and the *primary* accent, mark the word *final*: _____.

i a

■ In the word *final* the consonant *n* is between two vowels __ and __.

long

■ The *i* in *final* is _____ and accented.

i n

■ Because there is one consonant between two vowels, the first of which is long and accented, the word *final* is divided into syllables between the letters __ and __.

fi/nal

■ Using the slash mark, divide the word *final* into syllables: _____.

does

■ Now look at the word *rival*. It [does, does not] have one consonant between two vowels.

accented

■ The vowel *i* in *rival* is long and _____.

v

■ You would divide the word *rival* between *i* and __.

ri/val

■ Using the slash mark, divide the word *rival* into syllables: _____.

When a consonant comes between two vowels, the first of which is long and accented, the consonant usually goes with the second vowel.

■ The word *favor* is divided into syllables in this manner: fa/vor. State the generalization used.

Generalization 3

■ In syllabication, a consonant which comes between two vowels, the first of which is *long* and accented, usually goes with the *second* vowel. On the other hand, a consonant coming between two vowels, the first of which is *short* and accented, will usually not go with the second vowel but with the _____ vowel.

first

■ For example, take the word *modest*. The consonant *d* comes between the vowels __ and __.

o e

■ In pronouncing the word *modest* (mod'est) the primary accent would come on the [first, last] part of the word.

first

■ The *o* in *mŏdest* has the _____ sound of *o*.

short

■ Using the correct symbol for a short vowel, mark the first vowel in the word *modest*: _____.

mŏdest

■ Inasmuch as the *o* in *modest* is a short *o*, and the primary accent falls on the first part of the word, the consonant *d* between the two vowels *o* and *e* goes with the [o, e].

o

■ Using the slash mark, divide the word *modest* into syllables: _____.

mod/est

■ Using the correct symbols for the *short o* and the *primary* accent, mark the word *modest* accordingly.

mŏd'est

■ In the word *palace*, the first *a* has a _____ sound.

short

■ The consonant *l* in *palace* comes between the vowels *a* and __.

a

■ The accent in *palace* comes on the [first, last] part of the word.

first

l a

■ Therefore, you would divide the word *palace* into two syllables between the ___ and second ___.

pal/ace

■ Using the slash mark, divide the word *palace* into syllables: _____.

is

■ The generalization by which you divided the word *palace* [is, is not] the same for the word *solid*.

l o i

■ In the word *solid* there is one consonant ___ between two vowels ___ and ___.

does not

■ Say the word *solid*. The first vowel *o* [does, does not] have a long sound.

does

■ In pronouncing the word *solid,* the accent [does, does not] come on the first part of the word.

short

■ The first vowel in the word *solid* is [long, short] and accented.

first

■ Because the *l* in *solid* comes between the two vowels *o* and *i*, and the *o* is short and accented, the *l* goes with the [first, second] vowel.

sol/id

■ Using the slash mark, divide the word *solid* into syllables: _____.

short

■ Look at the word *preference*. Now say the word to yourself. The first vowel in *preference* has a [long, short] sound.

*pref*erence

■ In the word *preference* the consonant *f* comes between two *e*'s. The accent comes in the first part of the word. Therefore the first syllable would be _____.

pref/er/ence

■ Remembering that each syllable should have a pronounced vowel, you would divide the word *preference* into syllables like this: _____.

■ If a consonant comes between two vowels, the first of which is *short* and *accented,* the consonant will usually go with the _____ vowel.

first

■ If a consonant comes between two vowels, the first of which is *long* and *accented,* the consonant will usually go with the _____ vowel.

second

■ In the words *silent, final, local,* and *rival,* the first syllable ends with the [vowel, consonant].

vowel

■ In the words *palace, modest,* and *solid,* the first syllable ends with the [vowel, consonant].

consonant

Generalization 4

■ If a word ends in *le,* the consonant preceding it usually goes with the *le* to form a syllable. For example, look at the word *purple.* The *le* at the end of the word is preceded by *p.* The complete syllable is _____.

pur/*ple*

■ The word *purple* can be divided into syllables like this: *pur/*_____.

pur/*ple*

■ The second *d* in the word *middle* goes with the letters _____ to form a syllable.

le

■ Using the slash mark, divide the word *middle* into syllables: _____.

mid/dle

■ As in the word *middle,* the second *d* in the words *puddle, riddle,* and *cuddle* forms the syllable d_____.

d*le*

■ Divide the word *puddle* into syllables: _____.

pud/dle

■ Divide the word *riddle* into syllables: _____.

rid/dle

■ Divide the word *cuddle* into syllables: _____.

cud/dle

■ Divide the word *castle* into two syllables: _____.

cas/tle

tle

■ In the word *turtle* the consonant *t* which precedes the *le* begins the syllable *t*_____.

tur/tle

■ Divide the word *turtle* into syllables: _____.

bun/dle

■ Divide the word *bundle* into syllables: _____.

If a word ends in le, the consonant preceding it goes with the le to form a syllable.

■ The word *people* is divided into syllables like this: peo/ple. State the generalization used.

Review and Practice

long

■ The *a* in *paper* has the _____ sound of *a*.

short

■ The *e* in *pencil* has the _____ sound of *e*.

petter
potter
putter

■ The jingle which gives you the short sounds of the vowel is *pitter, patter,* _____, _____, _____.

a vowel alone or a vowel with one or more consonants

■ A syllable is a part of a word consisting of _____ _____

_____.

between

■ In syllabication, when two consonants come between two vowels, you divide [before, after, between] the consonants.

accent

■ Special stress or emphasis which is placed on one or more syllables in a word is called _____.

primary

■ The main accent is called the _____ accent.

secondary

■ The symbol ' indicates the primary accent, whereas the symbol ' indicates the _____ accent.

second

■ If a single consonant comes between two vowels, the first of which is long and accented, the consonant usually goes with the [first, second] vowel.

first

■ If a single consonant comes between two vowels, the first of which is short and accented, the consonant usually goes with the _____ vowel.

le

■ If a word ends in *le* the consonant which precedes it goes with the _____ to form a syllable.

syl/la/ble

■ Divide the word *syllable* into syllables: _____.

car/pen/ter

■ Using the generalizations on syllabication, divide the word *carpenter* into syllables: _____.

vowel

■ Look at the word *city* and say it to yourself. The *y* in this word acts as a [vowel, consonant].

two

■ Remembering that a *y* can be used as a vowel, there are _____ pronounced vowels in the word city.

two

■ There are _____ syllables in the word *city*.

short
accented

■ Look at the word *cit'y,* and pronounce it. The *t* comes between two vowels *i* and *y* and the first vowel *i* is _____ and _____.

cit/y

■ The word *city* is divided into syllables like this: _____.

four

■ Look at the word *necessary* and pronounce it. Remember that the final *y* acts as a vowel in this word, so the word has _____ syllables.

first

■ Look again at the word *necessary* and say it to yourself. The primary accent comes on the [first, last] part of the word.

last

■ The secondary accent in *necessary* comes in the [first, last] part of the word.

short

- The first *e* in *necessary* is a _____ *e*.

short

- The consonant *c* in *necessary* comes between two vowels *e* and *e*, the first of which is _____ and accented.

first

- The *c* in *necessary* goes with the [first, second] vowel.

nec/essary

- Put a slash mark in *necessary* to show the end of the first syllable: _____.

two

- Look again at the word *necessary*. There are two consonants between _____ vowels.

nec/es/sary

- Put a slash mark in *nec/essary* to show the end of the second syllable: _____.

nec/es/sar/y

- Remember that a *y* often acts as a vowel, and a syllable can consist of a vowel alone. Now put slash marks throughout the entire word *necessary* to show all the syllables: _____.

nec/es/sar/y

- Divide the word *necessary* into syllables: _____.

syl*lable*

- Now take the word *establishment*. The ending *ment* is a suffix meaning act or state of, and it forms a noun from a verb. In other words, *establishment* is the state of being established. Usually a suffix, such as *ment*, forms a whole syl___.

four

- There are _____ syllables in *establishment*.

es/tab/lish/ment

- Applying the generalizations we have discussed, divide the word *establishment* into syllables: _____.

four

- Now say the word *temperament*. Notice that there is an *a* in the middle of the word and it should be counted as a pronounced vowel. There are ___ syllables in this word.

■ Look at the word *temperament* again. The generalization about two consonants between two vowels and dividing between the consonants [does, does not] apply to this word.

does

■ The suffix *ment* in *temperament* constitutes _____ syllable.

one

■ Now divide the word *temperament* into syllables: _____.

tem/per/a/ment

■ Now look at the word *government* and pronounce it carefully. There are _____ syllables in this word.

three

■ The suffix *ment* in *government* forms the last _____.

syllable

■ The *o* in *gov′ernment* is _____ and _____.

short
accented

■ Divide the word *government* into syllables: _____ _____.

gov/ern/ment

■ Now look at the word *accommodate* and pronounce it. There are _____ syllables in this word.

four

■ The generalization about two consonants between two vowels [does, does not] apply to the word *accommodate*.

does

■ Divide the word *accommodate* into syllables: _____ _____.

ac/com/mo/date

■ A syllable can consist of a vowel alone. The word *privilege* contains a syllable consisting of a vowel _____.

alone

■ Look at the word *privilege* and pronounce it carefully. The second vowel stands alone and forms a _____.

syllable

■ The first *i* in the word *privilege* has a short sound and is accented, so the *v* goes with the [first, second] *i*.

first

priv/i/lege	■ Divide the word *privilege* into syllables: _____.
syllable	■ The word *suicide* is another word that has a vowel alone forming a _____.
three	■ Look at the word *suicide* and pronounce it carefully. There are _____ syllables in this word.
su/i/cide	■ Divide the word *suicide* into syllables: _____.
ad/ven/ture	■ Applying the generalizations we have discussed, divide the word *adventure* into syllables: _____.
one	■ Look at the word *du'plicate* and pronounce it. There are three pronounced vowels and _____ unpronounced vowel.
three	■ In the word *duplicate* there are _____ syllables.
first	■ The accent in *duplicate* comes on the [first, second, third] vowel.
long	■ The first vowel in *duplicate* has a _____ sound.
p l	■ Look again at the word *duplicate* and say it to yourself. When you pronounce the word, the consonants *pl* blend together and should not be thought of as two separate sounds. Two consonants in this word that blend together are __ and __.
du/pli/cate	■ Now divide the word *duplicate* into syllables: _____.
b r	■ If you pronounce the word *umbrella,* you will notice that two consonants in this word blend together. They are __ and __.
three	■ There are _____ syllables in *umbrella.*
um/brel/la	■ Divide the word *umbrella* into syllables: _____.

■ The word *manufacture* has one syllable that consists of a vowel alone. That vowel is ___.

u

■ *Manufacture* has _____ syllables.

four

■ Divide the word *manufacture* into syllables: _____.

man/u/fac/ture

■ Now look at the word *performance*. The ending *ance* is a suffix and is a complete syllable. Divide the word *performance* into syllables: _____.

per/form/ance

■ The word *disappear* has a prefix *dis*, which means away or from. As you can see, the prefix is a syllable which is added to the beginning of the word and which modifies the word in some way. The prefix forms an entire syl___.

syl*lable*

■ Look again at *disappear* and pronounce it. Now divide it into syllables: _____.

dis/ap/pear

■ Divide the word *disappoint* into syllables: _____.

dis/ap/point

■ Divide the word *disarrange* into syllables: _____.

dis/ar/range

■ Divide the word *disapprove* into syllables: _____.

dis/ap/prove

■ Applying your generalizations for syllabication, and sounding out this word to yourself, divide the word *magazine* into syllables: _____.

mag/a/zine

■ Now look at the word *dictionary* and say it to yourself. Using the slash marks, divide it into syllables: _____.

dic/tion/ar/y

■ Following the same *look* and *pronounce* pattern, divide the word *system* into syllables: _____.

sys/tem

■ Now divide the word *liberal* into syllables: _____.

lib/er/al

con/trib/ute

■ Look at the word *contribute* carefully. Pronounce it carefully. Now divide it into syllables: _____.

con/tin/u/ous

■ In the word *continuous* the suffix *ous* forms an entire syllable. Now divide the word into syllables: _____.

■ Before we leave this unit on syllables, let us take a quick review of what we have learned. The letters of the alphabet are used in written English to represent the spoken sounds. The five letters *a, e, i, o,* and *u* represent

vowels

vowel sounds and are called _____.

consonants

■ The other twenty-one letters of the alphabet represent consonant sounds and are called _____.

semivowels

■ Four of the consonants, *h, r, w,* and *y,* can be used as vowels and are properly called _____.

short

■ The word *nut* is an example of the [long, short] sound of the vowel *u.*

long

■ The *a* in *table* has a _____ sound.

līght

■ Say the word *light.* Write it and mark the *i* to show whether it has a long or short sound.

long

■ The *o* in *Moses* has a _____ sound.

short

■ The word *pitter* is the key word in our jingle for the _____ sound of *i.*

drĕss

■ Say the word *dress.* Write the word and place the proper mark over the *e* to show what sound it has.

mūsic

■ Say the word *music.* Write the word and place the proper mark over the *u* to show what sound it has.

syllable

■ A part of a word consisting of a vowel alone or a vowel with one or more consonants is called a _____.

accent

■ Special stress or emphasis on one or more syllables in a word is called _____.

third

■ In the word *prep'a ra'tion,* the primary accent is on the [first, second, third] syllable.

first

■ In the word *prep'o si'tion,* the secondary accent is on the [first, second, third, fourth] syllable.

sig/nal

■ Now divide the word *signal* into syllables: _____.

When two consonants come between two vowels, divide between the consonants.

■ State the generalization used in dividing the word *signal* into syllables: sig/nal.

no/tice

■ Divide the word *notice* into syllables: _____.

When one consonant comes between two vowels, the first of which is long and accented, the consonant goes with the second vowel.

■ State the generalization used in dividing the word *notice* into syllables.

lib/er/ty

■ Divide the word *liberty* into syllables: _____.

When one conso-
nant comes be-
tween two vowels,
the first of which
is short and ac-
cented, the conso-
nant goes with
the first vowel.
When two conso-
nants come be-
tween two vowels,
divide between
the consonants.

■ State the generalizations used in dividing the word *liberty* into syllables.

le

■ When a word ends in *le*, the consonant which precedes it usually goes with the ____ to form a syllable.

par/a/ble

■ Divide the word *parable* into syllables: _____.

chapter 2

Doubling the Final Consonant

Numerous errors in spelling are caused by not knowing when to double the final consonant. You may be relieved to know that if you follow the generalizations stated in this chapter, you will eliminate many mistakes in spelling from your written work. No longer will you wonder whether to double the *r* in *occur* when writing *occurrence,* or the *t* in omit when writing *omitting.*

In studying about doubling, remember to pronounce the words of more than one syllable. Accent plays an important role in determining whether or not the final consonant is doubled.

Test for Chapter 2

Add the suffixes indicated to the words listed below.

1. skim	ing	_____	14. plan	er	_____
2. control	ed	_____	15. hop	ing	_____
3. rebel	ion	_____	16. occur	ed	_____
4. swim	ing	_____	17. excel	ed	_____
5. omit	ed	_____	18. allot	ing	_____
6. transfer	ing	_____	19. hope	ing	_____
7. prefer	ence	_____	20. conceal	ed	_____
8. chagrin	ed	_____	21. gossip	y	_____
9. gallop	ing	_____	22. pin	ing	_____
10. design	er	_____	23. recur	ence	_____
11. trap	er	_____	24. benefit	ing	_____
12. rebel	ing	_____	25. confer	ence	_____
13. equip	ed	_____			

Generalization 1

■ In a word of *one* syllable ending in a single consonant preceded by a single vowel, you double the final consonant before adding a suffix or ending which begins with a vowel or the suffix *y*. For example, *club* has one syllable and ends in a consonant *b* which is preceded by the vowel ___.

u

■ The word *club* ends in a consonant preceded by a single vowel. Therefore, in adding a suffix beginning with a vowel, such as *ed*, to the word *club*, you double the final consonant ___.

b

■ When a word of one syllable ends in a single consonant preceded by a single vowel, you double the final consonant before adding a suffix beginning with a [vowel, consonant] or the suffix *y*.

vowel

■ When you add a suffix beginning with a vowel to a word of one syllable which ends in a single consonant preceded by a single vowel, you [do, do not] double the final consonant.

do

■ In adding a suffix beginning with a vowel to a word of one syllable, you double the final consonant if the word ends in a single _____ preceded by a single _____.

consonant
vowel

■ Look again at the word *club*. It ends in a single consonant *b* preceded by a single vowel *u*. Therefore, if you add the suffix *ing* you [do, do not] double the consonant *b*.

do

■ Add the suffix *ing* to the one-syllable word *club:* _____.

clubbing

■ When you add a suffix beginning with a vowel to a one-syllable word which ends in a single consonant preceded by a single vowel, you [do, do not] double the final consonant.

do

t i

■ The word *sit* has one syllable. It ends in the consonant ___ preceded by the vowel ___.

t

■ If you add a suffix beginning with a vowel, like *er* or *ing*, to the word *sit*, you double the final consonant ___.

sitting

■ Add the suffix *ing* to the word *sit:* _____.

sitting

■ The two cousins were _____ [sit + ing] across from each other.

e

■ The word *beg* is also a one-syllable word, ending in the consonant *g* preceded by the vowel ___.

consonant

■ To add a suffix beginning with a vowel, like *ed* or *ing*, to the one-syllable word *beg*, you double the final _____.

begged

■ Add the suffix *ed* to the word *beg:* _____.

begging

■ The old man was put in jail because he did not have a license for _____ [beg + ing] on street corners.

begged

■ The little dog sat up and _____ [beg + ed] for something to eat.

consonant

■ The word *plan* is also a one-syllable word. It ends in a single [vowel, consonant].

vowel

■ The word *plan* ends in a single consonant which is preceded by a single _____.

do

■ Because the word *plan* ends in a single consonant preceded by a single vowel, you [do, do not] double the final *n* when you add a suffix beginning with a vowel.

n

■ When you add a suffix like *ed, er,* or *ing* to the word *plan*, you double the final consonant ___.

planned	■ Add the suffix *ed* to the word *plan:* _____.
planner	■ Add the suffix *er* to the word *plan:* _____.
planning	■ Add the suffix *ing* to the word *plan:* _____.
planning	■ The new department store to be built on the corner of Chestnut and Main is still in the _____ [plan + ing] stage.
skimming	■ Add the suffix *ing* to the word *skim:* _____.
skimmed	■ Add the suffix *ed* to the word *skim:* _____.
skimming	■ The teacher instructed the students in the skill of _____ [skim + ing] an article.
skimmer	■ One who skims can be called a _____ [skim + er].
preceded	■ If you add the suffix *ing* to the word *scrub,* you double the final *b* because the word ends in a single consonant [preceded, followed] by a single vowel.
do	■ In adding *ing* to the word *scrub,* you [do, do not] double the final *b*.
scrubbing	■ Mary spent her holiday _____ [scrub + ing] the floors of the cabin.
scrubber	■ The brush company is advertising a new kind of _____ [scrub + er] for the busy housewife.
hopping	■ Add the suffix *ing* to the word *hop:* _____.
hopping	■ I watched the children skipping and _____ [hop + ing] down the path.
hopped	■ Add the suffix *ed* to the word *hop:* _____.

hopped

■ The oriole _____ [hop + ed] on the windowsill.

one

■ The word *swim* is a [one, two] syllable word.

vowel

■ The word *swim* ends in a single consonant preceded by a single _____.

do

■ Before you add a suffix beginning with a vowel to the word *swim,* you [do, do not] double the final consonant.

swimming

■ All the boys went _____ [swim + ing].

swimmer

■ Either a girl or a boy can be a good _____ [swim + er].

vowel

■ In a word of one syllable ending in a single consonant preceded by a single vowel, you double the final consonant before adding the suffix *y* or a suffix beginning with a [vowel, consonant].

clammy

■ Add the suffix *y* to the word *clam:* _____.

clammy

■ When I took her hand it was cold and _____ [clam + y].

skinning

■ Add the suffix *ing* to the word *skin:* _____.

skinner

■ Add the suffix *er* to the word *skin:* _____.

skinny

■ Add the suffix *y* to the word *skin:* _____.

consonant

■ When you add the suffix *y* or a suffix beginning with a vowel to the word *skin,* you double the final _____.

If a one-syllable
word ends in a
single consonant
preceded by a
single vowel, you
double the final
consonant before
adding a suffix
beginning with a
vowel or the suffix
y.

■ Look at the word *knit*. When you add the suffixes *ing* and *ed* to this word, you spell it *knitting* and *knitted*. State the generalization used.

Generalization 2

■ Now look at the word *equip* and pronounce it. This word has two syllables (e/quip), and the accent comes on the last syllable. In other words, when you say the word *equip,* you put more stress on the [first, last] syllable.

last

■ The word *equip* has two syllables and the accent is on the last syllable. The *u* which follows the *q* does not serve as a vowel because it has the sound of a *w*, which combined with *q* gives a *kw* sound (*e-kwip*). Therefore, this word ends in a single consonant *p* which is preceded by the single vowel ___.

i

■ The word *equip* has two syllables and ends in a single consonant preceded by a single vowel, and the stress is on the [first, last] syllable.

last

■ Now you can form the next generalization: Words of *more than one* syllable, if accented on the *last* syllable and ending in a single consonant preceded by a single vowel, will double the final [vowel, consonant] before adding a suffix beginning with a vowel.

consonant

■ In adding a suffix beginning with a vowel to a word of more than one syllable which is accented on the last syllable and ends in one consonant preceded by one vowel, you [do, do not] double the final consonant.

do

■ When you add a suffix beginning with a vowel to a word of more than one syllable, you must look for these characteristics of the word: the accent must fall on the [first, last] syllable and the word must end in a single _____ preceded by one vowel.

last
consonant

■ If you add the suffix *ed* to the verb *equip,* you must double the final consonant __.

p

■ Add the suffix *ing* to the two-syllable verb *equip:* _____.

equipping

■ Add the suffix *ed* to the verb *equip:* _____.

equipped

■ The accent in the verb *equip* comes on the [first, last] syllable.

last

■ The troops were _____ [equip + ed] with the best guns and ammunition.

equipped

■ Look at the word *control* and pronounce it. This word has two syllables and the accent comes on the [first, last] syllable.

last

■ The verb *control* has more than one syllable, is accented on the last syllable, and ends in the consonant __ preceded by the vowel __.

l o

■ If you add the suffix *ing* to the verb *control* you [do, do not] double the final *l.*

do

■ Add the suffix *ing* to the verb *control:* _____.

controlling

■ Add the suffix *ed* to the verb *control:* _____.

controlled

■ Add the suffix *able* to the verb *control:* _____.

controllable

■ The nurse had a difficult time _____ [control + ing] the patient.

controlling

controllable

■ The doctor realized that her hysterical laughter was not _____ [control + able].

controlled

■ Even though the two brothers hated each other, they _____ [control + ed] their tempers very well.

consonant
vowel

■ The verb *occur* ends in a single _____ preceded by a single _____.

last

■ Say the word *occur*. The accent falls on the [first, last] syllable.

do

■ Because the word *occur* is accented on the last syllable and ends in the consonant *r* which is preceded by the vowel *u*, you [do, do not] double the final *r* before adding a suffix beginning with a vowel.

occurred

■ Add the suffix *ed* to the verb *occur:* _____.

occurring

■ Add the suffix *ing* to the verb *occur:* _____.

r

■ Before you add the suffix *ence* to the word *occur*, you must double the final consonant __.

occurring

■ World-shattering events are _____ [occur + ing] every day.

occurred

■ This same situation has _____ [occur + ed] many times.

occurrence

■ An event or happening is an _____ [occur + ence].

equipped

■ The kitchen was _____ [equip + ed] with all the latest electrical devices.

controlling

■ Watching the antics of the two clowns, I had difficulty _____ [control + ing] my laughter.

occurrence

■ An event or a happening is an _____ [occur + ence].

last

■ Now look at the word *compel* and say it to yourself. The accent is on the [first, last] syllable.

l e

■ The verb *compel* ends in one consonant ___ preceded by one vowel ___.

vowel

■ The word *compel* meets the three requirements for doubling: the accent is on the last syllable and the word ends in a single consonant preceded by a single [vowel, consonant].

do

■ Before you add a suffix beginning with a vowel to the word *compel,* you [do, do not] double the final consonant.

compelled

■ Add the suffix *ed* to *compel:* _____.

compelling

■ Add the suffix *ing* to *compel:* _____.

compellable

■ Add the suffix *able* to *compel:* _____

compellent

■ Add the suffix *ent* to *compel:* _____.

compelled

■ The liberal candidate for office was _____ [compel + ed] to withdraw from the race.

compellable

■ That which is capable of being compelled is _____ [compel + able].

compelling

■ I fear that Lucy's parents are _____ [compel + ing] her to leave town.

last

■ Like the verb *compel,* the verb *omit* is accented on the [first, last] syllable.

one

■ The verb *omit* ends in one consonant which is preceded by _____ vowel.

■ If you add a suffix like *ed* or *ing* to the verb *omit*, you double the final consonant ___.

t

■ Add the suffix *ed* to the verb *omit*: _____.

omitted

■ Add the suffix *ing* to the verb *omit*: _____.

omitting

■ The sentence was not complete because the verb was _____ [omit + ed].

omitted

■ John has a habit of _____ [omit + ing] the period at the end of a declarative sentence.

omitting

■ Say the word *transfer′*. The accent in the verb *transfer* is on the last syllable. The word also ends in the single consonant *r* which is preceded by the single vowel ___.

e

■ To add the suffix *ed* or *ing* to the verb *transfer*, you must double the final consonant ___.

r

■ Add the suffix *ed* to *transfer*: _____.

transferred

■ Add the suffix *ing* to *transfer*: _____.

transferring

■ My uncle was very disappointed when he was _____ [transfer + ed] to the West.

transferred

■ I spent most of my time _____ [transfer + ing] from one bus to another.

transferring

■ Like the verb *control,* the accent in the verb *rebel′* falls on the [first, last] syllable.

last

■ The verb *rebel* ends in one consonant preceded by _____ vowel.

one

■ If you added the suffix *ed, ing,* or *ion* to the verb *rebel,* you _____ the final consonant *l.*

double

■ Add the suffix *ed* to *rebel*: _____.

rebelled

rebelling

■ Add the suffix *ing* to *rebel:* _____.

rebellion

■ Add the suffix *ion* to *rebel:* _____.

rebellion

■ It is not unusual for the natives of the area to rise in _____ [rebel + ion].

rebelled

■ No matter how much the father pleaded with his son, the son _____ [rebel + ed].

rebelling

■ The inmates spent much of their time _____ [rebel + ing] against the rules of the prison.

last

■ Say the word *recur'*. The accent falls on the [first, last] syllable.

vowel

■ *Recur* ends in a single consonant preceded by a single [consonant, vowel].

do

■ Because the accent in *recur* is on the last syllable and the word ends in one consonant preceded by one vowel, you [do, do not] double the final consonant before adding a suffix beginning with a vowel.

recurred

■ Add the suffix *ed* to *recur:* _____.

recurring

■ Add the suffix *ing* to *recur:* _____.

recurrence

■ Add the suffix *ence* to *recur:* _____.

recurring

■ The invalid was plagued by a _____ [recur + ing] fever.

recurred

■ Although Mr. Jones tried to avoid the subject of taxes, it _____ [recur + ed] time and time again.

recurrence

■ That which returns time after time is called a _____ [recur + ence].

■ The professor wished to avoid a _____ [recur + ence] of the same situation.

recurrence

■ Words of *one* syllable that end in a single consonant preceded by a single vowel [do, do not] double the final consonant before adding the suffix *y* or a suffix beginning with a vowel.

do

■ I wanted to buy an old-fashioned _____ [spin + ing] wheel.

spinning

If a word of more than one syllable is accented on the last syllable and ends in a single consonant preceded by a single vowel, you double the final consonant before adding a suffix beginning with a vowel.

■ Look at the word *equipping*. The *p* has been doubled before adding the suffix *ing*. State the generalization used.

■ Thunderstorms are _____ [occur + ing] more frequently in the North.

occurring

■ The municipal police department does a fine job of _____ [patrol + ing] the city.

patrolling

■ When the new manufacturing plant was built, it was _____ [equip + ed] with all the latest fire prevention devices.

equipped

■ Mr. Smith has the _____ [control + ing] interest in the company.

controlling

■ Add the suffix *ing* to *transfer:* _____.

transferring

■ The basic salary was _____ [omit + ed] from the contract.

omitted

compelled

■ The sudden snowstorm _____ [compel + ed] the travelers to seek shelter.

rebellion

■ This uprising is the worst _____ [rebel + ion] the country has ever seen.

forbidden

■ Chewing gum is _____ [forbid + en] in all classrooms.

excelled

■ Johnny was awarded a gold medal because he _____ [excel + ed] in scholastic achievement.

trimming

■ Lucy bought red and white ribbon for _____ [trim + ing] her straw hat.

recurrence

■ Occasionally Tom suffers a _____ [recur + ence] of the old malady.

last

■ Say the words *prefer, defer, refer,* and *confer.* They are all accented on the [first, last] syllable.

r e

■ The verbs *prefer, defer, refer,* and *confer* all end in the consonant __ which is preceded by the vowel __.

do

■ If you add the suffix *ed* or *ing* to the verbs *prefer, defer, refer,* and *confer,* you [do, do not] double the final consonant.

preferred

■ The banker bought several shares of _____ [prefer + ed] stock.

deferred

■ The final decision to take the trip was _____ [defer + ed] until Monday.

referred

■ Mr. Smith's letter was _____ [refer + ed] to Miss Jones for reply.

conferred

■ The two presidents _____ [confer + ed] for an hour.

■ It was impossible to interrupt the area manager because he was _____ [confer + ing] with his district chiefs.

conferring

■ Instead of giving his own opinion, the student spent his allotted time _____ [refer + ing] to what others had said.

referring

■ In response to Mr. Brown's request for clarification, Jim answered, "I am _____ [defer + ing] the decision until tomorrow."

deferring

preferring

■ Add the suffix *ing* to *prefer:* _____.

■ One exception to the generalization you have just learned is the word *chagrin,* which means mental distress. You do not double the final consonant. Add the suffix *ed* to the word *chagrin:* _____.

chagrined

■ Add the suffix *ing* to *chagrin:* _____.

chagrining

■ If a person is suffering from mental distress caused by failure, he is _____ [chagrin + ed].

chagrined

Generalization 3

■ If the accent in a word does *not* fall on the last syllable, or if the word ends in a single consonant which is *not* preceded by a single vowel, then you [do, do not] double the final consonant before adding a suffix beginning with a vowel.

do not

■ Look at the word *differ* and say it to yourself. Although it ends in a single consonant preceded by a single vowel, it does *not* have the accent on the last syllable. Therefore, if you add the suffix *ed* to *differ,* you spell it: _____.

differed

■ Add the suffix *ed* to the verb *differ:* _____.

differed

■ Add the suffix *ing* to the verb *differ:* _____.

differing

difference

■ Add the suffix *ence* to the verb *differ:* _____.

differed

■ The jurors could not reach a verdict because they _____ [differ + ed] in their judgments of the case.

difference

■ The two sides could not continue their negotiations because of the _____ [differ + ence] in their viewpoints.

last

■ Say the word *conceal*. The accent falls on the [first, last] syllable.

is not

■ Although the accent in the word *conceal* falls on the last syllable and the word ends in a single consonant, this last consonant [is, is not] preceded by a single vowel.

do not

■ If you add a suffix beginning with a vowel to the verb *conceal* you [do, do not] double the final *l*.

concealed

■ Add the suffix *ed* to *conceal:* _____.

concealing

■ Add the suffix *ing* to *conceal:* _____.

concealable

■ Add the suffix *able* to *conceal:* _____.

concealing

■ The maid is _____ [conceal + ing] information about the robbery.

concealed

■ When the officers pounded on the door, Mary ran upstairs and _____ [conceal + ed] herself behind the screen.

concealable

■ Because the package is so large, it could not be considered _____ [conceal + able].

does not

■ Although the verb *adapt* is accented on the last syllable, it [does, does not] end in a single consonant preceded by a single vowel.

adapted

■ Add the suffix *ed* to the verb *adapt:* _____.

adapting

■ Add the suffix *ing* to the verb *adapt:* _____.

adaptable

■ Add the suffix *able* to the verb *adapt:* _____.

adapted

■ The orphan boy has _____ [adapt + ed] him-self to his new surroundings.

adaptable

■ Joseph is a very _____ [adapt +able] person.

adapting

■ The stray dog is _____ [adapt + ing] itself to its new owner.

do not

■ Before adding a suffix beginning with a vowel to a word in which the accent does not fall on the last sylla-ble or which does not end in a single consonant preceded by a single vowel, you [do, do not] double the final consonant.

does not

■ The verb *design* [does, does not] end in a single consonant preceded by a single vowel.

designed

■ Add the suffix *ed* to the word *design:* _____.

designed

■ John and his cousin _____ [design + ed] their own boat.

designing

■ The artist spends many hours a day _____ [design + ing] children's clothes.

first

■ Like the verb *differ,* the verb *gallop* has the accent on the [first, last] syllable.

galloped

■ Add the suffix *ed* to the verb *gallop:* _____.

galloping

■ Add the suffix *ing* to the verb *gallop:* _____.

galloped

■ The horses _____ [gallop + ed] across the fields.

galloping

■ The children pretended they were _____ [gallop + ing] ponies.

■ Just as the verb *gallop* has the accent on the first syllable, the accent in the word *gossip* is on the _____ syllable.

first

■ Although the verb *gossip* ends in one consonant preceded by one vowel, the accent is on the first syllable. Therefore, before you add a suffix beginning with a vowel or the suffix *y,* you [do, do not] double the final conso-nant.

do not

■ The afternoon teas were usually attended by women who _____ [gossip + ed] for hours about their neighbors.

gossiped

■ Whenever I looked out of the window I would see the two women talking and _____ [gossip + ing] about the elderly recluse.

gossiping

■ Grandma's worst fault was that she was too _____ [gossip + y].

gossipy

Generalization 4

■ Now look at what happens when you add the suffix *ence* to *prefer, defer, confer,* and *refer.* Say these words to yourself: *preference, reference, deference,* and *confer-ence.* The accent in the last four nouns falls on the [first, last] syllable.

first

■ Look again at the spelling of these words: *preference, reference, deference,* and *conference.* There is only *one r* because the accent in these words falls on the [first, last] syllable.

first

■ Let us make a generalization. If the accent of the root word (like *prefer, refer, confer,* and *defer*) falls back on another syllable when the suffix *ence* is added, then you [do, do not] double the final consonant.

do not

first

■ The accent in the word *preference* falls on the [first, last] syllable.

first

■ There is only one *r* in the word *deference* because the accent in this word falls on the [first, last] syllable.

first

■ In the noun *conference*, the accent falls on the [first, last] syllable.

is not

■ The accent in the verb *refer* falls on the last syllable. However, when the suffix *ence* is added to *refer*, forming the noun *reference*, the accent falls back on the first syllable. The final consonant therefore [is, is not] doubled.

reference

■ Combine the suffix *ence* and the verb *refer:* _____.

conference

■ Add the suffix *ence* to *confer:* _____.

deference

■ Add the suffix *ence* to *defer:* _____.

preference

■ Add the suffix *ence* to *prefer:* _____.

Review

A word of one sylla-
ble ending in a
single consonant
preceded by a
single vowel dou-
bles the final con-
sonant before
adding a suffix be-
ginning with a
vowel or the suffix
y.

■ When you add the suffix *ing* to *skip* you write *skipping*. State the generalization used.

deferred

■ The secretary agreed to have the meeting _____ [defer + ed].

conference

■ Three officers of the company were present at the _____ [confer + ence].

planned

■ What have you _____ [plan + ed] to do for the summer?

compelled

■ The judge _____ [compel + ed] the prisoner to answer all the questions.

In a word of more than one syllable, if it is accented on the last syllable and ends in a single consonant preceded by a single vowel you double the final consonant before adding a suffix beginning with a vowel or the suffix *y*.

■ Look at the word *beginning*. Before the suffix *ing* is added to the root word *begin*, you must double the *n*. State the generalization used.

do not

■ The word *chagrin* is an exception to this generalization about doubling the final consonant. When you add suffixes like *ed* and *ing* to the word *chagrin*, you [do, do not] double the final consonant.

committing

■ The boy admitted that he had spent most of his young life _____ [commit + ing] crimes of one kind or another.

adapting

■ Add the suffix *ing* to the verb *adapt:* _____.

designer

■ The lady next door was a dress _____ [design + er].

concealed

■ Susan's mother asked, "What have you _____ [conceal + ed] behind the door?"

galloping

■ The pony went _____ [gallop + ing] around the arena.

witty

■ Mr. Churchill was a very _____ [wit + y] man.

trapper	■ Young Billy decided that he wanted to go to the north woods to become a _____ [trap + er].
pinned	■ Instead of basting the seams together, Jane _____ [pin + ed] them.
allotted	■ Two tickets are _____ [allot + ed] to each graduate.
patrolled	■ The streets are _____ [patrol + ed] every night by the sheriff's deputies.
If the accent in a word does not fall on the last syllable or if the word ends in a single consonant which is not preceded by a single vowel, you do not double the final consonant before adding a suffix beginning with a vowel or the suffix *y*.	■ Look at the italicized word in this sentence: The enemy is *retreating* across the river. State the generalization used for not doubling the final consonant.
gossipy	■ She was known as a _____ [gossip + y] old woman.
omitted	■ The index was _____ [omit + ed] from the book.
chagrined	■ When his plans did not succeed, my uncle was very much _____ [chagrin + ed].
labeling	■ The clerk spent all her time _____ [label + ing] the packets.

chapter 3

Final e

Like the problem of whether to double the final consonant, the problem of whether to drop the final *e* of a word in adding a suffix is often perplexing.

Do you keep the *e* in *write* when you add *ing?* Do you keep the *e* in *desire* when you add *ing* or *ous?* There are definite generalizations concerning the dropping of the final *e* which will help to eliminate many spelling errors in this category. Study each one carefully as well as the spelling of the words in this chapter, and you will find your correct spelling average higher than ever before.

Test for Chapter 3

Combine the suffixes indicated in each part with the words listed in that part.

A. *ing*

1. desire	_____	11. dye	_____
2. come	_____	12. use	_____
3. singe	_____	13. argue	_____
4. pursue	_____	14. achieve	_____
5. write	_____	15. praise	_____
6. dine	_____	16. advise	_____
7. surprise	_____	17. purchase	_____
8. hoe	_____	18. love	_____
9. receive	_____	19. judge	_____
10. lose	_____	20. canoe	_____

B. *able*

1. love	_____	6. service	_____
2. receive	_____	7. manage	_____
3. advise	_____	8. achieve	_____
4. pleasure	_____	9. amuse	_____
5. imagine	_____	10. notice	_____

C. *ful, ly, ness,* and *ment*

1. whole	ly	_____	9. remote	ness	_____
2. use	less	_____	10. advertise	ment	_____
3. fierce	ness	_____	11. due	ly	_____
4. true	ly	_____	12. age	less	_____
5. argue	ment	_____	13. manage	ment	_____
6. commence	ment	_____	14. judge	ment	_____
7. use	ful	_____	15. achieve	ment	_____
8. grace	ful	_____			

Generalization 1

is not

■ Some words, such as *write* and *desire,* end with a silent *e.* The *e* at the end of such words as *write* or *desire* [is, is not] pronounced.

t

■ Say the word *write* softly to yourself. In pronouncing this word, the *e* is silent because the last sound you hear is represented by the letter ___.

e

■ Now, whenever you add a suffix (or ending) which begins with a vowel to a word ending in a silent *e,* you usually drop that *e* before adding the suffix. For example, if you add *ing* to the word *write,* you drop the ___ before adding *ing.*

drop

■ Whenever you add a suffix beginning with a vowel to a word ending in a silent *e,* you usually [drop, keep] the silent *e* before adding the suffix.

e

■ If you add a suffix beginning with a vowel like *ing,* to the word *write* which ends in a silent *e,* you drop the ___ before adding *ing.*

drop

■ Just as you drop the final *e* in *write* before adding *ing,* so you also _____ the final *e* in *desire* before adding *ing.*

silent

■ The word *write* ends in a silent *e;* the word *desire* also ends in a _____ *e.*

■ When you add *ing* to the word *desire,* you drop the *e* because the suffix *ing* begins with the vowel ___.

i

■ When you add the suffix *able* to the word *desire,* you drop the *e* because the suffix begins with the vowel ___.

a

■ Look at the word *desire.* The last *e* is not pronounced; therefore, when you add the suffix *ing* to this word you spell it _____.

desiring

■ Look again at the word *write.* It also ends in a silent *e.* When you add *ing* to this word, you spell it _____.

writing

■ When a person writes something, he is said to be _____.

writing

■ When a person desires something, it can be said that he is de___ it.

desiring

■ Like the words *write* and *desire,* the verb *come* also ends in a silent ___.

e

■ If you add the suffix *ing* to the verb *come,* you drop the silent *e* because *ing* begins with the vowel ___.

i

■ When you add *ing* to the verb *come,* which ends in a silent *e,* you spell it this way: _____.

coming

■ When a person is in the process of appearing or arriving at a scene, he is said to be _____ [come + ing].

coming

■ When you add the suffix *ing* to the word *write,* you spell it _____.

writing

■ When you add *ing* to the verb *desire,* you spell it _____.

desiring

coming

■ When you add *ing* to the verb *come*, you spell it
_____.

i

■ Look at the verb *choose*. Because it ends in a silent
e, you drop this *e* before adding the suffix *ing* which
begins with the vowel ___.

choosing

■ When you add *ing* to the verb *choose* you spell it
_____.

choosing

■ When someone chooses something, he is said to be
in the process of _____.

ach*ing*

■ Now look at the verb *ache*. If you add the suffix *ing*
to the verb *ache,* you would spell it ach_____.

aching

■ An *ache* is a pain. If you are suffering pain in your
arm, you could say that your arm is _____.

aching

■ When you add *ing* to the verb *ache,* you spell it
_____.

coming

■ Mr. Jones asked his secretary, "Are you _____
[come + ing] to the picnic tomorrow?"

aching

■ Mabel asked her aunt why she was lying down, and
Mrs. Atlin said that her back was _____ [ache +
ing].

writing

■ John watched his sister's pen move rapidly across
the paper and said, "What are you _____ [write +
ing]?"

losing

■ Spell the word that results from adding *ing* to the
verb *lose:* _____.

drop

■ When you add a suffix beginning with a vowel to a
word ending in a silent *e,* such as *lose,* you [drop, keep]
the *e* before adding the suffix.

losing

■ When Janie lost her glasses, her mother said, "You children are always _____ [lose + ing] something."

dining

■ Combine the verb *dine,* which ends in a silent *e,* and the suffix *ing:* _____.

dining

■ When we walked into the restaurant, we saw Miss Nash _____ [dine + ing] with her cousin.

using

■ Add the suffix *ing* to the verb *use:* _____.

using

■ When Susan looked for the red and blue coloring pencils, she asked her brother, "Are you _____ [use + ing] the red and blue ones?"

silent

■ Look at the word *argue.* The last vowel is not pronounced; therefore, it is called a _____ *e.*

arguing

■ When you add *ing* to the verb *argue,* you spell it _____.

arguing

■ The men were _____ [argue + ing] about the results of the election.

e

■ When you add the suffix *ing* to the verb *pursue,* you drop the silent __ before adding the suffix which begins with the vowel *i.*

drop

■ When you add *ing* to the word *surprise,* you _____ the *e* because the suffix begins with a vowel.

e

■ The word *judging* does not have an *e* before the *ing* because you drop the silent __ before adding *ing.*

pursuing

■ After the holdup the two detectives spent several hours _____ [pursue + ing] the thieves.

surprising

■ When one thinks of the hazards involved in a trip through the thick underbrush, it is _____ [surprise + ing] that any club members volunteered to go.

judging

■ Lucian wondered how long the art critics would spend _____ [judge + ing] his paintings.

■ The publisher interviewed several teachers in the high school to find out what science textbooks they were _____ [use + ing].

using

■ When you add *ing* to the verb *receive,* you spell it _____.

receiving

■ Just as you drop the silent *e* before adding the suffix *ing,* you also _____ the silent *e* before adding suffixes like *able, ance, ed, ence, ity,* and *ous.*

drop

■ Like the suffix *ing,* the suffixes *able, ance, ed, ence, ity,* and *ous,* are examples of endings that begin with a [vowel, consonant].

vowel

■ Usually when you add the suffix *able* to a word ending in a silent *e,* you drop the __ before adding the suffix.

e

■ The verb *love* ends in a silent *e.* When you add *able* to the verb *love,* you spell it *lov____.*

lov*able*

■ His two little daughters had *lov____ dispositions.*

lov*able*

■ Because of his _____ [love + able] nature, John made his grandmother very happy.

lovable

■ When you add the suffix *able* to the word *receive,* you drop the __ before adding *able.*

e

■ When you add the suffix *able* to the verb *receive,* you spell it _____.

receivable

■ Audrey had a very difficult time understanding the term "_____ [receive + able] goods."

receivable

■ The verb *advise* ends in a silent *e.* If you add *able* to *advise,* you spell it _____.

advisable

■ Considering all the circumstances, I thought it would not be advis _____ to discuss politics when my nephew came to visit us.

advis*able*

■ Because it started to rain, we did not think that it was _____ [advise + able] to go to the fair.

advisable

■ When you add the suffix *able* to the noun *pleasure,* you _____ the *e* because the suffix begins with a vowel.

drop

■ Add the suffix *able* to the noun *pleasure:* _____.

pleasurable

■ Sleigh riding is one of the most pleasur _____ winter sports.

pleasur*able*

■ Add the suffix *able* to the verb *imagine:* _____.

imaginable

■ The verb *imagine* ends in a silent *e*. Therefore, you drop the *e* before adding the suffix *able* which begins with the vowel ___.

a

■ When you add *able* to the verb *imagine* you spell the result like this: _____.

imaginable

■ The locksmith tried every _____ [imagine + able] combination to open the vault.

imaginable

■ The word *purchase* ends in a silent *e*. Therefore, you drop the *e* before adding the suffix which begins with the vowel ___.

a

■ If you add the suffix *able* to the verb *purchase,* you spell it this way: _____.

purchasable

■ Add the suffix *able* to the verb *purchase:* _____.

purchasable

■ I was very much surprised to learn that an individual who is open to bribery or corrupt influence could be called _____ [purchase + able].

purchasable

lovable

■ When you add the suffix *able* to the verb *love* you spell it: _____.

receivable

■ The word which means capable of being received is _____ [receive + able].

advisable

■ The personnel officer did not think it was _____ [advise + able] to keep open the office on Saturday.

pleasurable

■ A word which means giving pleasure is _____.

imaginable

■ Capable of being imagined is the definition of the word _____.

purchasable

■ When an item is capable of being purchased, it is called _____.

choosing

■ Mary was provoked because her mother spent so much time _____ [choose + ing] patterns.

dining

■ The smallest room in the house is the _____ [dine + ing] room.

losing

■ The children are always _____ [lose + ing] their mittens.

arguing

■ Her brother wasted an hour _____ [argue + ing] about the qualifications of the candidates.

judging

■ It seems as though the panel of experts has been _____ [judge + ing] the contest for hours.

receiving

■ For several weeks Mr. Green has been _____ [receive + ing] mysterious phone calls.

surprising

■ The fact that he has only an eighth-grade education is indeed _____ [surprise + ing].

pursuing

■ Tim asked the French exchange students about the college courses they were _____ [pursue + ing].

When you add a suffix beginning with a vowel to a word ending in a silent *e*, you usually drop the *e* before adding the suffix.

■ When you add the suffix *ing* to the word *become*, you spell the result this way: *becoming*. State the generalization used.

density

■ Now, using the generalizations you have learned about dropping the final *e*, form the noun by adding the suffix *ity* to the adjective *dense*: _____.

*dens*ity

■ The quality or state of being dense is called _____*ity*.

density

■ We could not see the dome of the Capitol because of the _____ [dense + ity] of the fog.

immensity

■ Form the noun which results from adding *ity* to the adjective *immense*: _____.

*immens*ity

■ The state or quality of being immense or huge is called _____ *ity*.

immensity

■ The farmer was impressed by the _____ [immense + ity] of the packing plant.

rarity

■ The noun which results from adding the suffix *ity* to the adjective *rare* is _____.

rarity

■ The state or quality of being rare is called _____.

rarity

■ Finding three yolks in one egg is quite a _____ [rare + ity].

vowels

■ Suffixes like *able, ance, ed, ence, ing, ity,* and *ous* are examples of suffixes that begin with [consonants, vowels].

judged
judger
judging

■ Using the word *judge* as the root word, form three words by adding the suffixes *ed, er,* and *ing:* _____ [ed], _____ [er], _____ [ing].

advisable
advised
advising

■ Using the word *advise* as the root word, form three words by adding the suffixes *able, ed, ing:* _____ [able], _____ [ed], _____ [ing].

rarity

■ It is a _____ [rare + ity] to see an orange-colored rose.

scarcity

■ The heavy rains caused a _____ [scarce + ity] of berries.

immensity

■ The state or quality of being immense is called _____.

density

■ In the poorer sections of the city, the _____ [state of being dense] of the population is increasing steadily.

Before adding a suf-
fix which begins
with a vowel to
a word ending in
a final *e,* you usu-
ally drop the *e.*

■ Look at the root word *adventure.* When you add the suffix *ous,* you spell the result this way: *adventurous.* State the generalization used in adding the suffix.

Generalization 2

oe

■ However, if a word ends in *oe,* you must keep the *e* to retain the pronunciation before adding the suffix *ing* or *ist.* Keep the *e* in a word that ends in _____.

keep

■ Look at the word *canoe.* It ends in *oe;* therefore, you [drop, keep] the *e* before adding *ing* or *ist.*

canoeing

■ If you add the suffix *ing* to the word *canoe,* you spell the resulting word this way: _____.

canoeing

■ June and Dick went _____ [canoe + ing] at Lake Harriet.

canoeist

■ Tom's brother won first place as a _____ [canoe + ist].

canoeing

■ The three couples swam for an hour and then went _____ [canoe + ing] around the lakes.

oe

■ *Hoe* is another word that ends in _____.

e

■ If you add *ing* to the word *hoe,* you must retain the pronunciation by keeping the ___.

hoeing

■ Maxine's father spent the entire morning _____ [hoe + ing] in the garden.

keep

■ When you add *ing* to the word *hoe,* you must [drop, keep] the *e.*

hoeing
canoeing

■ While the three boys spent the afternoon _____ [hoe + ing] in the fields, the girls went _____ [canoe + ing].

Generalization 3

e

■ Just as you keep the *e* in *hoe* and *canoe* before adding *ing,* so do you retain the ___ in *dye* and *singe.*

■ The word *dye* retains the *e,* to avoid confusion with another word. For example, to *dye* means to color. If you drop the *e* before adding *ing,* you would spell *dying,* which means to become dead. Therefore, to spell *dyeing,* the process of coloring, you must [drop, keep] the *e.*

keep

■ When you add the suffix *ing* to the word *dye,* you spell it _____.

dyeing

■ The process of putting coloring permanently into fibers of cotton or wool is known as _____ [dye + ing].

dyeing

dyeing

■ Millie's mother spent an hour _____ her spring coat.

singing

■ To *singe* means to burn or scorch. If you dropped the *e* in *singe* before adding *ing,* you would spell an entirely different word _____.

soft

■ The sound of *g* has two main sounds, hard and soft. The word *get* has a *hard* sound, but the word *singe* has a _____ *g* sound.

e

■ In order to keep the soft sound of the *g* in the word *singe,* you must keep the __ before adding *ing.*

singeing

■ If you singe or scorch a garment, you are _____ it.

singeing

■ The cook would always sing a southern ballad while _____ [singe + ing] the hair from the chickens over the open fire.

keep

■ When adding the suffix *ing* to the words *canoe, hoe, dye,* and *singe,* you [drop, keep] the final *e.*

e

■ In order to avoid confusion with other words or to retain the pronunciation of the basic word, you must keep the final __ in words like *canoe, dye, hoe,* and *singe.*

hoeing
dyeing
canoeing
singeing

■ By adding the suffix *ing* to the following words you can form these words: _____ [hoe], _____ [dye], _____ [canoe], and _____ [singe].

Generalization 4

soft

■ Say this word softly to yourself: *change.* Like the word *singe,* the word *change* has a [hard, soft] sound of *g.*

■ To emphasize the difference between the hard and soft sound of *g*, say the word *get*. This *g* has the [hard, soft] sound of *g*.

hard

■ Whenever the suffix *able*, which begins with a vowel, is added to a word which ends in *ge*, you keep the *e* to retain the soft sound of the ___.

g

■ For example, if you add *able* to the verb *change*, you [drop, keep] the *e* before adding *able*.

keep

■ By adding the suffix *able* to the word *change*, you spell the word _____.

changeable

■ The adjective which means capable of being changed is _____.

changeable

■ His attitude toward his uncle was extremely _____ [capable of being changed].

changeable

■ Say the word *manage* to yourself. The words *change* and *manage* have the same [hard, soft] sound of *g*.

soft

■ When you add the suffix *able* to the word *manage*, you keep the *e* and add _____.

able

■ By adding the suffix *able* to the word *manage*, you spell the word _____.

manageable

■ When children are well disciplined, they are quite _____ [capable of being managed].

manageable

■ The word which means capable of being managed is _____.

manageable

■ Just as the sound of *g* can be hard or soft, so can the sound of *c* be hard or _____.

soft

■ Say the word *cat* softly to yourself. The sound of the *c* in *cat* is a hard *c*. Say the word *notice*. Unlike the hard sound of *c* in *cat*, the sound of the *c* in *notice* is _____.

soft

soft

■ Whenever you add the suffix *able* to a word which ends in *ce,* you must keep the *e* to retain the [hard, soft] sound of the *c.*

noti*ce*able

■ If you add the suffix *able* to the verb *notice,* you spell this word *notic___.*

no*tice*able

■ If something is worthy of being observed or noticed, it is said to be no ____able.

noticeable

■ John's disapproval of his brother's actions was very _____ [worthy of being noticed].

keep

■ To retain the soft sound of the *c* or *g* in words that end in *ce* or *ge,* you must [drop, keep] the *e* before adding the suffix *able.*

Special Words

ly

■ Now look at the word *truly.* This word, which means honestly, accurately, comes from the word *true* and the suffix ____.

tru*ly*

■ Remember that when you spell *truly* it does *not* have an *e.* This is an exception to the generalization you have just learned. *Truly* is spelled tru____.

truly

■ The word that means honestly, accurately is _____.

truly

■ The fact the hardware store was forced to move from its present location is _____ [true + ly] regrettable.

e

■ Just as *truly* is spelled without an *e,* the word *duly* is also spelled without an ___.

ly

■ The word *duly* is the combination of the word *due* and the suffix ____.

duly

■ When you write *duly* always spell it _____.

duly	■ The word *duly* can mean in an appropriate way, as this sentence: The visitors were _____ treated as representatives of a foreign country.
duly	■ The word *duly* can also mean in a regular or lawful way, as in this sentence: The criminals were _____ punished for their crimes.
e	■ *Wholly* is another word like *truly* and *duly*. Even though the word *wholly* is a combination of the word *whole* and the suffix *ly*, there is no __ in the word *wholly*.
wholly	■ The word *wholly* means entirely or completely. Completely has the same meaning as _____.
wh*olly*	■ Entirely is another word for wh_____.
wholly	■ My parents were not _____ satisfied with my excuse for being late.
wholly	■ His actions were _____ unforgivable.
e	■ The words *truly, duly,* and *wholly* have this point in common: there is no __ in *truly, duly,* and *wholly*.
wholly	■ The program was performed _____ [entirely] for the students.
du*ly*	■ The newly elected commissioner will begin his reform program within a du_____ specified time.
tr*uly*	■ When the boy was questioned, he said that he was tr_____ sorry about his part in the robbery.
judgment argument	■ Although the noun *judgment* can be spelled with an e after the g, the preferred spelling is without the e: _____. The noun *argument* is also spelled without the e after the u: _____.

■ When you add the suffix *ment* to the word *argue,* you [drop, keep] the final *e* before adding *ment.*

drop

■ A discourse which is designed to convince or to persuade is called an argu____.

argu*ment*

■ Add the suffix *ment* to the verb *argue:* _____.

argument

■ Both sides of the debate ended their discussion in a bitter _____.

argument

■ A discourse which is meant to convince or to persuade is called an _____.

argument

■ The preferred spelling of the word *judgment* [does, does not] have an *e* after the *g.*

does not

■ An opinion or a decision is called a judg____.

judg*ment*

■ Combine the verb *judge* and the suffix *ment:* _____.

judgment

■ The counselor showed good ju____ when he appointed a self-governing committee.

ju*dg*ment

■ An opinion or a decision can be called a _____.

judgment

■ There is no *e* in the nouns argu____ and judg____.

argu*ment*
judg*ment*

■ There is no *e* in these words: tru____, ____, and ____.

truly
duly
wholly

Review

■ Before adding a suffix beginning with a vowel to a word ending in a final *e,* you usually [drop, keep] the final *e.*

drop

achiever
achieved
achieving
achievable
achievement

■ Using the verb *achieve* as your root word, add the following suffixes to it: _____ [er], _____ [ed], _____ [ing], _____ [able], _____ [ment].

received
receiver
receiving
receivable

■ Using the word *receive* as your root word, add the following suffixes to it: _____ [ed], _____ [er], _____ [ing], _____ [able].

keep

■ When you add the suffix *able* to words ending in *ce* or *ge*, like *service* or *manage*, you [drop, keep] the final *e* to retain the soft sound of the *c* or *g*.

amuser
amused
amusing
amusable
amusement

■ Using the verb *amuse* as your root word, add the following suffixes to it: _____ [er], _____ [ed], _____ [ing], _____ [able], _____ [ment].

serviceable

■ Those shoes are very _____ [service + able].

judged
judgment
judging
judger

■ Using the verb *judge* as your root word, add the following suffixes to it: _____ [ed], _____ [ment], _____ [ing], _____ [er].

manageable

■ In spite of their fear of strangers, the children were quite _____ [manage + able].

keep

■ Words ending in *oe* [drop, keep] the *e* before adding the suffixes *ing* or *ist*.

insured
insurable
insurance
insurer

■ Using the verb *insure* as your root word, add the following suffixes to it: _____ [ed], _____ [able], _____ [ance], _____ [er].

hoeing

■ Mr. Hamilton told Mike to stop _____ [hoe + ing] and milk the cows.

woeful

■   The child had an extremely _____ [woe + ful]
look on his face.

judgment
argument

■   An opinion or decision is called a _____; a discourse to persuade or to convince is called an _____.

chapter 4

Final y

In dealing with the final *y* of a word, you can learn very specific ways in which to solve any difficulties arising from the use of this semivowel.

Without generalizations to follow, it is difficult to know when to keep the *y* or when to change it to *i* before adding a suffix. For example, when you form the plural of *fly* do you add *s* or change the *y* to *i* and add *es?* When you add *ing* to the word *study,* do you keep the *y* or change it to *i?* If you keep the *i,* why? When you form the present tense of verbs ending in *y* (such as *cry* or *try*) for the third person singular, do you change the *y* to *i* and add *es?* These and other questions can be answered by the careful study of this chapter.

Test for Chapter 4

Add the suffixes indicated to the words listed below.

1. chimney   plural ending s   _____
2. annoy   ing   _____
3. survey   plural ending s   _____
4. deny   ing   _____
5. pity   ful   _____
6. busy   ly   _____
7. destroy   ed   _____
8. tragedy   plural ending es   _____
9. accompany   ed   _____
10. cemetery   plural ending es   _____
11. cozy   ly   _____
12. mercy   ful   _____
13. study   ing   _____
14. society   plural ending es   _____
15. portray   al   _____

Test for Chapter 4 (Continued)

16. annoy   ance   _____
17. beauty   ful   _____
18. copy   ed   _____
19. enemy   plural ending es _____
20. trolley   plural ending s   _____

Generalization 1

alleys

■ If a word ends in *y* which is preceded by a vowel, you keep the *y* and add the suffix or ending. For example, if you add the plural ending *s* to the word *alley,* you write the word this way: _____.

y

■ A word ending in *y* preceded by a vowel usually keeps the ___ before adding the suffix.

vowel

■ The word *alley* ends in *y* preceded by a _____.

y

■ If you add a suffix to a word ending in *y* preceded by a vowel, you keep the ___ and add the suffix.

s

■ Suffixes that can be added to words ending in *y* preceded by a vowel might include *ed, ing, ance, ment,* and the plural ending ___.

e

■ The noun *alley* ends in *y* preceded by the vowel ___.

alleys

■ If you add the plural ending *s* to the noun *alley* you spell it _____.

vowel

■ Whenever you add a suffix to a word ending in *y* preceded by a [vowel, consonant], you keep the *y*.

keep

■ Because the word *alley* ends in *y* preceded by the vowel *e,* you [keep, drop] the *y* before adding the suffix.

alleys

■ Form the plural of the noun *alley:* _____.

vowel

■ The noun *trolley* ends in *y* preceded by a _____.

■ Before adding any suffix except *ing,* you change the *y* to *i* in words that end in *y* preceded by a _____.

consonant

■ The verb *deny* ends in *y* preceded by the consonant *n.* When you add the suffix *ed,* you must change the __ to __.

y i

■ When you add the suffix *ed* to the verb *deny* you write _____.

denied

■ When you add the suffix *al* to the verb *deny,* you write _____.

denial

■ The captured enemy tried to establish his innocence when he _____ [deny + ed] any responsibility for the raids.

denied

■ The manager's request for a two-week leave of absence was met with a firm _____ [deny + al] by his supervisor.

denial

■ If you wish to add the suffix *ing,* which begins with an *i,* to a word ending in *y* preceded by a consonant, then you must *keep* the *y.* For example, *ing* added to *deny* would be deny _____.

deny*ing*

■ Because the suffix *ing* begins with an *i,* you [do, do not] change the *y* to *i* in words ending in *y* preceded by a consonant.

do not

■ Charlie was faced with the hard task of _____ [deny + ing] his guilt.

denying

■ Like the verb *deny,* the word *beauty* ends in *y* preceded by a [vowel, consonant].

consonant

■ Therefore, before adding the plural ending, you change the *y* to *i* and add *es.* The plural of *beauty* would be *beaut*_____.

beaut*ies*

■ In the Miss America contest, the judges had difficulty in selecting a winner among all the _____ [plural form of *beauty*].

beauties

■ If you add the suffix *ful* to the noun *beauty*, you change the __ to __ and add *ful*.

y i

■ Add the suffix *ful* to the noun *beauty:* _____.

beautiful

■ The reigning queen is very _____ [beauty+ful].

beautiful

■ Form the plural of the noun *beauty:* _____.

beauties

■ The verb *occupy* ends in *y* preceded by a [consonant, vowel].

consonant

■ When adding the suffix *ed* to the verb *occupy,* you [do, do not] change the *y* to *i* before adding *ed*.

do

■ The suffix *ing* begins with the vowel __.

i

■ Because *ing* begins with an *i*, you must [drop, keep] the *y* in *occupy* before adding the *ing*.

keep

■ Add the suffix *ing* to *occupy:* _____.

occupying

■ Two elderly ladies _____ [occupy + ed] the space reserved for Mr. Brown and his wife.

occupied

■ In the evening the parents occupy themselves in reading; the boy occup__es himself in playing the piano.

i

■ The study of plane geometry is _____ [occupy + ing] most of Jim's time this summer.

occupying

■ Now look at the word *pity*. It ends in *y* preceded by the consonant __.

t

■ When you add any suffix except *ing* to the word *pity*, you must change the __ to __.

y i

Third Person Singular Verb Form

■ The present tense of verbs ending in *y* for the third person singular is formed by changing the *y* to *i* and adding *es*. For example, he *tries;* she _____.

tries

■ He _____ [present tense of *try*] to earn as much money as he can.

tries

■ Gerald _____ [present tense of *try*] very hard.

tries

■ Look at the verb *cry*. Now write the present tense for the third person singular: _____.

cries

■ He *cries;* she _____; John _____; Nancy _____.

cries
cries
cries

■ Now look at the verb *pity*. Write the present tense for the third person singular: _____.

pities

■ The boy _____ [present tense of *pity*] his father.

pities

■ Add the suffix *able* to the verb *pity:* _____.

pitiable

■ It is indeed a _____ [pity + ful] situation.

pitiful

■ The manager _____ [present tense of *rely*] too much on his son.

relies

■ Write the present tense of the verb *carry* in the following sentence: He _____ the large cartons up the steep stairs to the attic.

carries

y Plus ly

■ *ly* is another example of a suffix that can be added to words to form adverbs. Look at the word *busy,* which ends in *y* preceded by a consonant. In adding the suffix *ly* to the adjective *busy,* you change the __ to __.

y i

busily

■ Add the suffix *ly* to the adjective *busy:* _____.

busily

■ The girls were _____ [busy + ly] engaged in housework.

consonant

■ Just as the adjective *busy* ends in *y* preceded by a consonant, so does the adjective *angry* end in *y* preceded by a _____.

y

■ If you add the suffix *ly* to *angry,* you must change the __ to *i* and add *ly.*

angrily

■ Add the suffix *ly* to the adjective *angry:* _____.

angrily

■ Joe turned around and spoke _____ [angry + ly] to his sister.

consonant

■ The adjective *cozy* is a word like *busy* and *angry.* It also ends in *y* preceded by a [vowel, consonant].

y i
ly

■ When you add the suffix *ly* to the adjective *cozy,* you must change the __ to __ and add _____.

cozily

■ Add the suffix *ly* to the adjective *cozy:* _____.

cozily

■ The two little girls were sitting _____ [cozy + ly] in the big chair.

cozily

■ The baby was snuggled _____ [cozy + ly] in its crib.

i

■ If you add the suffix *ness* to the same word *cozy,* you must change the *y* to __ and add *ness.*

coziness

■ Add the suffix *ness* to the adjective *cozy:* _____.

coziness

■ The state of being cozy is called _____ [cozy + ness].

Review

If a word ending in y is preceded by a consonant, you change the y to i before adding a suffix beginning with a vowel except ing.

■ Look at the underlined word in the following sentence: Shakespeare has written some of the world's greatest *tragedies*. State the generalization used in the spelling of this plural form.

denying

■ I am not _____ [deny + ing] that I was there.

occupied

■ The boy was _____ [occupy + ed] with his own thoughts.

beautiful

■ The red carnations and roses are _____ [beauty + ful].

angrily

■ The man spoke _____ [angry + ly] to the crowd.

cozily

■ We sat _____ [cozy + ly] at the edge of the water.

pitiless

■ His words were cruel and _____ [pity + less].

busily

■ He was _____ [busy + ly] engaged in building a house.

In adding the suffix ing to a word ending in y preceded by a consonant, you keep the y.

■ Look at the italicized word in this sentence: Nora has been *studying* very hard this semester. State the generalization used in adding the suffix.

business

■ My father left the electronics firm and went into _____ [busy + ness] for himself.

accompanying

■ Social studies teachers are _____ [accompany + ing] the winners of the contest to Washington, D.C.

Words ending in *y* preceded by a vowel keep the *y* before adding a suffix.

■ State the generalization used in spelling the italicized word in the following sentence: The high school seniors who had the leading parts in the class play were commended for their fine *portrayal* of President Jackson and his wife.

do

■ Words ending in *y* preceded by a consonant [do, do not] change the *y* to *i* before adding any suffix except *ing*.

displayed

■ During the Thanksgiving holidays, the department stores _____ [display + ed] their Christmas items.

journeys

■ The plural form of *journey* is _____.

dismayed

■ When my father heard the news of the crash, he was _____ [dismay + ed].

tragedies

■ The plural form of the noun *tragedy* is _____.

tragedies

■ Aristotle laid down certain requirements for Greek _____ [plural of *tragedy*].

clumsily

■ He laid the box down very _____ [clumsy + ly].

copying

■ I spent a great deal of time _____ [copy + ing] my notes.

enemies

■ The newspaper stated that the dead man had many _____ [plural of *enemy*].

merciful

■ When the native was captured, he screamed, "Be _____ [mercy + ful]."

employing

■ The lumber company is now _____ [employ + ing] five hundred workers.

steadying

■ David Cunningham has been a _____ [steady + ing] influence on my father.

relayed

■ The secretary _____ [relay + ed] my message.

accompanying

■ The manager asked whether my folks were _____ [accompany + ing] me on the trip to Florida.

societies

■ There are three _____ [plural of *society*] that a student can join.

salaries

■ Don earns good _____ [plural of *salary*] from both firms.

companies

■ The two _____ [plural of *company*] merged last year.

cemeteries

■ We visited four _____ [plural of *cemetery*] in the city.

dictionaries

■ Our library has both unabridged and abridged _____ [plural of *dictionary*].

copying

■ Ronald spent three hours in _____ [copy+ing] his notes.

allies

■ The pact for peace was made by the six _____ [plural of *ally*] of Europe.

consonant

■ Before adding any suffix except *ing*, you must change the *y* to *i* in words that end in *y* preceded by a _____.

vowel

■ Before adding a suffix, you must keep the *y* in words that end in *y* preceded by a _____.

keep

■ Before adding the suffix *ing* to a word ending in *y* preceded by a consonant, you [drop, keep] the *y*.

studying

■ Many students should do more _____ [study + ing] than they do.

chapter 5

Plurals

Do you have difficulty in deciding when to add *s* or *es* to form the plural from the singular? Do you know when to drop the *y* at the end of a word, or change the *y* to *i* and add *es* to form the plural?

This chapter on the formation of plurals will give you very definite information on when to add *s* or *es*, when to keep or drop the *y* at the end of a word, plus other workable and usable generalizations. Study them carefully.

Test for Chapter 5

In the spaces below, write the plural forms of the words listed.

1. addendum _____	21. knife _____
2. princess _____	22. speech _____
3. penalty _____	23. tragedy _____
4. tariff _____	24. cemetery _____
5. display _____	25. army _____
6. veto _____	26. tax _____
7. soprano _____	27. potato _____
8. prefix _____	28. plaintiff _____
9. attorney _____	29. diary _____
10. witness _____	30. brush _____
11. handkerchief _____	31. grief _____
12. mosquito _____	32. photo _____
13. ally _____	33. suffix _____
14. Negro _____	34. hero _____
15. datum _____	35. crisis _____
16. wife _____	36. church _____
17. alley _____	37. analysis _____
18. contralto _____	38. academy _____
19. pulley _____	39. parenthesis _____
20. ambush _____	40. thief _____

Singular and Plural

■ The word *singular* pertains to a word form denoting one person, thing, or instance. The word *plural* denotes more than _____ person, thing, or instance.

one

■ The word *clocks* designates more than one clock, and is the [singular, plural] form of the word *clock*.

plural

■ The word *strips* is the [singular, plural] form of the word *strip*.

plural

■ If you speak of just one *table,* you are using the [singular, plural] form.

singular

■ The word *chair* is the [plural, singular] form.

singular

■ When you denote one person or thing, you use the singular form. When you denote more than one person or thing, you use the _____ form.

plural

■ The word *chairs* is the _____ form of *chair*.

plural

■ The word *shoe* is the _____ form of *shoes*.

singular

■ The word *pencil* is the _____ form of *pencils*.

singular

■ The word *erasers* is the [singular, plural] form of *eraser*.

plural

Generalization 1

■ Generally, the plural of most nouns is formed by adding *s*. For example, the plural form of *book* is _____.

books

■ If Mr. Jones plans to buy more than one *lot* in the new suburb, he will buy several _____.

lots

■ The plural form of *house* is _____.

houses

screens

■ The plural form of *screen* is _____.

floors

■ If the singular form is *floor*, the plural form is _____.

Most plurals are
  formed by adding
  s.

■ The plural of *home* is formed in this way: *homes*. State the generalization used.

princes

■ The royal family consists of the king, the queen, a princess, and two prince___.

buildings

■ The architect asked the commissioner how many _____ [plural of *building*] were being built in the area.

rink

■ There is only one _____ [singular of *rinks*] in the city.

stables

■ The company owns several riding _____ [plural of *stable*].

Generalization 2

■ Sometimes the plural is formed by adding *es* instead of just *s*. Study carefully the following generalization: If the noun ends in *ch, sh, s, x*, or *z*, add the letters _____ to the singular form.

es

■ Nouns ending in *ch, sh, s, x*, or *z* take _____ to form the plural.

es

■ Add *es* to the singular form of nouns ending in *ch, sh, s, x*, or *z* to form the _____.

plural

■ The noun *church* ends in *ch*. To form the plural you add _____.

es

■ A large city has several _____ [plural of *church*].

churches

churches	■ Several denominations of _____ [plural of *church*] are uniting under one head.
es	■ Just as *church* takes *es* to form the plural, the noun *arch* also takes _____.
ch	■ You add *es* to form the plural of *arch* because it ends in _____.
arches	■ The dictionary shows an illustration of seven different _____ [plural of *arch*] used in building construction.
arch	■ When Mr. Thompson built his new house, he put an _____ [singular of *arches*] between the living room and the dining room.
es	■ The noun *bush* ends in *sh;* therefore it takes _____ to form the plural.
bushes	■ The gardener planted several kinds of _____ [plural of *bush*] along the side paths to the house.
bush	■ Mr. Day planned to transplant the _____ [singular of *bushes*] in his lot near the lake.
sh	■ Like *bush,* the noun *brush* also ends in _____.
es	■ To form the plural of *brush* you add _____.
brushes	■ Many housewives buy all their _____ [plural of *brush*] from the local brush company.
toothbrushes	■ Jim has two _____ [plural of *toothbrush*].
To form the plural of nouns ending in *ch, sh, s, x,* or *z,* you add *es.*	■ The plural of *wish* is *wishes;* of *bunch, bunches;* of *muss, musses;* of *buzz; buzzes.* State the generalization used in forming these plurals.

gases

■ Nouns ending in *s* take *es* to form the plural. The plural of gas is _____.

es

■ To form the plural of *gas,* you add ____.

gases

■ The plural of *gas* is _____.

es

■ The plurals of *princess* and *witness* are formed by adding ____ to the singular.

princesses

■ The company assembled in the ballroom of the royal palace bowed as the three _____ [plural of *princess*] came into the room.

witnesses

■ The plural of *witness* is _____.

witnesses

■ The prosecutor called several _____ [plural of *witness*] to the stand.

princesses

■ If the singular form is *princess,* the plural form is _____.

es

■ The word *tax* is an example of a word ending in *x.* To form the plural you add ____.

taxes

■ The government is trying to reduce personal income _____ [plural of *tax*].

taxes

■ A student of law must learn about various kinds of _____ [plural of *tax*].

es

■ Like the noun *tax,* the noun *fox* ends in *x* and forms its plural by adding ____.

foxes

■ When the company offered ten dollars for animal skins, the four boys brought in the pelts of five _____ [plural of *fox*].

es

■ The noun *buzz* ends in *z;* therefore, it takes ____ to form the plural.

buzzes

■ The plural form of the noun *buzz* is _____.

buzzes

■ The receptionist devised the following system: one buzz for a telephone call; two _____ [plural of *buzz*] for the arrival of a client.

waltz

■ The singular from of *waltzes* is _____.

addresses

■ The plural form of *address* is _____.

watches

■ The plural form of *watch* is _____.

address

■ The plural form of *addresses* is formed from the singular _____.

prefixes

■ The plural form of *prefix* is _____.

s

■ Generally, most nouns form their plurals by adding __ to the singular form.

es

■ To form the plural of nouns ending in *sh, ch, s, x,* or *z* you add _____.

Generalization 3

e

■ Now let us look at nouns that end in *y*. A noun that ends in a *y* which is preceded by a vowel takes *s* to form the plural. For example, the noun *monkey* ends in *y* preceded by the vowel __.

s

■ If a noun ends in *y* which is preceded by a vowel, you add __ to form the plural.

vowel

■ The nouns *toy, key,* and *buy* are examples of words which end in *y* preceded by a _____.

toys

■ The plural of *toy* is _____.

■ The plurals of the nouns *boy* and *toy* are formed by adding ___.

s

■ The plural form of the noun *guy* is _____.

guys

■ The locksmith made three _____ [plural of *key*] for the front door.

keys

■ The plurals of the nouns *bay* and *guy* are formed by adding ___.

s

■ If a noun ends in *y* preceded by a vowel, the plural of that noun is formed by adding ___.

s

Generalization 4

■ On the other hand, if a word ends in *y* preceded by a consonant, the plural is formed by changing the *y* to *i* and adding *es*. For example, the plural of the noun *sky* is *sk*___.

sk*ies*

■ When you form the plural of a noun ending in *y* preceded by a consonant, you change the *y* to ___ and add ___.

i
es

■ Look at the noun *army*. It ends in *y* preceded by the consonant ___.

m

■ When you form the plural of the noun *army,* you must change the ___ to ___ and add ___.

y i
es

■ The commander-in-chief suggested that the _____ [plural of *army*] of the three nations be placed under the control of one chief.

armies

■ Like the noun *army*, the noun *ally* ends in *y* preceded by a _____.

consonant

■ To form the plural of *ally,* you must change the *y* to *i* and add ___.

es

allies

■ Countries that are united by a treaty or league are called _____ [plural of *ally*].

alleys

■ The alderman of the Seventh Ward said that all the _____ [plural of *alley*] between Pleasant and Pillsbury Avenues will be paved this year.

change the *y* to *i* and add *es*

■ The noun *diary* ends in *y* preceded by a consonant. Therefore, you must _____ to form the plural.

diaries

■ A daily record of personal items or memos is called a *diary*. Several of these records would be _____.

diary

■ Authors of biographies usually use personal letters and a _____ [singular of *diaries*] to give color and interest to their stories.

penalty

■ The singular of *penalties* is _____.

es

■ To form the plural of the noun *penalty*, you change the *y* to *i* and add _____.

penalties

■ A *penalty* is a punishment for some crime or offense. More than one penalty would be _____.

penalties

■ Crimes and offenses are punished by _____ [plural of *penalty*] which are appropriate for the crimes.

The plural ending *s* is usually added to the singular form.

■ The plural of *street* is *streets*. State the generalization used.

Nouns ending in *ch, sh, s, x, z,* take *es* to form the plural.

■ The plural of *branch* is formed in this manner: *branches*. State the generalization used.

To form the plural add *es* to a word ending in *y* preceded by a consonant.

■ The plural of *salary* is *salaries*. State the generalization used in forming this plural.

To form the plural add *s* to a word ending in *y* preceded by a vowel.

■ The plural of *valley* is formed in this manner: *valleys*. State the generalization used.

Generalization 5

radios

■ Nouns ending in *o* preceded by a vowel add *s* to form the plural. For example, the plural of *radio* is _____.

vowel

■ You add *s* when a noun ends in *o* which is preceded by a [vowel, consonant].

vowel

■ To form the plural of *radio*, you add *s* because the *o* is preceded by a [vowel, consonant].

radios

■ The plural form of *radio* is _____.

radios

■ We have two television sets, one phonograph, and three _____ [plural of *radio*] in our house.

s

■ Like the noun *radio*, the plural of the noun *cameo* is formed by adding ___.

vowel

■ The noun *cameo* ends in *o* preceded by a [vowel, consonant].

cameos

■ When my brother was stationed in Europe, he purchased several beautiful _____ [plural of *cameo*].

s

■ Like the noun *cameo*, the noun *zoo* forms its plural by adding ___.

zoos

■ I have visited all the large _____ [plural of *zoo*] in the country.

s

■ The nouns *radio, cameo,* and *zoo* form the plural by adding ___.

Generalization 6

■ Most nouns ending in *o* preceded by a *consonant* take *es* to form the plural. For instance, the noun *echo* ends in *o* preceded by the consonant ___.

h

■ The plural form of the noun *echo* is _____.

echoes

■ The children loved to stand in the cave just to shout their names and hear the weird _____ [plural of *echo*].

echoes

■ The noun *mosquito* is another word that takes *es* to form the plural. Spell the plural of this word: _____.

mosquitoes

■ To form the plural of *mosquito,* you must add *es* because the word ends in *o* preceded by a _____.

consonant

■ Insect repellant must be used at outdoor picnics in the summer so that the _____ [plural of *mosquito*] will not drive the picnickers away.

mosquitoes

■ Like the nouns *echo* and *mosquito,* the noun *veto* takes ___ to form the plural.

es

■ The noun *veto* is one of the words ending in *o* that takes ___ to form the plural.

es

■ In the history of the United Nations, Russia has cast more _____ [plural of *veto*] than any other country.

vetoes

■ The nouns *potato* and *tomato* end in *o* preceded by a consonant. To form the plural you add ___.

es

■ The plural form of *potato* is _____.

potatoes

■ The plural form of *tomato* is _____.

tomatoes

■ This season the farmers planted two kinds of _____ [plural of *potato*].

potatoes

■ I bought three pounds of _____ [plural of *tomato*] at the supermarket.

tomatoes

■ The singular of *potatoes* is _____.

potato

■ The singular of *tomatoes* is _____.

tomato

■ The noun *hero* also ends in *o*, and like the noun *potato*, takes _____ to form the plural.

es

■ Many a young boy tries to copy the lives of _____ [plural of *hero*] from the past.

heroes

■ The noun *Negro* ends in *o* preceded by the consonant _____.

r

■ The singular form is *Negro;* the plural form is _____.

Negroes

■ When Sherman's troops marched through Georgia, many of the _____ [plural of *Negro*] followed the soldiers, hoping to find freedom from slavery.

Negroes

■ Just as the noun *Negro* adds *es* to form the plural, so does the noun *torpedo* add _____.

es

■ To form the plural of the noun *torpedo,* you add *es.* The plural is spelled _____.

torpedoes

■ When the officer sighted the enemy, he shouted, "Man the _____ [plural of *torpedo*]."

torpedoes

■ The noun *tornado* ends in *o* preceded by a consonant; therefore, it takes _____ to form the plural.

es

■ Whirling winds and funnel-shaped clouds are characteristics of _____ [plural of *tornado*].

tornadoes

■ The noun *photo* is an exception to the generalization you have just learned. Although it ends in *o* preceded by a consonant, it takes just *s* to form the plural. The plural of photo is spelled _____.

photos

■ His nephews amused themselves by looking at the _____ [plural of *photo*] in the family album.

photos

■ The newspapers printed several _____ [plural of *photo*] of the swirling floodwaters.

photos

Generalization 7

■ Some other nouns that end in *o* preceded by a consonant take *s* to form the plural, as, for example, nouns that are musical in nature. For instance, the plural of the noun *soprano* is _____.

sopranos

■ Nouns ending in *o* that are musical in nature just take ___ to form the plural.

s

■ The nouns *soprano, alto, contralto, piano,* and *solo* are musical in nature and therefore take the letter ___ to form the plural.

s

■ The plural of *soprano* is _____.

sopranos

■ The plural form of *alto* is spelled _____.

altos

■ The singular form of *contraltos* is spelled _____.

contralto

■ The plural of *piano* is _____.

pianos

■ The singular of *solos* is spelled _____.

solo

■ There were too many _____ [plural of *soprano*] in the choir.

sopranos

altos

■ Mr. Krieger, the choir director, pleaded for more
_____ [plural of *alto*] to join the glee club.

■ The music director preferred to have more instru-
mental duos and trios on the program, rather than all

solos

vocal _____ [plural of *solo*].

■ Marian Anderson is one of the leading _____

contraltos

[plural of *contralto*] of our times.

Review

■ Including the old-fashioned player piano in the base-
ment, there were four _____ [plural of *piano*] in
the Ball home.

pianos

Most nouns ending
in *o* preceded by
a consonant take
es to form the
plural.

■ The plural of *torpedo* is *torpedoes*. State the generalization used.

Nouns ending in *o*
that are musical
in nature take *s*
to form the plural.

■ The plural of *soprano* is formed in this way: sopranos.
State the generalization used.

es

■ Just as you add *es* to form the plural of *echo,* you add
_____ to the singular form of *potato* and *tomato.*

vetoes

■ The plural of the noun *veto* is _____.

contraltos

■ The plural form of *contralto* is _____.

heroes

■ There were many heroes of the past just as there are
many _____ [plural of *hero*] of the present.

Negro

■ The singular form of the noun *Negroes* is spelled
_____.

solos

■ Write the plural of *solo:* _____

tornadoes

■ There is always a danger of _____ [plural of *tornado*].

mosquito

■ The child was severely bitten by a _____ [singular of *mosquitoes*].

pianos

■ The plural form of the noun *piano* is _____.

penalties

■ The plural form of the noun *penalty* is _____.

change the *y* to *i* and add *es*.

■ To form the plural of *dairy,* you must _____.

allies

■ The plural form of the noun *ally* is _____.

army

■ The singular form of the noun *armies* is _____.

prefixes

■ For both reading and spelling, a knowledge of suffixes and _____ [plural of *prefix*] is very helpful.

compresses

■ The doctor ordered the nurse to put cold _____ [plural of *compress*] on the patient's arm.

screeches

■ The official's wife was frightened by the _____ [plural of *screech*] of the natives.

speeches

■ The candidates agreed to make only two _____ [plural of *speech*] on television.

squashes

■ There are usually three species of cultivated _____ [plural of *squash*].

attorneys

■ The case was handled by three famous _____ [plural of *attorney*].

academies

■ The city now has seven private _____ [plural of *academy*].

pulleys	■ The boy attached the box to a hook and then operated the _____ [plural of *pulley*] to lift it up.
cemeteries	■ On Memorial Day the widow attended services at two _____ [plural of *cemetery*].
chimneys	■ On a windy day the sky is filled with black smoke from the _____ [plural of *chimney*].
tragedies	■ William Shakespeare wrote some of the finest _____ [plural of *tragedy*] in English literature.
virtues	■ The elderly lady was embarrassed by the magazine article which told of her many _____ [plural of *virtue*].
photos	■ The plural form of photo is _____.

Generalization 8

s	■ Generally, nouns ending in *f, fe,* or *ff* form their plurals by adding *s*. For example, the nouns belie*f*, stri*fe*, and sheri*ff* take ___ to form the plural.
s	■ Generally nouns ending in *f, fe,* and *ff* form their plurals by adding ___.
beliefs	■ The plural of *belief* would therefore be written _____.
s	■ The noun *belief* is a word that ends in *f* and takes ___ to form the plural.
beliefs	■ The class is studying the historical background of several religious _____ [plural of *belief*].
s	■ Just as *belief* takes *s* to form the plural, the noun *grief* also takes ___.

plural

■ The noun *grief* takes *s* to form the [singular, plural].

griefs

■ The young widow had many sorrows and _____ [plural of *grief*] during her brief marriage.

s

■ The noun *handkerchief* also takes __ to form the plural.

handkerchiefs

■ Watch the spelling of this word as you write the plural form of *handkerchief:* _____.

handkerchiefs

■ Mary received several embroidered _____ [plural of *handkerchief*] for her birthday.

s

■ Just as *handkerchief* takes *s* to form the plural, the noun *proof* also takes __.

proofs

■ James showed us the _____ [plural of *proof*] of his graduation picture.

s

■ The noun *fife* is a good example of a word ending in *fe* and taking __ to form the plural.

fifes

■ The bandmaster was able to recruit thirty _____ [plural of *fife*] for the Spirit of '76 tableau.

s

■ The noun *strife* also ends in *fe* and takes __ to form the plural.

strifes

■ A *strife* is a conflict or fight. More than one conflict or fight would be called _____.

ff

■ The noun *tariff* ends in _____ and takes *s* to form the plural.

s

■ To form the plural of *tariff* you add __ because the noun ends in *ff*.

■ Systems of duties imposed by a government on goods imported or exported are called _____ [plural of *tariff*].

tariffs

■ To form the plural of *tariff* you add *s*. To form the plural of *sheriff* you also add __.

s

■ The next convention to be held at the hotel will be the meeting of the county _____ [plural of *sheriff*].

sheriffs

■ Like the noun *tariff*, the plural form of the noun *plaintiff* is formed by adding __.

s

■ In the suit brought against the drug manufacturer there were three _____ [plural of *plaintiff*].

plaintiffs

Most nouns ending in *f*, *fe*, or *ff* add *s* to form the plural.

■ The plural of *belief* is *beliefs*; of *strife*, *strifes*; of *buff*, *buffs*. State the generalization used to form these plurals.

■ A few nouns, however, change the *f* or *fe* into *ves* to form the plural. For instance, the plural of *calf* is *cal*____.

calves

■ There are several young _____ [plural of *calf*] on Mr. Brown's farm.

calves

■ Like the noun *calf*, the noun *elf* changes the *f* to _____ to form the plural.

ves

■ The story that the children liked best was the one about the fairies and the _____ [plural of *elf*].

elves

■ Like *elf*, the noun *half* changes the *f* to _____ to form the plural.

ves

■ Benny cut the apple into _____ [plural of *half*].

halves

f
ves

■ The noun *shelf* also forms its plural by changing the ___ to _____.

shelves

■ The storekeeper lined the _____ [plural of *shelf*] with red paper.

ves

■ The noun *thief* forms its plural by changing the *f* to _____.

thieves

■ My uncle chased the _____ [plural of *thief*] for two blocks.

kni*ves*

■ Three words ending in *fe* change the *fe* to *ves* to form the plural: *knife, wife,* and *life*. The plural of *knife* is *kni____*.

lives

■ In the last flood many _____ [plural of *life*] were lost.

wives

■ The ball was attended by all the officers and their _____ [plural of *wife*].

knives

■ Anne put forks and spoons on the table but forgot the _____ [plural of *knife*].

Most nouns ending in *f, fe,* or *ff* take *s* to form the plural.

■ The plural of *sheriff* is *sheriffs*. State the generalization used in forming this plural.

Generalization 9

■ Many foreign words are from the Latin and so Latin plurals are used. For instance, many Latin words which end in *um* take *a* to make the plural. The Latin word *datum* would be spelled *dat___* in its plural form.

data

■ If the plural of the Latin ending *um* is *a*, then the plural of the Latin word *datum* is *dat___*.

data

data

■ The word *datum* is a Latin word meaning a fact. A group of facts are called _____.

data

■ The researcher gathered the _____ [group of facts] by means of a questionnaire.

data

■ The educator decided that the students had not presented the _____ [group of facts] to prove their points.

addenda

■ Another Latin noun is *addendum,* which means an addition, like something added to a book. More than one addition, or *addendum,* are _____.

a

■ Like the noun *datum,* the Latin noun *addendum* ends in *um.* The plural of both words is formed by changing *um* to __.

addenda

■ The printers hope that there will not be too many _____ [plural of *addendum*] to the brochure.

addenda

■ Inasmuch as a great number of data were sent in after the official deadline, it will be necessary to publish several _____ [plural of *addendum*] to the report.

um
a

■ Just like *datum* and *addendum,* the Latin word *medium* forms its plural by changing the _____ to __.

media

■ The newspapers, radio, and television are three important _____ [plural of *medium*] for broadcasting the foreign and domestic news.

media

■ The store owner decided that the best way to increase his sales was to use all the _____ [plural of *medium*] of advertising.

Many Latin words ending in *um* take *a* to form the plural.

■ The plural of *bacterium* is *bacteria.* State the generalization used in forming this plural.

■ Latin words that end in *um* take ___ to form the plural.

a

■ The plural of *datum* is _____.

data

■ The singular of *addenda* is _____.

addendum

■ The plural of *medium* is _____.

media

Generalization 10

■ Some Latin nouns end in *is* in the singular form. To make these nouns plural the *is* is changed to *es*. A familiar word in this class of nouns is *crisis*. The plural of *crisis* would be *cris*___.

crise*s*

■ To form the plural of Latin nouns that end in *is*, change the *is* to ___.

es

■ The plural of *crisis* is written _____.

crises

■ The plural noun that means more than one turning point is _____.

crises

■ Almost every adult has had several _____ [plural of *crisis*] in his life.

crises

■ In the last decade there have been many _____ [plural of *crisis*] in the world.

crises

■ Like the Latin noun *crisis*, the noun *analysis* ends in *is*. To form the plural of *analysis* you change the *is* to ___.

es

■ The plural form of *analysis* is _____.

analyses

■ If you make an analysis of a theory or topic, you separate it into its parts or elements. When you make more than one *analysis*, you are making several _____.

analyses

■ Three scientists made separate _____ [plural of *analysis*] of the new theory.

analyses

■ The Latin noun *synopsis* also ends in *is* and forms the plural by changing the *is* to _____.

es

■ If you write a *synopsis* of a story, you write a condensed statement of it. If you write several of these condensed statements, you write several *synops*_____.

synops*es*

■ The plural form of *synopsis* is _____.

synopses

■ Before I chose the final books for the reading list, I read several _____ [plural of *synopsis*] of each one.

synopses

■ The English teacher instructed her students to write a _____ [singular of *synopses*] of a novel by Charles Dickens.

synopsis

■ The Latin word *parenthesis* also forms the plural by changing the *is* ending to _____.

es

■ A *parenthesis* is one of the curved marks ( ) which are used to enclose a word or phrase inserted in a sentence. The two curved marks are called *parenthes*_____.

parenthes*es*

■ The plural form of *parenthesis* is _____.

parentheses

■ Write the singular form of *parentheses:* _____.

parenthesis

■ The two curved marks used to show an inserted word or phrase in a sentence are called _____.

parentheses

■ The student always forgot to enclose the topic numbers in _____.

parentheses

Many Latin words
ending in *is*
change the *is* to
es to form the
plural.

■ The plural of *hypothesis* is *hypotheses*. State the generalization used in forming this plural.

hypothes*es*

■ A *hypothesis* is a tentative theory or explanation. Several tentative theories or explanations are called *hypothes_____*.

hypotheses

■ The plural form of *hypothesis* is _____.

hypotheses

■ Several tentative theories are _____.

hypotheses

■ Arguments can be started by stating tentative theories or _____ [plural of *hypothesis*].

Review

analysis

■ The singular form of *analyses* is _____.

es

■ To form the plural of the Latin noun *crisis,* you change the *is* to _____.

synopses

■ Condensed statements are called _____ [plural of *synopsis*].

hypotheses

■ The plural form of *hypothesis* is _____.

parentheses

■ The curved marks ( ) are called _____.

cutoffs

■ Applying the generalization of plurals of nouns ending in *f, fe,* or *ff,* write the plural form of the noun *cutoff:* _____.

tariffs

■ The plural of *tariff* is _____.

plaintiffs

■ The plural form of *plaintiff* is _____.

handkerchiefs	■ Bill bought his mother three white linen _____ [plural of *handkerchief*].
knives	■ Mrs. Browning asked Susan to put the forks and _____ [plural of *knife*] on the table.
halves	■ If you divide an apple in half, you will have two _____.
data	■ A group of facts are called _____ [plural of *datum*].
heroes	■ Every country has its long list of _____ [plural of *hero*].
media	■ The plural of *medium* is _____.
torpedo	■ Write the singular form of *torpedoes:* _____.
mosquitoes	■ Write the plural of *mosquito:* _____.
valleys	■ The plural of *valley* is _____.
academies	■ Write the plural of *academy:* _____.
es	■ To form the plural of nouns like *echo, Negro, veto,* or *potato,* you add ___ to the singular.
oases	■ Write the plural of the noun *oasis:* _____.
s	■ Generally, most nouns take ___ to form the plural.
es	■ Generally, nouns ending in *sh, ch, s, x,* or *z* take ___ to form the plural.
A noun ending in *y* preceded by a vowel takes *s* to form the plural.	■ The plural of *monkey* is *monkeys.* State the generalization used to form this plural.

A noun ending in *y* preceded by a consonant changes the *y* to *i* and adds *es* to form the plural.

■ The plural of *cemetery* is *cemeteries*. State the generalization used to form this plural.

If a noun ends in *o* which is preceded by a vowel, add *s* to form the plural.

■ The plural of *radio* is *radios;* of *cameo, cameos;* of *zoo, zoos*. State the generalization used to form these plurals.

s

■ Nouns ending in *o* that are musical in nature (like *alto, soprano,* and *basso*) take ___ to form the plural.

Most nouns ending in *f, fe,* or *ff* take *s* to form the plural.

■ The plural of *chief* is *chiefs;* of *strife, strifes;* of *bailiff, bailiffs*. State the generalization used to form these plurals.

Some nouns ending in *f* or *fe* change the *f* to *ves* to form the plural.

■ The plural of *thief* is *thieves*. State the generalization used to form this plural.

a

■ Many Latin nouns ending in *um* change the um to ___ to form the plural.

es

■ Many Latin nouns ending in *is* change the *is* to _____ to form the plural.

ie and ei

When should you use *ie* as in *chief* or *ei* as in *receive* or *weird*?

Most of you undoubtedly remember a little verse from your elementary school days:

i before *e*,
Except after *c*,
Or when sounded like *a*,
As in *neighbor* and *weigh*.

Sounds childish? Perhaps it does, but upon this little verse lies your success in spelling words with the combined letters *ie* or *ei*. Study the generalizations carefully, work out the spelling of all the words, and apply what you learn to the spelling of other words that contain the combination of *i* and *e*.

Test for Chapter 6

Fill in the missing letters in the words below:

1. To ease means to rel_____ve.
2. To regain or recover is to retr_____ve.
3. Vanity is another word for conc_____t.
4. To get means to rec_____ve.
5. The head of a tribe is usually called a ch_____f.
6. To see is to perc_____ve.
7. Our best friend is our n_____ghbor next door.
8. The postman offered to w_____gh all my packages.
9. Nancy bought a new v_____l for her hat.
10. Doc Adams has an enlarged v_____n in his right arm.
11. King Henry VIII r_____gned over thirty years.
12. To be lacking in something is to be defic_____nt.
13. The early settlers made their homes on the front_____r.

14. To be well versed in an art is to be profic_____nt.
15. We went on a sl_____gh ride yesterday afternoon.
16. To have enough is to have a suffic_____nt amount.
17. Odd or unusual is the meaning of the word w_____rd.
18. Free time is called l_____sure.
19. A forgery is a counterf_____t.
20. When you measure how tall you are, you are measuring your h_____ght.
21. An earthen mug is called a st_____n.
22. To accomplish means to ach_____ve.
23. To lose the right to something is to forf_____t it.
24. A quantity of yarn put up in a large loop is a sk_____n.
25. When the th_____f came around the corner, I tried to s_____ze him by the coat.

Generalization 1

retrieve

■ When *i* and *e* are combined to give the sound represented by the letter *e* (a long *e*), they are usually written *ie* after any letter *but c,* as in *relieve* and *retr_____ve.*

e

■ When *i* and *e* are combined to give the sound of a long ___, they are usually written *ie,* except after *c.*

relieve

■ To *relieve* means to ease; therefore, to ease means to _____.

retrieve

■ To *retrieve* means to recover or regain; therefore, to recover or regain means to _____.

retrieve

■ If a person will regain his freedom, he will _____ it.

rel*ie*ve

■ There are many new drugs on the market which help to *rel_____ve* discomfort and pain suffered by many people.

c

■ The verb *receive* is spelled with the *e* before the *i* because these two letters follow the letter ___.

rece*i*ve

■ To *relieve* means to ease; to get means to *rec_____ve.*

rece*ive* rel*ieve*	■ The patient will *rec*_____ a prescription from the doctor which will *rel*_____ the pain.
c	■ When *i* and *e* are combined to give the sound represented by the letter *e*, they are usually written *ie*, except after the letter ___.
rece*ive*	■ It is with a great feeling of relief that I shall *rec*_____*ve* the money.
relieve	■ To ease means to _____.
receive	■ To get means to _____.
dece*ive*	■ To mislead or cheat means to *dec*_____*ve*.
c	■ The verb *perceive* means to see. The *e* comes before the *i* because these two letters follow the letter ___.
perce*ive*	■ To see means to *perc*_____*ve*.
dece*ives*	■ A person who misleads or cheats another *dec*_____*ves* him.
retrieve	■ To recover or regain is to _____.
receive	■ To get is to _____.
perceive	■ To see is to _____.
retrieve	■ To recover or regain is to _____.
receive	■ My principal told me that I would _____ [get] a scholarship from the state college.
retrieve	■ Susan dropped her watch in the well and her brother climbed down to _____ [recover] it.

relieve

■ The patient begged the physician to give him a pill to _____ [ease] the pain.

receive

■ The clerk at the hardware store promised that we would _____ [get] the screens in two days.

deceive

■ To mislead or cheat is to _____.

perceives

■ If one sees a problem clearly, he *perc___ves* it.

retrieve

■ To recover or regain a lost article is to _____ it.

Generalization 2

ie
c

■ When *i* and *e* are combined to give the sound represented by the letter *e* (a long *e*), they are usually written ____ after any letter but __.

weigh

■ When *i* and *e* are combined to give the long sound of *a*, they are usually written *ei* as in *neighbor* and *w___gh*.

a

■ In the word *weigh* the *ei* has the sound of a long __.

long

■ In the noun *neighbor* the *ei* is pronounced as a _____ *a*.

weigh

■ The postman said that he would *w___gh* the package in a few minutes.

long

■ The *ei* combination in *weigh* and *neighbor* has the sound of a _____ *a*.

neighbor

■ The man who lives next door is my *n___ghbor*.

neighbor
weigh

■ Mr. Jones, my *n___bor*, offered to *w___* the packages I wanted to send to my cousin in Europe.

e i

■ When a word has a combination of *e* and *i* and these two letters have the sound of a long *a,* the ___ comes before the ___.

long

■ In the word *sleigh* the *e* comes before the *i* because the letters have the sound of a _____ *a.*

sleigh

■ One of the most pleasurable sports in the wintertime is a *sl____gh* ride.

sleigh

■ My grandfather asked us whether we wanted to go on a _____ ride.

a

■ The nouns *veil, vein,* and *skein* are spelled with the *ei* combination as they have the sound of a long ___.

veils

■ Women like *v____ls* on their hats.

veil

■ Joanne went downtown to buy a new _____ for her brown hat.

vein

■ A vessel which carries blood back to the heart is called a *v____n.*

vein

■ The student asked the anatomy teacher the location of the largest *v____n* in the human body.

skein

■ A quantity of yarn or silk which is put up in a large loop is called a *sk____n.*

skein

■ The homemaking instructor told her pupils to buy a *sk____n* of red yarn.

veil
skeins

■ Martha went to the store to buy a new *v____l* for her hat and three *sk____s* of yarn.

vein

■ Jim has an enlarged _____ in his leg.

long

■ The nouns *veil, skein,* and *vein* have the sound of a _____ *a.*

long

■ The verb *reign* also has the sound of a _____ *a*.

reign

■ The king will r_____gn for many years.

reign

■ The *r*_____ of King Henry VIII lasted about thirty-eight years.

Generalization 3

■ When *i* and *e* follow *c* and represent the sound of *sh*, they are written *ie*, as in *efficient* and *suffic*_____*nt*.

sufficient

■ *Sufficient* means enough, as in this sentence: We have _____ funds to meet all current expenses.

sufficient

■ There are three syllables in the word *sufficient:* suf/fi/cient. The first syllable is _____.

suf/fi/cient

■ The second syllable is suf/_____/cient.

suf/*fi*/cient

■ The last syllable is suf/fi/_____.

suf/fi/*cient*

■ This amount of money is _____ [enough].

sufficient

■ If I want to buy a new coat for $50 and have $75 in my spending account, then I have a *suf*_____ amount of money to pay for it.

suf*ficient*

■ If a person lacks a definite amount of something, it means he is *defic*_____*nt*.

deficient

■ The adjective *deficient* has three syllables: de/fi/cient. The first syllable is _____.

de/fi/cient

■ The second syllable is de/_____/cient.

de/*fi*/cient

■ The last syllable is de/fi/_____.

de/fi/*cient*

deficient

■ The adjective that means lacking or wanting is _____.

sufficient

■ The adjective that means enough is _____.

pro/fi/*cient*

■ Just as the adjectives *sufficient* and *deficient* end in *cient,* so does the adjective *proficient: profi*____.

proficient

■ *Proficient* means to be skilled or adept in an occupation as in this sentence: Susan is _____ in her administration of the nursery school.

pro/fi/cient

■ *Proficient* has three syllables: pro/fi/cient. Write the first syllable: ____.

pro/*fi*/cient.

■ The second syllable is pro/____/cient.

pro/fi/*cient*

■ The last syllable is pro/fi/____.

proficient

■ Write the word, saying it in syllables as you write: _____.

proficient

■ One who is well versed or skilled in his trade or occupation is called _____.

proficient

■ Mr. Hiram Jones has been nominated the most _____ worker in his trade.

Review

p*ie*ce

■ Aunt Mary divided the pie and gave each child a large *p*____*ce.*

y*ie*ld

■ On many occasions a driver has to *y*____*ld* the right of way to a pedestrian.

long

■ The noun *frontier* is a good example of the *i* before *e* giving the sound of a _____ *e.*

before	■ When *i* and *e* are combined to represent the sound of a long *a*, the *e* comes [before, after] the *i*.
long	■ The words *weigh, sleigh,* and *skein* all have the sound represented by *ā*: a _____ *a*.
e	■ The words *chief, niece,* and *achieve* are all pronounced with a long __.
thief	■ Someone who steals is a robber or a *th____f*.
brief	■ The instructor gave a very *br____f* lecture on tardiness.
receipt	■ I asked the mechanic for a *rec____pt* for the work done on the car.
ceiling	■ We plan to paint the *c____ling* of the living room tomorrow.
i before *e* except after *c;* also, the *ie* has the long sound of *e*.	■ State the *ie-ei* generalization used in the spelling of this word: *achieve*.
Write *ei* when these two letters represent the long sound of *a*.	■ State the *ie-ei* generalization used in spelling of *freight*.
i before *e* except after *c*.	■ State the *ie-ei* generalization used in the spelling of *deceive*.
When *i* and *e* are combined and follow *c* to represent the sound of *sh*, they are usually written *cie*.	■ State the *ie-ei* generalization used in the spelling of *efficient*.

Exceptions

■   There are exceptions, of course, to the generalizations you have just learned, and the best way to remember them is to practice spelling them. For example, the verb *seize* is always spelled this way: _____.

seize

■   To *seize* means to grasp; therefore to grasp means to _____.

seize

■   In the word which means to grasp, the *e* comes _____ the *i*.

before

■   When I came around the corner, the boy tried to _____ [grasp] my bag.

seize

■   When the girl began to kick and scream, he tried to _____ [grasp] her by the collar.

seize

■   *Either* and *n____ther* are also exceptions and are spelled with the *e* before the *i*.

neither

■   Two adjectives that are spelled with the *e* before the *i* are ____ther and *n____ther*.

either
neither

■   The teacher said that I had to choose ____ther one or the other.

either

■   We told Mrs. Brown that *n____ther* Susan nor Sandra found the gloves.

neither

■   The adjective *weird* is also spelled *w____rd*.

weird

■   Strange or fantastic is the definition of the adjective *w____rd*.

weird

■   The boy told a _____ tale of having been kidnapped for three hours.

weird

weird

■ An adjective which means strange or fantastic is
_____.

i

■ You will notice that the noun *leisure* also has the *e*
before the __.

leisure

■ *Leisure* can be defined as free time; therefore, time
during which one is not employed is called _____
time.

leisure

■ John asked me what I had planned to do in my
_____ [free] time.

leisure

■ Betty planned to read several novels during her
_____ [free] time.

before

■ The final *feit* in the words *forfeit* and *counterfeit* are
pronounced fit. You will notice that the *e* comes _____
the *i*.

for*feit*

■ The verb *forfeit* means to lose or lose the right to
something by some offense or crime. For example: The
King must *for*____ his claim to the throne.

forfeit

■ A verb which means to lose, or lose the right to, by
some error, offense, or crime, is _____.

forfeit

■ By the seriousness of his crime the traitor will
_____ [lose right to] his estate and all his personal
possessions.

counter*feit*

■ Another word that ends in feit is *counter*____.

counter*feit*

■ A *counter*____ is an imitation, also a forgery.

counterfeit

■ The prisoner admitted that he printed _____
money.

counterfeit

■ The ten-dollar bill was a poor piece of _____
money.

counterfeit

■ The two men printed illegal dollar bills. This illegal money is called _____.

e

■ The noun *height* is spelled with the __ before the *i*.

he*i*ght

■ If you measure how tall you are, you are measuring your *h___ght*.

height

■ As Tom had grown an inch this summer, his _____ was now 5 feet 6 inches.

height

■ When you measure how tall you are, you measure your _____.

stein

■ The word *height* is spelled with the *e* before the *i*, just as the noun which means an earthen mug: *st___n*.

ste*i*n

■ An earthen mug is called a *st___n*.

stein

■ The German bartender poured the ale into a large _____ [earthen mug].

*ei*der

■ The word *eider* is spelled ___*der*.

*ei*der

■ The soft down from the large female sea duck is called ___*der*.

eider

■ My pillow is filled with soft _____ down.

stein
he*i*ght

■ The *ei* combination in *eider* is the same as in *st___n* and *h___ght*.

height

■ When Joe measures how tall he is, he is measuring his _____.

weird

■ Robert had a _____ [strange] story about some ghosts in a haunted house.

stein

■ An earthen mug is called a _____.

eider

■ The soft down from a female sea duck is _____.

Review

counterfeit

■ An imitation or a forgery can be called a _____ .

forfeit

■ When Jack stole the money, he had to _____ [lose] his right to the scholarship.

receipt

■ When I paid my bill, I asked the dentist for a *rec____pt.*

seize

■ The three men attempted to _____ [grasp] the thief when he ran out of the house.

leisure

■ Mary requested that she be allowed to read during her _____ [free] hours.

achieve

■ To accomplish means to *ach____ve.*

priest

■ The girl visited the parish *pr____st* to discuss her wedding plans.

neighbor

■ The man who lives next door to us is our _____ .

relieve

■ To ease means to *re____.*

sleigh

■ If it snows tomorrow, our club will go on a _____ ride.

skein

■ A quantity of yarn put up in a large loop is called a *sk____.*

veil

■ Susie purchased a new *v____* for her hat.

receive

■ To get means to _____ .

deceive

■ To cheat or mislead is to _____ .

perceive

■ To see means to *perc____ve.*

retrieve

■ To recover or regain is to _____ .

neither

■ I will accept *n____ther* one nor the other.

chief

■ The main reason would be the *ch____f* reason.

achieve

■ To accomplish means to *ach____ve.*

conceit

■ Vanity is a word that means the same as *conc____t.*

sufficient

■ By the end of September I shall have _____ [enough] money to buy a new car.

deficient

■ To be lacking or wanting is the definition of the adjective _____.

proficient

■ To be skilled in a trade or occupation is the definition of the adjective _____.

seize

■ To grasp is to *s____ze.*

nieces

■ Mrs. Gray has one nephew and two *n____ces.*

weird

■ As I crossed the meadow I heard _____ [strange] sounds coming from the vacant house.

stein

■ An earthen mug is a _____.

veil

■ I need a new _____ for my blue hat.

reign

■ The commoners hope that the present king will *r____gn* for many years.

sleigh

■ Grandfather asked us if we wanted to go on a *sl____* ride.

leisure

■ Free time is called _____ time.

counterfeit

■ Imitation or forgery is the meaning of the word _____.

forfeit

■ To lose one's right to a claim is to _____ that claim.

brief

■ The speaker made his remarks *br____f.*

skein

■ A quantity of yarn or silk put up in a large loop is called a *sk____.*

either

■ When asked how I liked the two debaters, I replied that I did not like ____*ther* one.

neither

■ *N____ther* position interested me very much.

piece

■ Jimmy asked his mother for another *p____ce* of chocolate cake.

ie

■ When *e* and *i* are combined to represent the long sound of *e*, they are usually written ____ except after *c*.

i before e except after c.

■ *Receive* and *deceive* are spelled *ei*. State the generalization used.

When i and e are combined to represent the long sound of a, write them ei.

■ The words *sleigh* and *neighbor* are spelled *ei*. State the generalization used.

cie

■ When *i* and *e* are combined and follow *c* to represent the sound of *sh*, they are usually written *c____.*

counterfeit
forfeit

■ Two words whose last syllable is pronounced as *fit* are _____ and _____.

either
neither

■ Two exceptions to the *ie-ei* generalizations are spelled ____*ther* and *n____ther.*

seize
weird
height
leisure

■ The other exceptions we have studied are spelled *s____ze, w____rd, h____ght,* and *l____sure.*

chapter 7

Homonyms and Confused Words

Meaning is paramount in the spelling of homonyms and other words that are easily confused. In the first place, homonyms sound exactly alike: *principal, principle*. Other words are very similar in sound: *affect, effect*. The main difference, of course, is the meaning of each word. If you know that the word *principle* is a rule and the word *principal* means main or chief, you will cease to make these spelling errors.

This chapter is divided into two parts: homonyms and confused words. The explanation of each word is based on its meaning. In some cases several definitions have been given so that you may build up your vocabulary as well as your spelling. Study each word and use it appropriately in your daily work.

Test for Chapter 7

Choose the correct word from each set.

1. I placed the book [their, there, they're].　　　————
2. The material is very [course, coarse].　　　————
3. The students are writing their thank-you notes on their best [stationery, stationary].　　　————
4. The child asked [to, too, two] go along.　　　————
5. There were [to, too, two] men in the store.　　　————
6. "[Your, You're] right," she exclaimed.　　　————
7. We are [all ready, already] to leave for the coast.　　　————
8. The president of the company paid me a very high [compliment, complement].　　　————
9. The recommendations were presented by the city [counsel, council].　　　————
10. [Who's, Whose] book is this?　　　————
11. The dog wagged [its, it's] tail.　　　————

12. The usher escorted us down the center [isle, aisle]. _____
13. Rodney has difficulty in remembering the
    mathematical [principal, principle].   _____
14. We wanted lemon pie for [desert, dessert].   _____
15. The building where a state legislature meets is
    called a [capital, capitol].   _____
16. An island is an [isle, aisle].   _____
17. John had [all ready, already] gone to the beach.   _____
18. The clergyman was happy to [counsel, council]
    the couple.   _____
19. The children were told to remove [there, their]
    coats and hats.   _____
20. [Its, It's] going to rain.   _____
21. That is indeed a [morale, moral] question.   _____
22. The doctor said, "[Breath, Breathe] deeply."   _____
23. I am at a loss to know what to [advise, advice] him. _____
24. The question is whether I should [accept, except]
    the gift.   _____
25. Of the two solutions, the [later, latter] is the
    only sensible one.   _____
26. This has been [quite, quiet] a day!   _____
27. [Whether, Weather] you like it or not, I intend to
    go to the party.   _____
28. Mary put the [lose, loose] change in her purse.   _____
29. Great Britain is an [alley, ally] of the United States. _____
30. All the supervisors [accept, except] Mr. Johnson
    voted for the pay raise.   _____
31. The rain and snow will surely [affect, effect] the
    berry crop.   _____
32. What [advise, advice] can you give the newlyweds?   _____
33. The director spoke to all the [personal, personnel]
    of the plant.   _____
34. The [weather, whether] bureau predicted fair and
    sunny days.   _____
35. I hope that I will not [lose, loose] another pair of
    gloves this spring.   _____
36. The air you inhale and exhale is called [breath,
    breathe].   _____
37. The supply of ironing boards is in [access,
    excess] of the number needed for immediate sale.   _____
38. The patient must have a [quiet, quite] room.   _____
39. The dispute was a [personal, personnel] one.   _____
40. The [affect, effect] of his speech is unknown at
    this time.   _____

Homonyms

■ A *homonym* is any of two or more words alike in sound, but differing in meaning and spelling. The words *bear* and *bare* are pronounced the same but do not mean the same. They are called homo_____s.

homo*nym*s

■ If two words sound alike but do not have the same meaning or spelling, they are called _____nyms.

*homo*nyms

■ A *homonym* is any of two or more words that _____ alike but differ in meaning and spelling.

sound

■ A word that sounds like another but has a different meaning and spelling is called a _____.

homonym

■ Although the word *bear* has the same sound as *bare*, it does not have the same meaning and spelling. It is therefore called a _____.

homonym

■ The two words *herd* and *heard* are homonyms because they sound alike but [do, do not] have the same meaning and spelling.

do not

■ The noun *herd* signifies a group of animals assembled together, as in the sentence: The farmer had a large _____ of cattle on the farm.

herd

■ The past tense of the verb to hear is *heard,* as in this sentence: Yesterday I _____ the bells ring.

heard

■ As my cousin ran in the door, he shouted, "Have you _____ the news?"

heard

■ I watched the auctioneer trying to sell my father's _____ of cows.

herd

■ The sound of the whistle was [herd, heard] by all the workers in the fields.

heard

■ The shepherd watched his _____ of sheep all night.

herd

■ The two nouns *aisle* and *isle* sound alike and are often confused. However, they do not have the same meaning and spelling, so they can be called _____.

homonyms

■ The noun *aisle* is a passageway, as in the sentence: I went down the middle _____ of the theater looking for an empty seat.

aisle

■ An *isle* is an island: They sailed to an _____ on the Pacific Ocean.

isle

■ There was a narrow _____ between the rows of chairs.

aisle

■ The natives on the small _____ were very industrious.

isle

■ After the bridal couple walked down the center _____ of the cathedral, they left the church and boarded a ship to take them to the _____.

aisle
isle

■ The adverb *already* and the adjective phrase *all ready* sound alike. However, they are called homonyms because they differ in meaning and _____.

spelling

■ The adverb *already* means previously or earlier, as in this sentence: John had _____ left for the office.

already

■ The two words *all ready* are used as an adjective phrase, meaning all are ready or prepared. For example: When the whistle blew, the workers were ___ _____ to leave.

all ready

■ Some of the delegates had _____ left the convention hall.

already

■ The chauffeur asked us if we were _____ to leave.

all ready

■ Mary Adele tried to call Dick at the plant, but he had _____ left the building.

already

all ready

■ Susan called to friends, "Are you _____ to go?"

■ When Aunt Sarah arrived to take her brother's family to the lake, she found that her nephew had _____ gone with his friend, John Davis, but the rest of the family were _____ to go.

already
all ready

■ A certain kind of rough cloth is called *canvas.* This noun is confused with the word *canvass,* which means to solicit. The two words differ in meaning and spelling but are alike in sound. They are therefore called _____.

homonyms

■ *Canvas* (with one *s*) is a rough kind of cloth, as in this sentence: The heavy sacks were made of _____.

canvas

■ *Canvass* (with two *s*'s) can be used as a verb or noun. As a noun it means a gathering of votes or orders, as in this sentence: Volunteers started a campaign for the governor by making a door-to-door _____ of votes.

canvass

■ *Canvass* can be used as a verb, meaning to seek votes or orders, as in the following sentence: He asked us to _____ the neighborhood for votes.

canvass

■ Our school plans to _____ the business firms in the immediate vicinity.

canvass

■ The party members, carrying their campaign literature in _____ bags, made a _____ of the neighborhood to solicit votes for Mr. Jones.

canvas
canvass

■ The two nouns *capital* and *capitol* are pronounced the same, but do not have the same meaning and spelling. The capitol (spelled with an *o*) is the building in which a state legislature meets. Think of a dome on the *top* of a capit__l.

capit*ol*

■ The building in which a state legislature meets is called a *capi*___.

capi*tol*

Capitol

■ When the word *capitol* is spelled with a capital C, it usually refers to the building in Washington, D.C., where Congress meets: During my visit to Washington, D.C., I visited the _____.

capitol

■ I drove to the _____ [state legislature building] in twenty minutes.

capital

■ The noun *capital* (with an *a*) has several meanings. First, it means the major city of a state or nation, as in this sentence: St. Paul is the _____ of the state of Minnesota.

capital

■ The noun *capital* can also mean a stock of wealth, as in this sentence: Mr. Smith needed a great deal of _____.

capital

■ Jim Brown put all his _____ into the new business.

capital

■ The word *capital* can also be used as an adjective, meaning chief, main, or foremost, as in this sentence: Kidnapping is regarded as a _____ offense.

capital

■ Nashville is the _____ of Tennessee.

capital

■ The ability to speak extemporaneously is of _____ importance to an orator.

capital

■ The adjective *capital* also means first-rate or excellent, as in this sentence: Mr. Smith said to his lawyer, "That is a _____ idea."

capital

■ Lima is the _____ of Peru.

capital
capitol

■ It is of [capitol, capital] importance that I go to the [capitol, capital] Thursday morning.

capital

■ Mr. Merriwether borrowed ten thousand dollars to have enough _____ to expand his grocery business.

capital

■ The opera performances were [capital, capitol].

Capitol

■ The workmen have just finished renovating the [capitol, Capitol] of the United States.

meaning
spelling

■ The homonyms *coarse* and *course* sound alike but differ in _____ and _____.

coarse

■ The adjective *coarse* means rough or harsh, as in this sentence: The lady chose a very _____ material for her drapes.

course

■ The noun *course* means a way to be followed, as in this sentence: Richard decided which _____ of action to take.

coarse

■ The adjective *coarse* can also mean vulgar, as in the sentence: His manners were very _____.

coarse

■ Mrs. Green finally found a good way to stop her husband from using _____ language.

course

■ Mary chose a vocational _____ in high school.

coarse

■ The boys were warned not to use _____ language.

course

■ I have not succeeded in deciding on the best _____ to follow.

coarse

■ Burlap is a _____ material used in making bags and curtains.

homonyms

■ Now look at the words *complement* and *compliment*. These words sound much alike but differ in meaning and spelling. They can be called _____.

complement

■ The word *complement* (with an *e*) can be used as a noun or verb. The noun means something that fills up or completes, as in the sentence: The new _____ of soldiers saved the fort from being besieged.

■ *Complement* (with an *e*) can also be used as a verb, as in this sentence: The two courses in French literature will _____ the courses in English literature to satisfy the requirements for graduation.

complement

■ The word *compliment* (with an *i*) is a noun meaning an expression of admiration or praise, as in this sentence: He paid me a very nice _____.

compliment

■ Compliment (with an *i*) is also a verb meaning to praise, or pay a compliment to, as in this sentence: I know that Joe will _____ his brother on his new job.

compliment

complement

■ Something which completes another is a *compl___ment*.

complement

■ If you complete or fill up you will *compl___ment*.

compliment

■ If a person performs well in a play, you will undoubtedly *compl___ment* him.

compliment

■ If you give praise to a person, you pay him a *compl___ment*.

compliment

■ The President received a great _____ from the premier of a foreign country.

complement

■ In order to finish the design Mrs. Jones decided to _____ the row of brown figures with a row of red figures.

compliment

■ The teacher's _____ made Harry work harder in his English class.

complement

■ When the fresh [complement, compliment] of men arrived, the general complimented the soldiers on their fine appearance.

sel

■ The two homonyms *council* and *counsel* sound much alike. However, they do not mean the same and they are not spelled the same: *council* ends in *cil* and *counsel* ends in ___.

■ The noun *council* is a group of men who are appointed or elected to be an advisory or legislative body. A group of men who would advise the governor would be called a *coun_____*.

coun*cil*

■ The word *counsel* can be used as a noun or verb. The noun means advice, as in this sentence: After many hours of consultation, Dick said that he has received very good *coun_____*.

coun*sel*

■ The verb to *counsel* means to advise or to recommend, as in the sentence: My best friend tried to _____ me about entering the race.

counsel

■ A legislatory or advisory body of men is called a _____.

council

■ To advise or recommend means to _____.

counsel

■ The doctor's _____ was to move to a warmer climate.

counsel

■ The mayor called the city _____ into special session.

council

■ The noun *counsel* also means an attorney, as shown in this sentence: Sam's _____ told him to plead guilty.

counsel

■ Mr. Rittenhouse has been engaged as _____ for the defendant.

counsel

■ Jerome Countryman was elected to the city _____.

council

■ After making a careful analysis of the problem, I tried to give the best _____ I could.

counsel

■ When Mr. Olson needed some information about foreign exchange in Norway, he asked his cousin, who was a member of the city _____, for _____.

council
counsel

consul

■ Now look at the word *consul*. It does *not* have the same pronunciation, meaning, or spelling as *council* or *counsel,* but it is similar enough to be confusing. A *consul* is an official who represents his country in a foreign nation, as in this sentence: Renee's husband was appointed the French _____ at St. Paul.

con*sul*

■ An official who represents his country in a foreign nation is called a *con*_____.

*con*sul

■ Anne went to see the German _____*sul* about arrangements to visit her relatives in Germany.

consul

■ Mr. Olaf Andersen has been appointed a _____ for the Norwegian government.

counsel
consul

■ The mayor will _____ the Austrian _____ about the tax laws.

dessert

■ The two nouns *desert* (one *s*) and *dessert* (two *s*'s) are sometimes confused. The noun *dessert* is the ice cream, pastry, or fruit course served at the end of the meal. Finish the spelling of the word that means the fruit course at the end of the meal: *de*_____*ert.*

dessert

■ Nancy's mother baked a lemon pie for _____.

dessert

■ What would you like for _____: ice cream, chocolate cake, or tapioca pudding?

desert

■ The word *desert* can be used as a noun or verb. As a noun it means dry, barren ground, as in this sentence: When we traveled through Arizona we had to go through the _____.

Desert

■ The Gobi *De*_____*ert* is located in Central Asia.

desert

■ The verb to *desert* means to leave behind, as in this sentence: Some men _____ their wives and children.

de*sert*	■ To leave behind means to *de*____.
desert	■ Dry, barren ground is called a _____.
dessert	■ The fruit or pastry course at the end of a meal is called _____.
desert	■ It is a crime to _____ one's family.
desert desert	■ When the army division reached the vast _____, a few soldiers tried to _____ by making their way to a small village some miles away.
dessert	■ The Jones family stayed at a roadside inn for dinner, and each one had a different _____.
ple	■ Two homonyms which cause a great deal of confusion are *principal* and *principle*. The spelling differs in the last three letters: *pal* and ____.
pal	■ The noun *principal* (*pal*) can mean a leader or a head of something. For instance, the head of a high school is called a principal. Remember that this principal could be a ____ [last three letters of the word].
principal	■ Mr. Wiggington has been named the _____ of the new school.
principal	■ The noun *principal* can also mean a capital sum of money placed at interest and used as a fund: Mr. Raymond's account totaled $1,000, of which approximately $900 was the _____.
principal	■ *Principal* used as an adjective means main or important, as in this sentence: It is usually not very difficult to find the _____ causes of war.
principal	■ A noun is a _____ [main] part of speech.
principal	■ In doing an arithmetic problem in interest, you must remember that the _____ is the sum of money on which the interest is computed.

principal

■ The speaker emphasized the _____ points of his discussion.

■ The noun *principle* means a rule in conduct or in science or mathematics. An easy way to remember that this word ends in *le* is this: The word *rule* ends in *le* and so does the word *principle,* which means ru____.

ru*le*

■ Although Jud would recite a mathematical *princi*____ from memory, he could not apply the rule in practical situations.

princi*ple*

■ The noun that means a rule is spelled _____.

principle

■ The noun that means a chief or head of an organization is spelled _____.

principal

■ The adjective that means main or important is _____.

principal

■ The noun that means a sum of money placed at interest and used as a fund is _____.

principal

■ The _____ reason that Mr. Brown was appointed _____ of the school was that he was a good administrator.

principal
principal

■ The entire community knew him as a man of high [principles, principals].

principles

■ An easy way to correctly spell the word meaning a head of a school is to remember that this person could be a *p*____.

p*al*

■ An easy way to correctly spell the word meaning a rule is to remember that this word and the word *rule* both end in ____.

le

■ Paper used in correspondence is called *stationery.* If you cannot remember that this noun ends in *ery,* think of the noun letter, written on stationery. The word letter ends in *er* and so does *station*____*y* on which a letter is written.

station*ery*

stationery

■ A reliable paper company usually makes several grades of *station*_____.

stationery

■ Jane received two boxes of *station*_____.

stationery

■ Are you going to write your thank-you notes on the blue or the white _____?

stationary

■ The homonym which is confused with the noun *stationery* is the adjective *stationary* which means fixed, as in this sentence: The pews in the church are _____.

ary

■ The noun *stationery* ends in this way: *ery,* whereas the adjective *stationary* is spelled ___*ry.*

station*ary*

■ In designing the new school the architect stressed the use of movable furniture; in other words, he did not recommend the installation of *station*_____ furniture.

stationary

■ When Joe heard his name, he remained in a _____ position for several seconds.

stationery

■ Mavis wrote to me on her best _____.

stationery

■ A shop that sells paper, pens, pencils, ink, et cetera, is called a _____ store.

stationary

■ The economy showed no sign of improvement or decline; therefore, the expert said the present economic condition could be called _____.

homonyms

■ These three words, *there, their,* and *they're,* which sound alike but do not have the same meaning or spelling, should be studied well. They can be called _____.

ere

■ The adverb *there* is an adverb of place. It is the opposite of here. Notice that *here* and *there* end in exactly the same way: _____.

there

■ I put the blankets *th*_____ [in that place].

there

■ Kent Donaldson cannot go today, but he will go _____ [to that place] tomorrow.

their

■ The adjective *their* is the possessive case of they. *Their* shows possession, as in this sentence: The lawyer proved beyond a doubt that it was _____ property.

boys

■ In the sentence, The boys put on their swim suits, the adjective *their* shows that the swim suits belonged to the _____.

their

■ You use the adjective *their* to show possession: They did not like _____ seats in the balcony.

there

■ The adverb which means in that place is _____.

their

■ The adjective which is the possessive case of they is _____.

there

■ Mary looked here, _____, and everywhere.

their

■ Mr. and Mrs. Davis entered _____ horses in the big race.

there
their

■ The contraction *they're* sounds the same as *th____e* and *th____r*.

a

■ A contraction is a shortened form made by taking out letters in the middle of a combination of words. The word *they're* is a contraction and stands for *they are*. The one letter that is omitted is the __.

a

■ When a letter is omitted, it is replaced by an apostrophe (*'*). The apostrophe in the word *they're* takes the place of the __ in *they are*.

They're

■ *They're* is a contraction and stands for the pronoun *they* and the verb *are*. This word should then be used as the subject and verb of a sentence or clause, as in this sentence: _____ here!

■ *They're* should be used as the subject and verb of a clause or sentence as it is a contraction and stands for _____.

they are

■ Mary looked out the window and said, "_____ the same couple who walked down the street an hour ago."

They're

■ When I picked up the clock and set it _____, I did not know it was broken.

there

■ It was _____ prized possession.

their

■ Jimmy took out the suitcases and placed them _____.

there

■ If the boys want to read, they will have to go to the library and get _____ own books.

their

■ I replied, "_____ no better than we are."

They're

■ The couple insisted that we were camping on _____ [possessive of they] property.

their

■ Nancy shouted, "_____ here." "Where?", I replied. "Over _____," she said, "holding _____ suitcases."

They're
there
their

■ The next three words should be studied very carefully: *to, too,* and *two.* They sound alike but are different in meaning and spelling. They are called _____.

homonyms

■ The word *to* (one *o*) is a preposition which can be used with a noun or pronoun as in this sentence: I told him to give the money to her (pronoun) or _____ Father (noun).

to

■ Send the book _____ Mabel.

to

■ The preposition *to* can also be used with a verb to form an infinitive: Mother told him *to give* it to her. *Give* is a verb, and when the preposition *to* is used with it, as in _____ *give,* this forms an infinitive.

to

■ I promised _____ go to the movie on Thursday.

to

■ John gave his tickets _____ Julie.

to

■ Form an infinitive using *go* as the verb: _____ *go.*

to

■ Use the preposition *to* with the pronoun him: I gave it _____ him.

to

■ Use the preposition *to* with the noun Virginia: He decided not to send it _____ Virginia.

to

■ The word *too* (two *o*'s) is an adverb meaning also, as in this sentence: He wanted to go _____ .

too

■ I, _____ [also], was offered a job at the bakery.

too

■ The adverb *too* also means more than enough, as shown in this sentence: There are _____ many people in the elevator.

too

■ We had _____ many problems _____ worry about Jim's ball game.

too
to

■ Billy arrived late for the ceremony _____ .

too

■ Don't give it _____ him.

to

■ There is _____ much noise on the playground.

too

■ Norma does not intend _____ wear a ballet costume.

to

■ The last word that sounds like *to* and *too* is *two,* meaning the numeral 2, as in this sentence: There is room for _____ more.

two

■ The carpenter received a wage increase of _____ dollars a day.

two

■ We stayed at the party until _____ o'clock in the morning.

two

■ We saw the beautiful display of fireworks _____.

too

■ Richard's father arrived _____ late to see the President.

too

■ My sister felt that she was too old _____ enter the contest.

to

■ She gave the entry blank _____ me.

to

■ There were three women in the living room and _____ men in the dining room.

two

■ The homonyms *who's* and *whose* sound alike but differ in meaning and spelling. Like the word *they're,* the word *who's* is a contraction. The apostrophe in *who's* stands for the omitted letter ___.

i

■ The contraction *who's* stands for two words: *who* _____.

is

■ The contraction *who's* stands for _____.

who is

■ Jerry shouted, "_____ [contraction of *who is*] going to ride with me?"

Who's

■ When the orchestra met at the school auditorium, the director asked, "_____ going to drive his car to the concert hall?"

Who's

Whose

■ The word *whose* is the possessive pronoun of who, as in this sentence: _____ shoe is this?

whose

■ We tried to find out _____ books were left on the table.

whose

■ I wonder _____ entry will win first prize.

who's

■ The officers of the club would like to know _____ going to the fair.

Who's

■ Glaring at us the teacher rose and said, "_____ responsible for this drawing?"

whose

■ I did not dare admit _____ fault it was.

whose

■ It took two hours to discover _____ clothes had been left in the locker.

its

■ The next two homonyms are *it's* and *its*. *Its* is the possessive form of *it*, as in the sentence: The dog wagged _____ tail.

its

■ The possessive form of *it* is _____.

is

■ The homonym of *its* is *it's*, which is the contraction of *it* _____.

it's

■ The contracted form of *it is* is _____.

i

■ The apostrophe in *it's* stands for the letter ___.

It's

■ _____ going to rain.

its

■ We watched the mother bird feeding _____ young.

it's

■ When John hears about the new procedure, he will try to find out which division _____ going to affect.

its

■ Minnesota is known for _____ ten thousand lakes.

you

■ The last two homonyms are *your* and *you're*. Like *their*, which is the possessive form of *they*, the word *your* is the possessive form of _____.

your

■ The possessive form of *you* is _____.

are

■ Like *who's* and *they're*, the word *you're* is a contraction. It stands for *you* _____.

a

■ The apostrophe in the contraction *you're* stands for the omitted letter ___.

You're

■ Jim looked at me in amazement and gasped, "_____ not going!"

your

■ When you leave the university, what do you intend to do with _____ books?

your

■ He is _____ friend, not mine.

You're

■ As I hesitated in the doorway, Robert screamed, "_____ crazy!"

Review

to

■ His mother shouted, "Go [to, too, two] bed."

to

■ If you don't want to keep it, give it [to, too] me.

too

■ He never cared for [to, too] many new toys at one time.

Two

■ [To, Too, Two] people boarded the train at Dunningham.

whose

■ Mary did not have to ask [whose, who's] candy it was.

principal

■ My cousin was named [principle, principal] of the new elementary school.

aisle

■ There was a narrow [aisle, isle] between the rows of chairs.

desert

■ The commander shouted, "Don't [desert, dessert] the ship!"

counsel

■ I told the judge that I did not need a [council, counsel] for my defense.

capital

■ Kidnapping is considered a [capital, capitol] crime.

stationery

■ Jane asked her friend to meet her at the [stationary, stationery] store.

to

■ The warden allowed me [to, too] visit the prisoner once a month.

already

■ Jerry has [already, all ready] promised Mary to go with her.

heard

■ Have you [herd, heard] the latest rumor?

There

■ As soon as she saw the plane, June exclaimed, "[Their, They're, There] it is!"

course

■ The man spent hours trying to decide what [course, coarse] to take.

complement

■ The new [compliment, complement] of men will help restore the prestige of the troops.

council

■ An advisory or legislative body is called a [council, counsel].

canvass

■ Do you have time to [canvas, canvass] for votes?

whose	■ I tried to find out [who's, whose] pen it was.
you're	■ The contracted form of *you are* is _____.
consul	■ An official who represents his government in a foreign country is a [consul, counsel].
dessert	■ I prefer banana cream pie for [dessert, desert].
canvas	■ Heavy socks can be made of [canvas, canvass].
herd	■ The boy watched the [heard, herd] of cattle in the pasture.
coarse	■ The fabric was too [coarse, course] for a dress.
principle	■ A rule can be called a [principal, principle].
stationary	■ Chairs that are not movable are called [stationery, stationary].
their	■ Tell them to hang up [their, there] coats.
your	■ The possessive form of *you* is _____.
two	■ We shall leave at [to, two, too] o'clock tomorrow afternoon.
Who's	■ [Whose, Who's] going to the theater tonight?
too	■ There are [to, too] many stray dogs in the city.
too	■ My parents will be arriving tomorrow [to, too].
They're	■ [They're, There, Their] really not to blame for what happened at the picnic.

principal

■ This is the [principle, principal] reason for my decision.

compliment

■ My employer paid me a very high [complement, compliment].

capitol

■ James asked me to drive to St. Paul to see the [capital, capitol].

all ready

■ The bus driver asked whether we were [already, all ready] to resume our trip.

isle

■ A small island is an [aisle, isle].

capital

■ He could not raise enough [capitol, capital] to start in business for himself.

it's

■ The company is afraid [its, it's] going to turn into a riot.

its

■ The state of Florida stresses [its, it's] warm climate.

Confused Words

advice

■ The words *advice* and *advise* are often confused. The noun is *advice,* and it rhymes with "mice." The noun we are talking about is _____.

advise

■ The verb *advise* differs in both spelling and pronunciation from the noun *advice. Advise* rhymes with "arise." The verb we are talking about is _____.

advice
advise

■ The noun *advice* means counsel. The verb *advise* means to give counsel to someone. The noun counsel is another word for _____, and the verb to counsel means to _____.

advice

■ The noun which can be defined as counsel and which rhymes with "mice" is _____.

advise

■ The verb which means to counsel and rhymes with "arise" is _____.

advice

■ The noun that means counsel is _____.

advise

■ The verb meaning to counsel is _____.

advice

■ We wondered what _____ Mr. Brown would give Howard.

advise

■ My teachers are always willing to _____ me.

advise

■ Robert will [advise, advice] you about the car.

advice

■ Ruby asked her father for [advice, advise].

noun

■ The words *device* and *devise* are similar to *advice* and *advise.* Like *advice,* the word *device* is a [noun, verb].

verb

■ Like the verb *advise,* the word *devise* is also a _____.

device

■ The noun *device* is a contrivance or appliance, as in this sentence: Jim should patent the _____ he has just invented.

device

■ The noun *device* is also a scheme, as in this sentence: He tried to think of a _____ that would prevent a successful campaign.

de*vice*

■ We became interested in a *de*___ [contrivance] to remove weeds.

devise

■ The verb *devise* means to invent or contrive, as in this sentence: The inventor will continue to _____ new designs.

devise

■ Mr. Jones asked if I could _____ [contrive] a new scheme for better publicity.

devise

■ The two boys planned to _____ a flying machine.

devise

■ It is his intention to _____ a better method to measure the density.

■ The two words *alley* and *ally* are confusing words because they look somewhat similar. However, they are not pronounced the same. The word that rhymes with "valley" is [alley, ally].

alley

■ The noun *alley* rhymes with "valley." The word that rhymes with "rely" is [ally, alley].

ally

■ The word *ally* can be used as a noun and as a verb. The noun *ally* means one united to another, as in this sentence: Great Britain is an _____ of the United States.

ally

■ The verb to *ally* means to unite or to make a connection between, as in this sentence: The congressman will _____ himself with the farm bloc.

ally

■ The verb meaning to unite, which rhymes with "rely" is _____.

ally

■ One can usually depend on France to _____ herself with Great Britain and the United States.

ally

■ One country usually becomes an _____ of another country through the ratification of a treaty.

ally

■ The noun *alley* (spelled *ey*) is a narrow lane between houses or buildings or a walk in a park: You are probably familiar with the _____ behind your house.

alley

■ The noun which means a narrow lane and rhymes with "valley" is _____.

alley

■ I ran down the _____ and into the garage.

alley

alley

■ A walk in a garden, bordered by bushes and trees, is also called an _____.

alley

■ The city engineer informed us that the _____ behind our house will be paved next fall.

ally

■ The senator announced that he would _____ himself with the Republicans on this issue.

ally

■ France was an _____ of the United States during the last war.

ally

■ One who is united to another is an _____.

alley

■ A narrow lane between buildings is called an _____.

verb

■ *Breath* is a noun defined as air which is inhaled and exhaled. The word is different from the verb to *breathe,* which is defined as to inhale and exhale. In the sentence, I *inhale and exhale,* you can substitute the [noun, verb] for the italicized words.

breath

■ The noun *breath* is pronounced with a short *e,* and rhymes with "death." The noun meaning air which is inhaled and exhaled and rhyming with "death" is _____.

breathe

■ The verb *breathe* is pronounced with a long *e* and the *th* has the same sound as the *th* in *these*. The verb meaning to inhale and exhale, which has a long *e* and the same *th* sound as *these* is _____.

breath

■ The doctor asked the patient to take a deep _____.

breathe

■ I have a pain in my chest when I _____.

noun

■ *Breath* is the [noun, verb].

verb

■ *Breathe* is the [noun, verb].

breathe	■ When the athletes finished the race, they could not _____ deeply.
breath	■ He ran so fast that his _____ came in short gasps.
accept	■ The verb to *accept* means to receive with favor or consent, as in this sentence: I shall _____ the gift.
accept	■ You will notice that the verb *accept* has a double *c*: a___ept.
s	■ Look at the word *accept* and pronounce it. The first *c* has a hard *c* sound, as in *cat*. The second *c* has the same sound as in the word *set*, or an ___ sound.
c	■ The verb *accept* has two ___'s.
accept	■ The verb *accept* means to receive with favor or consent: I will happily _____ the title bestowed on me.
except	■ The preposition *except* can be used in this way: All went to the party _____ John.
except	■ The preposition *except* means with the exclusion of. In other words, the person or thing that is excepted is left out: All the girls went to the game _____ Mary.
*ac*cept	■ You will notice that the two words *accept* and *except* are similar in spelling. They differ in the first syllables: *ex*cept and ___cept.
except	■ Everyone left the theater _____ Joe.
accept	■ Howard could not _____ the job.
except	■ Every supervisor volunteered to work on Saturday _____ Mr. Hanes.
accept	■ The issue is whether the students should _____ the offer of part-time scholarships.

■ Another pair of confusing words are *access* and *excess*. Like *accept* and *except,* the word *access* has *ac* as its first syllable, and *excess* has _____ as its first syllable.

ex

■ The first syllable of word *access* (ac) has a hard __ sound.

c

■ In the second syllable of the word *access* (cess), the *c* has the sound of __.

s

■ The noun *access* is defined as a way of approach or admittance, as in this sentence: The student has _____ to the supply cabinet.

access

■ The corridor offers good _____ to all the music rooms.

access

■ The noun *excess* is like *except* in that the first syllable is spelled _____.

ex

■ The money turned in was in _____ of one hundred dollars.

excess

■ Do you have _____ to the drawing materials?

access

■ In looking through the cabinets, he found an _____ of mimeographed booklets.

excess

■ The location of the kitchen gives easy _____ to every room in the house.

access

■ To have a number of pencils beyond that specified by the teacher is to have an _____ of pencils.

excess

■ The words *affect* and *effect* are often confused because they are similar in spelling. Only one letter differs, the first. The verb *affect* begins with *a* and the noun *effect* begins with __.

e

affect

■ The verb *affect* means to change, to influence, as in this sentence: The heavy snows will _____ the fruit crop this winter.

*af*fect

■ To change or influence is to ____fect.

affect

■ To change or influence something is to _____ it.

affect

■ The mood of the speaker will _____ his listeners.

a

■ The noun *effect* begins with *e,* whereas the verb *affect* begins with __.

effect

■ The noun *effect* means result, or fulfillment, as in this sentence: We shall never know the full _____ of his speech.

*ef*fect

■ The result can be called the ____fect.

e

■ A good way to remember that the noun *effect* begins with *e* is to think of the meaning, a result. The first syllable of r*e*sult has an __.

effect

■ Remember that the word *affect* can never be used as a noun. The noun is always spelled _____.

effect

■ The supply of a certain item may have an _____ on the price.

effect

■ The _____ of the speech was visible on the faces of the audience.

affect

■ The beauty of the scene will surely _____ his indifference.

later

■ *Later* is an adverb and the comparative form of the adverb *late.* Inasmuch as there are three degrees of comparison [late, later, latest], the word *later* would be the second degree of comparison: late, _____, latest.

later

■ Because of the snowstorm we arrived much _____ [comparative of *late*] than usual.

one

■ The adverb *later* is spelled with only _____ *t*.

later

■ I shall go to the store _____ in the day.

later

■ Nancy arrived much _____ than Sue.

latter

■ The word *latter* is an *adjective* and can be defined as the second of two things mentioned, as in this sentence: If the manager asks whether you prefer to sit downstairs or in the balcony, tell him you prefer the _____.

one

■ The adjective *latter* has two *t*'s, whereas the adverb *later* has only _____ *t*.

latter

■ When two things are mentioned and you refer to the second, you call it the la_____er.

latter

■ Of the two kinds of pie, chocolate cream or lemon, I chose the _____.

later

■ I arrived at the bank much _____ than I had expected.

latter

■ Of the two solutions proposed by the union, the _____ is the more workable.

lose

■ To *lose* is a verb and can be defined as to miss from one's possession, as in this sentence: Rachel always manages to _____ one pair of gloves every spring.

lose

■ The verb *lose* has only one *o* and rhymes with "whose." The verb which means to miss from one's possession and rhymes with "whose" is _____.

lose

■ Because Jack does not carry a pencil case, he must l_____ two or three pencils a day.

lose

■ My father does not dare go to the races because he is afraid to _____ any more money.

loose

■ The word *loose* is an adjective, meaning free, not fastened down tight, as in this sentence: The _____ board in the floor is a hazard.

loose

■ The adjective *loose* has two *o*'s and rhymes with "goose." The adjective that means not fastened down tight and rhymes with "goose" is _____.

verb

■ Whereas *loose* is an adjective, *lose* is a _____.

loose

■ The buttons on the dress were not firmly attached, so they became _____.

loose

■ After the car crashed into the tree, the officers discovered that a bolt was _____.

lose

■ He does not wish to _____ any more time.

loose

■ The witness testified in court that the screws in the chair had been _____ for several days.

does not

■ The two words *moral* and *morale* have several differences. For instance, *morale* has a final *e*; *moral* [does, does not] have a final *e*.

moral*e*

■ The word *moral* can be used as a noun or adjective; the word *moral___* is a noun.

ale

■ Remember the accent in the word *moral* comes on the *mor*. The accent in the word *morale* comes on the ___.

moral

■ The word *moral* can be defined as right and proper. If we speak of a law pertaining to the right and good, we are speaking of a _____ law.

moral

■ The adjective *moral* can be used in this way: A son who wants to take care of his parents when they are old feels a _____ obligation to do so.

moral	■ The noun *moral* signifies the inner meaning of a lesson or experience, as in this sentence: What is the _____ of this story?
morale	■ The noun *morale* signifies the state of well-being of one or more individuals, as in this sentence: The _____ of the troops is high.
morale	■ The manager of the baseball team is worrying about the _____ of the players.
moral	■ He is a man of high _____ character.
moral	■ There are two kinds of law: man-made and _____.
personal	■ The word *personal* is an adjective meaning private or pertaining to a particular person, as in this sentence: This is a _____ argument.
adjective	■ The word *personal* is an [noun, adjective].
per*sonal*	■ If a grievance pertains to a particular person, it is a *per*_____ grievance.
personal	■ Private or pertaining to a particular person is the meaning of the adjective _____.
personnel	■ The noun *personnel* can be defined as a body of persons employed in some service, as shown in this sentence: The office workers and the mechanics comprise the _____ of the firm.
noun	■ The word *personal* is an adjective; the word *personnel* is a [noun, adjective].
perso*nal* person*nel*	■ There are other differences between *personal* and *personnel*. Look at the endings of the words: the adjective *person*_____ and the noun *person*_____.
personal	■ The adjective which means pertaining to a particular person is _____.

personnel

■ The noun which means a body of persons employed in some service is _____.

nel

■ The accent in the word *personal* is on the syllable *per,* whereas the accent in *personnel* falls on the last syllable _____.

personnel

■ The body of persons working for a company is known as the _____ of the firm.

personal

■ Inasmuch as it is a _____ dispute, we cannot intervene.

personal

■ Pertaining to a particular person is the definition of the word _____.

personnel

■ All large companies have a director of _____.

quite

■ The adverb *quite* means completely and wholly, as in this sentence: Through all her grief, the widow stood _____ alone.

adverb

■ Look at the italicized word in this sentence: The president of the bank is *quite* ill today. This word is an [adjective, adverb].

qui*te*

■ The adverb that means completely and wholly is *qui*____.

quite

■ Although he was badly hurt, Jimmy was _____ conscious of everything about him.

quiet

■ *Quiet* is an adjective meaning free from noise, as in the following sentence: There is a _____ zone around the hospital.

qui*et*

■ The adjective that means free from noise is *qui*____.

qui*et*

■ The spelling of the words *quite* and *quiet* differs in the last two letters: The adverb is *quite* and the adjective is *qui*____.

■ The word *whether* is a conjunction which introduces an indirect question, as in this sentence: He asked _____ he should carry the basket.

whether

■ The conjunction *whether* can also introduce an alternative condition, as in this sentence: I shall go to the theater _____ you go or not.

whether

■ The conjunction *whether* introduces an [direct, indirect] question.

indirect

■ The conjunction *whether* also introduces an alternative condition, as in this sentence: Do you know _____ he is going to school or not?

whether

■ _____ it rains or shines, we will start on our trip to Canada tomorrow.

Whether

■ How far we drive the first day will depend on the _____.

weather

■ The _____ bureau predicted rain for the next five days.

weather

■ I don't care _____ you learn to drive or not.

whether

Review

■ The teacher asked the class to be [quite, quiet] because some students were trying to study.

quiet

■ Bill refused to discuss the matter as it was a [personnel, personal] quarrel.

personal

■ The group of persons employed in the water department of the city government can be called the [personnel, personal] of that department.

personnel

■ Bob wondered [weather, whether] his brother had heard about their father.

whether

whether

■ The game will go on [whether, weather] it rains or not.

accept

■ My family urged me to [except, accept] the position in Florida.

access

■ All students in the music school should have [excess, access] to the library.

advise

■ The counselor offered to [advice, advise] the students, but they did not accept his offer.

later

■ Why don't you study your English lesson [latter, later] when it is quiet?

lose

■ The children were told to put their mittens in their pockets so that they would not [loose, lose] them.

breath

■ The air which is exhaled and inhaled is known as [breath, breathe].

morale

■ Even though the soldiers were deprived of many comforts, their [moral, morale] was very good.

personnel

■ The credit manager spoke to the [personnel, personal] about paying their bills promptly.

affect

■ The damp weather will always [effect, affect] my rheumatism.

devise

■ When the enemy guessed our intention to ambush them, we had to [device, devise] another scheme.

alley

■ You can get to the store on time if you go through the [ally, alley].

moral

■ It is very difficult to make a [moral, morale] decision.

loose

■ Judith put all the [lose, loose] change in her purse.

latter

■   Mrs. Cones had to choose between a blue coat and a tan car coat, so she chose the [later, latter].

■   When Joe considers his extensive training and education, he cannot [quite, quiet] understand his inability to obtain employment.

quite

Breathe

■   The doctor said, "[Breathe, Breath] deeply."

■   When the announcement of Jane's marriage appeared in the paper, I could well imagine the [effect, affect] it would have on John Walsh.

effect

quiet

■   The patient is very calm and [quite, quiet].

■   What kind of [device, devise] are you working on now?

device

ally

■   One who is united to another is known as an [alley, ally].

except

■   All the residents on Hawthorne Street [except, accept] the Johnsons were ordered to fix their sidewalks.

weather

■   The broadcaster announced that this area would have sunny and clear [whether, weather] for three days.

excess

■   Because of the low consumer demand for berries, the farmers predicted they would have an [excess, access] of fruit this summer.

Whether

■   [Whether, Weather] it rains or snows, the mailmen deliver the mail.

chapter 8

Demons

There are a number of words that have so-called trouble spots, such as the first *e* in de*s*cribe, the first *a* in sep*a*rate, the second *a* in gramm*a*r, or the *u* in s*u*rprise. Professor W. Franklin Jones, in his *Concrete Investigation of the Material of English Spelling,* November, 1913, named these specific troublemakers "demons," and this word has become standard terminology. These trouble spots are common to many people, usually because they have not corrected their ingrained bad spelling habits.

It will be to your advantage to study these words diligently so that you can spell them properly and use them in your written work. For your convenience in learning to spell these demons, those words with similar difficulties have been grouped together: those with *a, e, i, o,* and *u* trouble; double consonants; silent letters; etc. By studying the demons in this chapter you will not only learn a number of useful words but will also develop a good foundation for learning other words that are difficult for you to spell.

Test for Chapter 8

Fill in the dashes or blanks as appropriate.
1. Apart or not connected means sep_____.   _____
2. Having ability is the definition of the adjective cap__ble.   _____
3. The degree of hotness or coldness as measured on a definite scale is called tem_____.   _____
4. A scoundrel is a vil_____.   _____
5. A good knowledge of gramm__r is always helpful.   _____
6. An adjective that means having a general likeness is sim_____.   _____
7. A record of the days of the year is a calen_____.   _____

8. I am positive that I shall __njoy the ice skating. _____
9. A foe or a hostile person is an en_____. _____
10. To profit means to ben__fit. _____
11. We were annoyed by the incessant rep__tition of his childish phrases. _____
12. A plant cultivated for food is a veg_____. _____
13. The opposite of the word temporary is the word per_____. _____
14. Please close this letter with the phrase, Sin_____ly yours. _____
15. To sever, to separate means to d__v__de. _____
16. Clear, apparent is the definition of the word ev__dent. _____
17. To be sure or self-reliant is to be conf__dent. _____
18. A grant of a special right is called a priv_____. _____
19. If you pause undecidedly, you hes_____. _____
20. Giving up something for an end that is regarded as better is to sac_____. _____
21. A plan that is clearly defined is a def_____ plan. _____
22. A person who has strange ideas might be called pecul_____. _____
23. A face that is well known to you is a famil_____ face. _____
24. The child was forced to write an _____ [expression of regret]. _____
25. Painstaking preparations are elab_____ preparations. _____
26. To chase is to p_____sue. _____
27. To collect a fortune is to ac_____late it. _____
28. The players made three ap_____ances on the stage. _____
29. To buy for a price is to p_____chase. _____
30. To oblige is to ac_____date. _____
31. To come upon a person without warning is to s_____prise him. _____
32. The teacher asked the student about his p_____pose in requesting the library books. _____
33. The alderman requested permission to _____point his own secretary. _____
34. The verb that means to be thankful for is ap_____ate. _____
35. To put in order is to _____range. _____
36. To reach a place means to a_____ive. _____
37. The start or origin is the begin_____. _____
38. Graduation exercises are called com_____ment. _____
39. The child embar_____ed his parents by his temper tantrums. _____
40. Two words that mean indispensable are es_____tial and nec_____ary. _____
41. To leave without delay is to leave im_____iately. _____

42. The bars in the gym were placed in a para____el position.   _____
43. The cousins live on op____site sides of the street.   _____
44. To own is to po____ess.   _____
45. The council suggested that the mayor recom____ the best solution.   _____
46. To work or to function is the meaning of the verb op____ate.   _____
47. The second month of the year is called Feb____.   _____
48. The games and sports for athletes are known as ath____ics.   _____
49. The state of being grateful is grat__tude.   _____
50. The result of his speech was disas____ous.   _____
51. We ordered a new vac__um cleaner.   _____
52. A reply is an ans__er.   _____
53. I sincerely dou__t your honesty.   _____
54. It is necessary for our neighbor to mor__gage his house.   _____
55. Sound reasoning is the definition of the word sen____.   _____
56. Formal permission from authorities to do something is called a lic____.   _____
57. He must pay all his de__ts before he can get any more credit.   _____
58. Protection from attack is called defen____.   _____
59. The actress' life was one of pret____ [false show].   _____
60. One who guards is called a g____ian.   _____

"a" Difficulty

a

■ Some words that are difficult to spell have "a" trouble. In other words, a person substitutes another letter for the necessary ____.

a

■ The word *separate* has a great deal of "a" trouble. You spell sep*a*rate with two ____'s.

separate

■ The word *separate*, which is used as a verb or as an adjective, means apart or not connected, as in this sentence: The dresses were put in _____ piles according to the various sizes.

sep/a/rate

■ The word *separate* has three syllables: sep/a/rate. The first syllable is ____.

■ The second syllable is sep/*a*/rate. This syllable has the troublesome ___.

a

■ The third syllable is sep/a/_____.

sep/a/*rate*

■ The three syllables are _____/__/_____.

sep/a/rate

■ Write the entire word, saying it in syllables as you write: _____.

separate

■ The boys and girls were housed in _____ buildings.

separate

■ The instructor told us to _____ the yellow flash cards from the red ones.

separate

■ Because the two secretaries had to screen many telephone calls for their superiors, the office manager decided to give them _____ phones.

separate

■ Remember that the second syllable of *separate* is _____.

a

■ The second word with the "a" difficulty is *capable,* which is spelled cap___ble.

a

■ The adjective *capable* means having ability or fitness, as in this sentence: Mr. Davis' nephew is a very _____ young man.

capable

■ If you have ability you are *cap*_____ of doing something.

cap*able*

■ The adjective *capable* has three syllables: ca/pa/ble. The first syllable is _____.

ca/pa/ble

■ The second syllable is ca/_____/ble.

ca/*pa*/ble

■ The third syllable is ca/pa/_____.

ca/pa/*ble*

ca/pa/ble

■ The three syllables are ____/____/____.

capable

■ Write the entire word, saying it in syllables as you write: _____.

capable

■ Having ability or fitness is the definition of the adjective _____.

capable

■ Although the young girl has not had much formal training in art, she seems very _____.

capable

■ Joe did not get the job because the employment office did not believe that he was _____ of doing the advanced work in engineering.

a

■ Another "a" word is *temperature*. You need an __ in temper*a*ture.

temperature

■ The noun *temperature* can be defined as the degree of hotness or coldness measured on a definite scale, as in the following sentence: In July and August the _____ can rise to the low 100's.

tem/per/a/ture

■ Now look at the whole word *temperature* and then at the noun divided into syllables: tem/per/a/ture. The first syllable is ____.

tem/*per*/a/ture

■ The second syllable is tem/____/a/ture.

tem/per/*a*/ture

■ The third syllable is tem/per/__/ture.

tem/per/a/*ture*

■ The last syllable is tem/per/a/____.

tem/per/a/ture

■ Divide the word into four syllables: ____/____/__/____.

temperature

■ Write the entire word, saying it in syllables as you write: _____.

temperature

■ The weather bureau predicted that the _____ would drop to 32 degrees by six o'clock.

temperature

■ It is not uncommon for the _____ to rise to 110 degrees in parts of California.

a

■ Remember that the third syllable of *temperature* is __.

a

■ Like the words *separate, capable,* and *temperature,* the adjective pleas*a*nt has a troublesome __.

pleasant

■ The adjective *pleasant* can be defined as pleasing, giving pleasure, as in this sentence: We had a very _____ time.

pleas/ant

■ There are two syllables in the adjective *pleasant:* pleas/ant. The first syllable is _____.

pleas/*ant*

■ The second syllable is pleas/_____.

pleas/ant

■ Divide the word into two syllables: _____/_____.

pleasant

■ Write the entire word, saying it in syllables as you write: _____.

pleasant

■ Pleasing, or giving pleasure, is the definition of the adjective _____.

pleasant

■ If a person has pleasing manners he could be called a _____ fellow.

pleasant

■ The weather has been very _____ this summer.

pleasant

■ In spite of her disappointment, Aunt Mabel greeted us in her usual _____ manner.

villain

■ The noun *villain* signifies a scoundrel, a person who is guilty of great crimes, as shown in this sentence: In Shakespeare's drama *Othello,* Iago is the _____.

a

■ The noun villain has a troublesome ___.

vil/lain

■ The noun *villain* has two syllables: vil/lain. The first syllable is _____.

vil/*lain*

■ The second syllable is vil/_____.

vil/lain

■ The two syllables are _____.

villain

■ Write the entire word, saying it in syllables as you write: _____.

vil*lain*

■ A *villain* is usually caught and sometimes slain. The word *slain* ends in the same way as the word *vil*_____.

villain

■ The audience booed and hissed when the _____ appeared on the stage.

villain

■ A scoundrel is a _____.

villain

■ One who is guilty of a great crime is called a _____.

pleasant

■ Pleasing or giving pleasure is the definition of the word _____.

a

■ Some words have the "a" difficulty in the last syllable. One of these words is gramm___r.

grammar

■ *Grammar* is the science which deals with words and their arrangement in writing, speaking, and reading, as in this sentence: We study about simple and compound sentences in _____.

gram/mar

■ Look at the whole word *grammar* and then look at the syllables: gram/mar. The first syllable is _____.

gram/*mar*

■ The second syllable is gram/_____.

gram/mar

■ The two syllables are _____/_____.

grammar

■ The science that deals with words and their arrangement in writing, speaking, and reading is _____.

gram*mar*

■ Many years ago the textbook used in English classes was known as a *gram*___.

gram*mar*

■ When the teacher saw the boy marking up his book, she said, "John, don't *mar* your *gram*___."

grammar

■ The science of words and their arrangement in writing is called _____.

a

■ The adjective *similar* also has the "a" difficulty in the last syllable. The word *similar* ends in l__r.

similar

■ The adjective *similar* can be defined as having a general likeness, as in this sentence: The two books are very _____ in format.

sim/i/lar

■ The adjective *similar* has three syllables: sim/i/lar. The first syllable is ___.

sim/*i*/lar

■ The second syllable is sim/___/lar.

sim/i/*lar*

■ The third syllable is sim/i/___.

sim/i/lar

■ The three syllables are ___/___/___.

similar

■ Write the entire word, saying it in syllables as you write: _____.

similar

■ The two dresses are very _____.

similar

■ Having a general likeness is the definition of the adjective _____.

similar

■ The new cars are _____ to those manufactured last year.

■ If one table resembles another, it is _____ to the other.

similar

■ The last "a" word is *calendar*. Remember that there is an *a* at the beginning of the word, and one near the _____ of the word.

end

■ A record of the days of the year is called a *calendar,* as in this sentence: I always forget to turn the pages of the _____ on the first day of each month.

calendar

■ There are three syllables in the noun *calendar:* cal/en/dar. The first syllable is _____.

cal/en/dar

■ The second syllable is cal/_____/dar.

cal/*en*/dar

■ The third syllable is cal/en/_____.

cal/en/*dar*

■ The three syllables are _____/_____/_____.

cal/en/dar

■ Write the entire word, saying it in syllables as you write: _____.

calendar

■ Remember that the noun *calendar* has two *a*'s: c__lend__r.

calendar

■ A record of time is known as a _____.

calendar

■ My brother works for an advertising firm that specializes in making religious _____.

calendars

■ In checking the _____ I find that there are only twenty-five days until Christmas.

calendar

■ Having a general likeness means to be _____.

similar

■ Fill in the missing letter: *sep__rate*.

separate

capable

■ Fill in the missing letter: *cap___ble.*

temperature

■ Fill in the missing letter: *temper___ture.*

pleas*ant*

■ Fill in the missing letters: *pleas_____.*

vil*lain*

■ Complete the spelling of the word that means a scoundrel: *vil_____.*

gram*mar*

■ Complete the spelling of *gram_____.*

simi*lar*

■ Complete the spelling of *simi_____.*

calen*dar*

■ Complete the spelling of *calen_____.*

temperature

■ The degree of hotness or coldness measured on a definite scale is called _____.

capable

■ When an individual has ability to do something he is considered _____.

pleasant

■ A person with pleasing manners can be called _____.

separate

■ If you place blue and red beads in different boxes, you would put them in _____ boxes.

villain

■ A person who is guilty of a great crime is a _____.

calendar

■ A record of the days of the year is a _____

grammar

■ The science of words and their arrangement in speaking, writing, and reading is called _____.

similar

■ When two objects have a general likeness, they are called _____.

"e" Difficulty

■ Some very useful words have "e" difficulty, that is, people have trouble remembering to put in the necessary ___ in the right place.

e

■ The verb *enjoy* begins with ___.

e

■ The verb *enjoy* means to have satisfaction in experiencing, as in this sentence: I _____ symphony concerts.

enjoy

■ Look at the whole word *enjoy*. It has two syllables: en/joy. The first syllable is _____.

en/joy

■ The second syllable is en/_____.

en/*joy*

■ The two syllables are _____/_____.

en/joy

■ Write the entire word, saying it in syllables as you write: _____.

enjoy

■ To have satisfaction in experiencing something is to _____.

enjoy

■ In the wintertime we _____ ice skating and skiing.

enjoy

■ The noun *enemy* also has "e" trouble: ___n___my.

enemy

■ A foe or one who is hostile to another is an *enemy*, as in this sentence: In the field of politics, it is easy for an individual to make an _____.

enemy

■ Look at the entire word *enemy*. Now look at its division into syllables: en/e/my. The first syllable is _____.

en/e/my

■ The second syllable is en/___/my.

en/*e*/my

en/e/*my*	■ The last syllable is en/e/_____.
en/e/my	■ The three syllables are _____/___/_____.
enemy	■ Write the entire word, saying it in syllables as you write: _____.
enemy	■ Remember that the noun *enemy* is spelled ___n___my.
enemy	■ A foe could be called an _____.
enemy	■ The father of the murdered boy stated that he did not think the boy had an _____ [hostile person].
benefit	■ The word *benefit* is spelled with two *e*'s: b___n___fit.
benefit	■ The word *benefit* is a verb meaning to profit: We shall _____ by his mistakes.
ben/e/fit	■ *Benefit* has three syllables: ben/e/fit. The first syllable is _____.
ben/*e*/fit	■ The second syllable is ben/___/fit.
ben/e/*fit*	■ The third syllable is ben/e/_____.
ben/e/fit	■ The three syllables are _____/___/_____.
benefit	■ Write the entire word, saying it in syllables as you write: _____.
benefit	■ The postmaster said that his office will not _____ in any way from the establishment of the new methods.
benefit	■ A young person can usually _____ from his own mistakes.
benefit	■ The doctor does not expect to _____ from the new health insurance plan.

re*p*etition	■ The noun *repetition* can also be classified as having "e" trouble: r__p__tition.
repetition	■ The noun *repetition* can be defined as the act of repeating an act or performance, as in this sentence: The impact of the senator's speech was weakened by the constant _____ of the phrase "my worthy opponent."
rep/e/ti/tion	■ The noun *repetition* has four syllables: rep/e/ti/tion. The first syllable is _____.
rep/*e*/ti/tion	■ The second syllable is the troublesome rep/__/ti/tion.
rep/e/*ti*/tion	■ The third syllable is rep/e/_____/tion.
rep/e/ti/*tion*	■ The fourth syllable is rep/e/ti/_____.
rep/e/ti/tion	■ The four syllables are _____/__/_____/_____.
repetition	■ Write the entire word, saying it in syllables as you write: _____.
repetition	■ The act of repeating an act or performance is called _____.
repetition	■ Repeating a word in a theme is good for emphasis, but the constant _____ of the word becomes monotonous.
repetition	■ Purposeful _____ of an error sometimes helps one to overcome the fault.
vegetable	■ The noun *vegetable* can be defined as a plant which is cultivated for food, as in this sentence: We planted a _____ garden in the vacant yard.
veg/e/ta/ble	■ The noun *vegetable* has four syllables: veg/e/ta/ble. The first syllable is _____.
veg/*e*/ta/ble	■ The second syllable is veg/__/ta/ble.

veg/e/*ta*/ble

■ The third syllable is veg/e/_____/ble.

veg/e/ta/*ble*

■ The fourth syllable is veg/e/ta/_____.

veg/e/ta/ble

■ The word is divided into syllables like this: _____.

vegetable

■ Write the entire word, saying it in syllables as you write: _____.

vegetable

■ Marcy Ann will not eat any kind of _____ [plant for food].

vegetable

■ The one _____ I dislike is cauliflower.

e

■ The noun secretary also has "__" trouble.

secretary

■ There are two *e*'s in *secretary,* both near the beginning of the word: s__cr__tary.

sec/re/tar/y

■ There are four syllables in the noun *secretary:* sec/re/tar/y. The first syllable is _____.

sec/*re*/tar/y

■ The second syllable is sec/_____/tar/y.

sec/re/*tar*/y

■ The third syllable is sec/re/_____/y.

sec/re/tar/*y*

■ The last syllable is sec/re/tar/__.

sec/re/tar/y

■ The four syllables are _____/_____/_____/__.

secretary

■ Write the entire word, saying it in syllables as you write: _____.

secretary

■ A clerk or stenographer who attends to private or confidential correspondence and records is called a *secretary,* as in this sentence: The president's _____ checked the files for the missing bond.

secretary	■ A girl who handles correspondence of a private or confidential nature is usually called a _____.
secretary	■ Mavis was promoted to the position of _____ to the personnel manager.
permanent	■ The adjective *permanent* can be defined as lasting, continuing in the same state, as in this sentence: His lectures will have a _____ effect on the students.
per/ma/nent	■ The adjective *permanent* is easy to spell by syllables. This word is divided into syllables like this: per/ma/nent. The first syllable is ____.
per/*ma*/nent	■ The second syllable is per/____/nent.
per/ma/*nent*	■ The final syllable is per/ma/____.
per/ma/nent	■ The three syllables are ____/____/____.
permanent	■ Write the entire word, saying it in syllables as you write: _____.
permanent	■ Jack was forced to accept a temporary job because he could not find a _____ one.
permanent	■ The physician had to tell Mr. Brown that the paralysis in his arm was of a _____ nature.
e	■ The difficulty in spelling the adverb *sincerely* is the silent letter sincer__ly.
sincerely	■ The adverb *sincerely* can be defined as honestly, as in this sentence: He is _____ trying to be a better husband and father.
ly	■ The adverb *sincerely* is the combination of the adjective *sincere* and the suffix ____.

■ When you add *ly* to the word *sincere* to form the adverb *sincerely,* you [do, do not] drop the *e* at the end of sincere.

do not

■ When you add *ly* to the word *sincere* you write it

sincerely

_____.

■ There are three syllables in the adverb *sincerely:* sin/cere/ly. The first syllable is _____.

sin/cere/ly

■ The second syllable is sin/_____/ly.

sin/*cere*/ly

■ The last syllable is sin/cere/_____.

sin/cere/*ly*

■ The three syllables are _____/_____/_____.

sin/cere/ly

■ The adverb *sincerely* is also used as a complimentary close in writing correspondence: *Sin_____ yours.*

Sin*cerely*

■ At the public hearing on tax increases, the housewife stated her argument simply and _____ [honestly].

sincerely

■ The opposite of a temporary address is a _____ one.

permanent

■ As our car approached the woods, we could see the *en___my* guarding the border.

enemy

■ One should *ben___fit* from all his mistakes.

benefit

■ Nancy's ambition is to become a private *secr___tary*.

secretary

■ A plant cultivated for food is called a *veg___table*.

vegetable

■ Mrs. Smith took her daughter to the hairdresser for a *perman___nt* wave.

permanent

■ The act of repeating is called *rep___tition*.

repetition

Sincerely

■ It is customary to use the phrase *Sincer___ly yours* as a complimentary close in writing correspondence.

benefit

■ Although it was a bitter experience, Henry will _____ [profit] from it in many ways.

*en*joy

■ After reading all the critics' reviews, I expect to ___*joy* the stage production of *Little Women*.

vegetable

■ Spinach is the one _____ I do not like.

repetition

■ I was greatly disturbed by the constant _____ [act of repeating] of the hissing noise.

sincerely

■ The word honestly means the same as the adverb _____.

enemy

■ It is easy for a lawyer who prosecutes a criminal to make an _____ [hostile person] of him.

Sec*retary*

■ Gloria was thrilled when she saw the new sign on her desk *"Sec_____ to the President."*

permanent

■ The mover suggested that we put our furniture in _____ [lasting] storage.

"i" Difficulty

■ Although many students do not have eye trouble, they do have "i" trouble when it comes to spelling words. We shall now look at ten common and useful words that have "___" trouble.

i

■ The first word we shall study is the verb *divide*. To divide is to separate, to sever, as in this sentence: I will _____ the apple in three pieces.

divide

di*vi*de

■ The verb *divide* has two *i*'s: d___v___de.

di/vide

■ The verb *divide* has two syllables: di/vide. The first syllable is _____.

di/*vide*

■ The second syllable is di/_____.

di/vide

■ The two syllables are _____/_____.

divide

■ Write the entire word, saying it in syllables as you write: _____.

divide

■ The administrator tried to _____ the property into equal shares.

divide

■ The Hamiltons used a number of screens to _____ the one large room into smaller rooms.

divide

■ The president's remarks did not unite the two groups; in fact, they seemed to _____ the groups into two distinct factions.

ev*i*dent

■ The second word with "i" trouble is ev__dent.

evident

■ The adjective *evident* means clear, apparent, as in this sentence: His hostile attitude was _____ in his actions.

ev/i/dent

■ The adjective *evident* has three syllables: ev/i/dent. The first syllable is _____.

ev/*i*/dent

■ The second syllable is ev/__/dent.

ev/i/*dent*

■ The third syllable is ev/i/_____.

ev/i/dent

■ Divide the word into syllables: _____/__/_____.

evident

■ Write the entire word, saying it in syllables as you write: _____.

evident

■ From the demands of the workers it is _____ that the main issue is wages.

evident	■ Her hatred was _____ in her bitter and sarcastic comments.
confident	■ A person who is sure, self-reliant, is *confident,* as in this sentence: I am _____ that the plan will work.
con/fi/dent	■ The adjective *confident* has three syllables: con/fi/dent. The first syllable is _____.
con/*fi*/dent	■ The second syllable is con/_____/dent.
con/fi/*dent*	■ The third syllable is con/fi/_____.
con/fi/dent	■ The three syllables are _____/_____/_____.
confident	■ To be sure or self-reliant is to be _____.
confident	■ In spite of all his handicaps, Sam is _____ that he will win the race.
confident	■ From the moment she enters the room, Jeanne gives the impression of a very _____ young lady.
i	■ The noun bus*i*ness has an __ in the middle of the word.
business	■ The noun *business* can be defined as one's regular work, trade, or industry, as in this sentence: My father is in the plumbing _____.
bus/i/ness	■ The noun *business* can be divided into three syllables: bus/i/ness. The first syllable is _____.
bus/*i*/ness	■ The second syllable is the troublesome __.
bus/i/*ness*	■ The third syllable is bus/i/_____.
bus/i/ness	■ The noun has three syllables: _____/__/_____.

■ Write the entire word, saying it in syllables as you write: _____.

business

■ A large number of students who attend college enter some kind of _____ after graduation.

business

■ After three weeks' vacation it was difficult to attend to my _____ at the store.

business

■ A *privilege* is a grant of a special right or a right granted as a peculiar advantage or favor, as in this sentence: All upperclassmen in the college have the _____ of attending the science lectures.

privilege

■ Spelling the noun *privilege* is easier if you learn it by syllables. This word has three syllables: priv/i/lege. The first syllable is _____.

priv/i/lege

■ The second syllable is priv/___/lege.

priv/*i*/lege

■ The last syllable is priv/i/_____.

priv/i/*lege*

■ The three syllables are _____/___/_____.

priv/i/lege

■ Write the entire word, saying it in syllables as you write: _____.

privilege

■ The foreman granted Dick the _____ of going to trade school.

privilege

■ Our family considers it a _____ to worship as we please.

privilege

■ Because Lucy had a perfect attendance record, she was granted the _____ of going to Canada with her family during the final week of school.

privilege

■ The verb *hesitate* means to pause undecidedly, as in this sentence: The appearance of the professor caused John to _____ in the doorway.

hesitate

hes/i/tate

■ The verb *hesitate* is divided into three syllables: hes/i/tate. The first syllable is _____.

hes/*i*/tate

■ The second syllable is hes/___/tate.

hes/i/*tate*

■ The third syllable is hes/i/_____.

hes/i/tate

■ The three syllables are _____/___/_____.

hesitate

■ Write the entire word, saying it in syllables as you write: _____.

sacr*i*fice

■ The word *sacrifice* has a problem "i" right in the middle of the word: sacr___fice.

sacrifice

■ The verb *sacrifice* can be defined as giving up something for an end that is better or superior, as in this sentence: George is willing to _____ this year in order to go to college next fall.

sac/ri/fice

■ There are three syllables in *sacrifice:* sac/ri/fice. The first syllable is _____.

sac/*ri*/fice

■ The second syllable is sac/_____/fice.

sac/ri/*fice*

■ The third syllable is sac/ri/_____.

sac/ri/fice

■ The three syllables are _____/_____/_____.

sacrifice

■ Write the entire word, saying it in syllables as you write: _____.

sacrifice

■ To give up something for an end that is better or superior is the definition of the verb _____.

sacrifice

■ To reach the office of the presidency of the hardware concern, Tom Jones had to _____ a great deal during his early years.

sacrifice

■ Because some people are not willing to give up some of their luxuries, they cannot understand how others can _____ the necessities of life.

definite

■ When a plan is *definite*, it is clear and defined, not vague or general. The word can be used in a sentence like this: In the early stages of planning, the proposal was not very _____.

def*i*nite

■ Like the other words in this classification, the adjective *definite* has the troublesome def__nite.

def/i/nite

■ The adjective *definite* is divided into syllables as follows: def/i/nite. The first syllable is _____.

def/*i*/nite

■ The second syllable is def/__/nite.

def/i/*nite*

■ The third syllable is def/i/_____.

def/i/nite

■ The three syllables are _____/__/_____.

definite

■ Write the entire word, saying it in syllables as you write:

definite

■ I made a reservation for the Tuesday evening flight to San Francisco as soon as my plans were _____.

definite

■ Most of the debater's arguments are not _____ and properly presented.

famil*iar*

■ The last two words we shall study in the "i" classification end in the same way: *iar*. The first word is famil_____.

familiar

■ If something is well known to you it is *familiar* to you, as in this sentence: The student said he was _____ with Shakespearean tragedies.

fa/mil/iar

■ The adjective *familiar* can be divided into three syllables: fa/mil/iar. The first syllable is _____.

fa/*mil*/iar	■ The second syllable is fa/_____/iar.
fa/mil/*iar*	■ The third syllable is fa/mil/_____.
fa/mil/iar	■ The three syllables are _____/_____/_____.
familiar	■ Write the entire word, saying it in syllables as you write: _____.
familiar	■ As I looked around the crowded lobby, I found that many of the faces were _____ to me.
familiar	■ The adjective *familiar* also means closely acquainted, as in this sentence: Jim's uncle stated that he was _____ with the way Bob did not keep his promises.
familiar	■ Having lived in South America for several years, the minister was quite _____ with the customs of the various Indian tribes.
iar	■ Like the word *familiar,* the adjective *peculiar* also ends in _____.
peculiar	■ The adjective *peculiar* means strange, as in this sentence: The old recluse had _____ ideas about sanitation.
peculiar	■ The adjective *peculiar* can also mean not common, as in the following sentence: My mother always had her own _____ ideas about raising children.
pe/cu/liar	■ There are three syllables in *peculiar:* pe/cu/liar. The first syllable is _____.
pe/*cu*/liar	■ The second syllable is pe/_____/liar.
pe/cu/*liar*	■ The third syllable is pe/cu/_____.
pe/cu/liar	■ The three syllables are _____/_____/_____.

peculiar

■ Write the entire word, saying it in syllables as you write: _____.

peculiar

■ The whole town thought the boy who lived in the green house by the railroad tracks was a bit _____.

peculiar

■ When a person possesses a trait that is not common to everyone, that trait can be called _____ to this one person.

iar

■ Both adjectives *familiar* and *peculiar* end in __.

familiar

■ To be closely acquainted with is to be _____.

peculiar

■ Many strange ideas could be called _____.

divide

■ The teacher told us to _____ [separate] the circle into four equal parts.

confident

■ Howard had studied hard for all his examinations, and was _____ [sure] when he went to the testing room.

business

■ The manager of the loan company asked him what _____ [trade or industry] he was in.

familiar

■ I saw many _____ [well known] faces in the audience.

definite

■ Joe asked, "Have you any _____ [clearly defined] plans for tomorrow?"

evident

■ From his boisterous conduct, it is _____ [clear] that he has been celebrating for many hours.

hesitate

■ As Susan neared the church, she seemed to _____ [pause undecidedly] before entering the side door.

sacrifice

■ To give up something for an end regarded as better or superior is to _____.

peculiar	■ Because the young lad had some strange ideas about life and death, he was thought to be _____.
privilege	■ A special right to be granted is called a _____.
famil*iar*	■ Finish the spelling of *famil*___.
pecul*iar*	■ Finish the spelling of *pecul*___.
ev*i*dent	■ Complete the spelling of *ev__dent*.
con*fi*dent	■ Complete the spelling: *con___dent*.
d*i*vide	■ To separate or sever is to *d__vide*.
hes*i*tate	■ To pause undecidedly is to *hes__tate*.
def*i*nite	■ Clearly defined is the meaning of _____.
sacrifice	■ Something that you give up is called a _____.
business	■ Your work or occupation is your _____.
privilege	■ Because Tom finished his lessons on time, he was granted the _____ of going home early.

"o" and "u" Difficulty

chocolate	■ Three useful words that have "o" trouble are elabo-rate, apol*o*gy, and choc___late.
choc/o/late	■ The noun *chocolate* has three syllables: choc/o/late. The first syllable is ___.
choc/*o*/late	■ The second syllable is choc/___/late.
choc/o/*late*	■ The third syllable is choc/o/___.

choc/o/late

■ The three syllables are _____/__/_____.

chocolate

■ Write the entire word, saying it in syllables as you write: _____.

chocolate

■ *Chocolate* consists of ground roasted cacao beans and is used chiefly in candy and as a beverage: Whenever Sue stops at the coffee shop, she asks for a cup of hot _____.

chocolate

■ For an evening snack my mother prefers a cup of hot _____ and vanilla wafers.

o

■ Another word in which there is a troublesome "o" is *elab__rate.*

elaborate

■ The adjective *elaborate* means studied, painstaking, as in this sentence: The committee made _____ preparations for the ball.

e/lab/o/rate

■ There are four syllables in *elaborate:* e/lab/o/rate. The first syllable is __.

e/*lab*/o/rate

■ The second syllable is e/_____/o/rate.

e/lab/*o*/rate

■ The third syllable is e/lab/__/rate.

e/lab/o/*rate*

■ The last syllable is e/lab/o/_____.

e/lab/o/rate

■ Divide the word into four syllables: __/___/__/__.

elaborate

■ Write the entire word, saying it in syllables as you write: _____.

elaborate

■ Plans that have been studied and made with great care are _____ plans.

elaborate

■ The committee asked Jack to be chairman of the event because he would make _____ [painstaking] preparations for the final program.

apology

■ The noun *apology* has two *o*'s: ap__l__gy.

apology

■ The noun *apology* can be defined as something said or written that expresses regret for some improper act, as shown in this sentence: Jim's mother made him write an _____ to Mr. Gallen for hitting him with a snowball.

a/pol/o/gy

■ The noun *apology* has four syllables: a/pol/o/gy. The first syllable is __.

a/*pol*/o/gy

■ The second syllable is a/_____/o/gy.

a/pol/*o*/gy

■ The third syllable is a/pol/__/gy.

a/pol/o/*gy*

■ The last syllable is a/pol/o/_____.

a/pol/o/*gy*

■ The four syllables are __/_____/__/_____.

apology

■ Write the entire word, saying it in syllables as you write: _____.

apology

■ The official did not proceed with the hearing until the speaker offered an _____ for his remarks.

apology

■ Before Tim returned to the store, he wrote an _____ to the manager.

pursue

■ Four common words which need the "u" are *surprise, purpose, purchase,* and *p__rsue.*

pursue

■ To *pursue* means to chase, to go after, as in this sentence: The police were forced to _____ the thieves across town.

pur/sue

■ The verb *pursue* has two syllables: pur/sue. The first syllable is _____.

pur/*sue*

■ The second syllable is pur/_____.

pur/sue

■ The two syllables are _____/_____.

pursue

■ Write the entire word, saying it in syllables as you write: _____.

pursue

■ The victim promised to _____ the criminals until they were brought to justice.

pursue

■ When the two boys ran into the thick woods, it was impossible for the farmer to _____ them any farther.

purchase

■ The second word with "u" trouble is p___rchase.

purchase

■ The verb *purchase* means to buy for a price, as in this sentence: I intend to _____ a new car.

pur/chase

■ The verb *purchase* has two syllables: pur/chase. The first syllable is _____.

pur/*chase*

■ The second syllable is pur/_____.

pur/chase

■ The two syllables are _____/_____.

purchase

■ Write the entire word, saying it in syllables as you write: _____.

purchase

■ The noun *purchase* can be defined as that which is obtained for a price, as in this sentence: Although we shopped for hours, we came home with only one _____.

purchase

■ The corporation tried to _____ the insurance company for five thousand dollars.

purchase

■ The best _____ I made today was a new hat.

*pur*pose

■ Another word whose first syllable is *pur* is _____*pose*.

purpose	■ A *purpose* is an intention, an aim or goal, as shown in this sentence: We wondered about Jack's _____ in destroying the papers.
p*u*rpose	■ To have an aim or goal is to have a *p__rpose*.
pur/pose	■ The noun *purpose* has two syllables: pur/pose. The first syllable is _____.
pur/*pose*	■ The second syllable is pur/_____.
pur/pose	■ The two syllables are _____/_____.
purpose	■ Write the entire word, saying it in syllables as you write: _____.
purpose	■ None of the employees could understand the manager's _____ in issuing the new directive.
purpose	■ In agreeing to fly to Chicago, Nancy had a definite _____ in mind.
s*u*r	■ The last "u" word is *surprise*. Be sure to watch the first syllable, s__r.
surprise	■ The verb *surprise* means to amaze, as in this sentence: When she entered the world affairs contest, Janie knew that she would _____ her parents with her knowledge of current events.
surprise	■ The verb *surprise* also means to come upon without warning, as in this sentence: Alvin sneaked around the east corner of the barn to _____ his sister.
sur/prise	■ There are two syllables in *surprise:* sur/prise. The first syllable is _____.
sur/*prise*	■ The second syllable is sur/_____.

sur/prise	■ The two syllables are ____/____.
surprise	■ Write the entire word, saying it in syllables as you write: ____.
surprise	■ The boy's intention was to ____ us with his new bicycle.
surprise	■ By entering the side door of the conference room, I hoped to ____ him.
purpose	■ The warden asked the prisoner about his ____ [intention] in requesting the law books from the library.
purchase	■ The real estate broker stated that this month was the best time to ____ [buy for a price] a new home.
pursue	■ To chase or to go after is to ____.
surprise	■ Because his family knew his miserly habits, Joe knew he would ____ [amaze] them by calling long distance.
chocolate	■ My favorite beverage is hot ____.
apology	■ An expression of regret for some improper act is known as an ____.
purchase	■ To buy for a price is to ____.
elaborate	■ If you make preparations that are studied, you make ____ preparations.
purpose	■ An aim or goal is called a ____.
surprise	■ To come upon someone without warning is to ____ him.
pursue	■ To chase or to go after means to ____.

chocolate

■ Although I enjoy a piece of chocolate cake, I do not like _____ creams.

apology

■ The parents of the disobedient boy suggested that he offer an _____ [expression of regret] to the owner of the grocery store.

purchase

■ We traveled to the next town to _____ [buy for a price] a new power mower.

pursue

■ The sheriff's men tried to _____ [chase] the hit-and-run driver through the loop district but were prevented by the heavy traffic.

elaborate

■ If you work painstakingly on certain plans, you are making _____ plans.

surprise

■ To amaze, or to come upon without warning, is to _____.

purpose

■ An aim in life can be called a _____ in life.

Double Consonant Difficulty

■ Many words are called "demons" because they contain a double consonant which students forget to put in. For example, the word *accommodate* has two *c*'s, and two __'s.

m

■ The verb *accommodate* means to oblige, to favor, as in this sentence: I hope that the hotel will be able to _____ our entire delegation.

accommodate

■ If you spell the verb *accommodate* by syllables, you will find the spelling much easier. There are four syllables: ac/com/mo/date. The first syllable is ____.

ac/com/mo/date

■ The second syllable is ac/____/mo/date.

ac/*com*/mo/date

■ The third syllable is ac/com/____/date.

ac/com/*mo*/date

ac/com/mo/*date*	■ The last syllable is ac/com/mo/_____.
ac/com/mo/date	■ Divide the verb into syllables: ____/____/____/__.
ac*com*modate	■ To oblige or to favor is to *ac*_____.
accommodate	■ We received a letter from the motel manager stating that he could not _____ [oblige] us for the Fourth of July.
accommodate	■ The small auditorium in the high school will _____ only 300 people.
m	■ Remember, in the word *accommodate* there are two *c*'s and two __'s.
c	■ The verb *accompany* also has a double consonant: two __'s.
accompany	■ The verb *accompany* means to escort, to attend, as in this sentence: Miss Blake, the social studies teacher, will _____ the students on their field trips.
ac/com/pa/ny	■ There are four syllables in the verb *accompany:* The first syllable is _____.
ac/*com*/pa/ny	■ The second syllable is ac/_____/pa/ny.
ac/com/*pa*/ny	■ The third syllable is ac/com/_____/ny.
ac/com/pa/*ny*	■ The final syllable is ac/com/pa/_____.
ac/com/pa/ny	■ The four syllables are ____/____/____/____.
accompany	■ Write the entire word, saying it in syllables as you write: _____.
accompany	■ To escort, to attend means to _____.

accompany	■ The wives of the officials will _____ their husbands on the world tour.
ac/com/mo/date	■ Divide the verb *accommodate* into syllables: ____/ ____/____/____.
accumulate	■ Another demon that has two *c*'s is the verb *a*____*umulate*.
accumulate	■ The verb *accumulate* can be defined as to amass, to collect, as in this sentence: If a person lives in the same house for thirty years, he will _____ a lot of mementos.
ac/cu/mu/late	■ The verb *accumulate* is divided into syllables like this: ac/cu/mu/late. The first syllable is ____.
ac/*cu*/mu/late	■ The second syllable is ac/____/mu/late.
ac/cu/*mu*/late	■ The third syllable is ac/cu/____/late.
ac/cu/mu/*late*	■ The last syllable is ac/cu/mu/____.
ac/cu/mu/late	■ The four syllables are ____/____/____/____.
accumulate	■ Write the entire word, saying it in syllables, as you write: _____.
accumulate	■ If you amass or collect a large fortune, you _____ it.
accumulate	■ Jane's father exclaimed, "How many books can you _____ in a year?"
accompany	■ To escort means to _____.
p	■ The verb *appear* has a double __.

■ The verb *appear* means to come or be in sight, as in this sentence: Dick listened intently to the cues so that he could _____ on stage on time.

appear

■ The verb *appear* has two syllables: ap/pear. The first syllable is _____.

ap/pear

■ The second syllable is ap/_____.

ap/*pear*

■ The two syllables are _____/_____.

ap/pear

■ Many parents look forward to seeing their children _____ on a stage.

appear

■ An actor's biggest thrill is to see his name _____ in lights.

appear

■ Like the verb *appear*, the verb *appoint* has _____ *p*'s.

two

■ The verb *appoint* means to assign or designate, as in this sentence: The official will _____ two new deputies.

appoint

■ There are two syllables in *appoint*: ap/point. The first syllable is _____.

ap/point

■ The second syllable is ap/_____.

ap/*point*

■ The two syllables are _____/_____.

ap/point

■ Write the entire word, saying it in syllables as you write: _____.

appoint

■ From the list of eligible candidates, the governor decided to _____ the person who had the most experience.

appoint

■ Before retiring, the agent expressed his desire to _____ his successor.

appoint

appoint	■ To designate is to _____.
p	■ Remember that there are two __'s in *appoint*.
a*pp*rove	■ Another word with two *p*'s is the verb *a____rove*.
approve	■ The verb *approve* can be defined as to confirm, to sanction, as in this sentence: Before the official can take office, the congress must _____ his appointment.
ap/prove	■ The verb *approve* has two syllables: ap/prove. The first syllable is _____.
ap/*prove*	■ The second syllable is ap/_____.
ap/prove	■ The two syllables are _____/_____.
approve	■ Write the entire word, saying it in syllables as you write: _____.
approve	■ In small communities it is customary for the members of the school board to _____ the appointment of the teachers.
approve	■ Although I can say nothing against the plan, I do not _____ of it in every way.
a*pp*reciate	■ Another word with a double *p* is the verb *a____re-ciate*.
appreciate	■ The verb *appreciate* means to be thankful for, as in this sentence: Aunt Mary wrote me a letter saying that she would _____ all my kindness for many years.
appreciate	■ The verb *appreciate* also means to be fully aware of, as in the following sentence: We can certainly _____ the problem of transportation in the suburbs.
ap/pre/ci/ate	■ The verb *appreciate* has four syllables: ap/pre/ci/ate. The first syllable is _____.

ap/*pre*/ci/ate	■ The second syllable is ap/_____/ci/ate.
ap/pre/*ci*/ate	■ The third syllable is ap/pre/_____/ate.
ap/pre/ci/*ate*	■ The last syllable is ap/pre/ci/_____.
ap/pre/ci/ate	■ The four syllables are _____/_____/_____/_____.
appreciate	■ Write the entire word, saying it in syllables as you write: _____.
appreciate	■ Children should be brought up to _____ what their parents do for them.
appreciate	■ Mr. Smith told his secretary that he could _____ the dilemma in which she found herself.
r	■ Whereas the word *appreciate* has a double *p,* the verb *arrange* has a double __.
arrange	■ The verb *arrange* can be defined as to put in order, as in this sentence: I must _____ my books in the bookcase.
arrange	■ The verb *arrange* also means to adjust, as in this sentence: The cook will _____ the menus to fit the diets of the inmates.
ar/range	■ The verb *arrange* has two syllables: ar/range. The first syllable is _____.
ar/*range*	■ The second syllable is ar/_____.
ar/range	■ The two syllables are _____/_____.
arrange	■ Write the entire word, saying it in syllables as you write: _____.

arrange

■ The supervisor ordered the clerks to _____ all the applications according to the last name of the clients.

arrange

■ It took John an hour to decide how to _____ the clippings on the bulletin board.

r

■ Like the verb *arrange,* the verb *arrive* has a double ___.

arrive

■ The verb *arrive* means to reach a place, as in this sentence: The boat is scheduled to _____ at the port on the tenth of August.

arrive

■ The verb *arrive* can also mean to attain a state or condition by effort or study, as in the following sentence: The professor told the students that it should not take them very long to _____ at the right conclusion.

ar/rive

■ There are two syllables in *arrive:* ar/rive. The first syllable is _____.

ar/*rive*

■ The second syllable is ar/_____.

ar/rive

■ The two syllables are _____/_____.

arrive

■ Write the entire word, saying it in syllables as you write: _____.

arrive

■ Before a final agreement can be reached, all the participants must _____ at the best solutions to the problem.

arrive

■ Although Lawrence and his wife left an hour earlier, we were able to _____ at the country club before they did.

arrive

■ The statistician asked the student how he could _____ at such a solution.

n

■   When you read a book, you usually start at the beginning. The word *beginning* has a double ___.

beginning

■   The noun *beginning* can be defined as the origin, or
the start, as in this sentence: It is difficult for many adults
to understand about the _____ of the world.

be/gin/ning

■   The noun *beginning* has three syllables: be/gin/ning.
The first syllable is _____.

be/*gin*/ning

■   The second syllable is be/_____/ning.

be/gin/*ning*

■   The third syllable is be/gin/_____.

be/gin/ning

■   The three syllables are _____/_____/_____.

beginning

■   Write the entire word, saying it in syllables as you
write: _____.

beginning

■   The psychologist asked the patient to describe the
_____ of his daydreaming.

beginning

■   We were delayed by traffic so long that we arrived
after the _____ of the play.

commence

■   The verb *commence* means to begin, as in this sentence: When does the program _____?

com/mence

■   The verb *commence* is divided into two syllables:
com/mence. The first syllable is _____.

com/*mence*

■   The second syllable is com/_____.

com/mence

■   The two syllables are _____/_____.

commence

■   Write the entire word, saying it in syllables as you
write: _____.

commence	■ Jim was not sure what time the exercises would _____ [begin].
commence	■ This summer the park recreation activities will _____ [begin] on the fifteenth of June.
committee	■ A body of persons chosen to act upon some matter is a *committee,* as in this sentence: The manager appointed a _____ to study the grievances of the workers.
com/mit/tee	■ The noun *committee* has three syllables: com/mit/tee. The first syllable is _____.
com/*mit*/tee	■ The second syllable is com/_____/tee.
com/mit/*tee*	■ The third syllable is com/mit/_____.
com/mit/tee	■ The three syllables are _____/_____/_____.
committee	■ Write the entire word, saying it in syllables as you write: _____.
committee	■ The governor appointed a _____ to study the rural unemployment situation.
committee	■ The chairman asked whether the _____ was ready to present its recommendations.
embarrass	■ The verb *embarrass* means to confuse or to perplex, as in this sentence: His remarks seemed to _____ the young women.
em/bar/rass	■ There are three syllables in *embarrass:* em/bar/rass. The first syllable is _____.
em/*bar*/rass	■ The second syllable is em/_____/rass.
em/bar/*rass*	■ The third syllable is em/bar/_____.

em/bar/rass

■ The three syllables are ____/____/____.

embarrass

■ Write the entire word, saying it in syllables as you write: _____.

embarrass

■ Modern ways of living tend to _____ [confuse] the older generation.

embarrass

■ When Sam stood up to speak about the rights of the minority group, he did not intend to _____ his family.

essential

■ The adjective *essential* means very important or indispensable, as in this sentence: Good study habits are _____ to success in college.

es/sen/tial

■ The adjective *essential* has three syllables: es/sen/tial. The first syllable is ____.

es/*sen*/tial

■ The second syllable is es/____/tial.

es/sen/*tial*

■ The last syllable is es/sen/____.

es/sen/tial

■ The three syllables are ____/____/____.

essential

■ Write the entire word, saying it in syllables as you write: _____.

essential

■ It is _____ that the board hold its first meeting on Monday.

essential

■ The speaker enumerated the _____ factors in the bribery case.

essential

■ A balanced diet is _____ to good health.

immediately

■ The adverb *immediately* can be defined as without delay, as in this sentence: His mother told him to go _____ into the house.

im/me/di/ate/ly	■ The adverb *immediately* has five syllables: im/me/di/ate/ly. The first syllable is _____.
im/*me*/di/ate/ly	■ The second syllable is im/_____/di/ate/ly.
im/me/*di*/ate/ly	■ The third syllable is im/me/_____/ate/ly.
im/me/di/*ate*/ly	■ The fourth syllable is im/me/di/_____/ly.
im/me/di/ate/*ly*	■ The last syllable is _____.
im/me/di/ate/ly	■ The five syllables are _____/_____/_____/_____/_____.
immediately	■ Write the entire word, saying it in syllables as you write: _____.
immediately	■ If you are asked to do something without delay, you will do it _____.
immediately	■ After Jane's father called to her several times, he said, "Jane, come here _____."
immediately	■ When the workmen heard the whistle, they put down their tools _____ and left for lunch.
necessary	■ The adjective *necessary* means essential or indispensable, as in this sentence: It is _____ for a teacher to be able to spell well.
nec/es/sar/y	■ There are four syllables in the adjective *necessary:* nec/es/sar/y. The first syllable is _____.
nec/*es*/sar/y	■ The second syllable is nec/_____/sar/y.
nec/es/*sar*/y	■ The third syllable is nec/es/_____/y.
nec/es/sar/*y*	■ The last syllable is nec/es/sar/__.

necessary

■ Write the entire word, saying it in syllables as you write: _____.

necess*ary*

■ Jane's mother told her it was *neces*_____ for her to go to the store.

s

■ Remember that there is a double __ in *necessary*.

necessary

■ Fill in the missing letters: *nece*_____*ary*.

nec*essary*

■ In baking most pastry, flour is a *nec*_____ ingredient.

ess*ential*
nec*essary*

■ Two words that mean indispensable are *es*_____ and *nec*_____.

occasion

■ The noun *occasion* can be defined as an occurrence or a happening as in this sentence: His daughter's birthday party was a very happy _____ for Jim Harrington.

oc/ca/sion

■ There are three syllables in *occasion:* oc/ca/sion. The first syllable is _____.

oc/*ca*/sion

■ The second syllable is oc/_____/sion.

oc/ca/*sion*

■ The last syllable is oc/ca/_____.

oc/ca/sion

■ The three syllables are _____/_____/_____.

occasion

■ Write the entire word, saying it in syllables as you write: _____.

occasion

■ Graduation is a joyous _____ for many young people.

one

■ Remember that there are two *c*'s and only _____ *s* in *occasion*.

opposite

■ The adjective *opposite* means opposed or hostile, as in this sentence: Even though they were brothers, each represented the _____ sides of the question.

op/po/site

■ The adjective *opposite* has three syllables: op/po/site. The first syllable is ____.

op/*po*/site

■ The second syllable is op/____/site.

op/po/*site*

■ The third syllable is op/po/____.

op/po/site

■ The three syllables are ____/____/____.

opposite

■ Write the entire word, saying it in syllables as you write: _____.

opposite

■ Although Mark and Steven are brothers, they are _____ in character and appearance.

opposite

■ The cousins live on _____ sides of the street.

opposite

■ The teachers thought the students would take the affirmative side of the question, but to their amazement, the pupils chose the _____ side.

para*ll*el

■ A word having a double *l* is *para____el.*

parallel

■ The adjective *parallel* means extending in the same direction without meeting, as in this sentence: The art instructor assigned a design that consisted of _____ lines.

parallel

■ The adjective *parallel* can also mean similar, or having a marked likeness, as in the following sentence: Floyd's experience in a Paris cafe was _____ to the one I had in Venice.

par/al/lel

■ *Parallel* has three syllables: par/al/lel. The first syllable is ____.

par/*al*/lel

■ The second syllable is par/_____/lel.

par/al/*lel*

■ The third syllable is par/al/_____.

par/al/lel

■ The three syllables are _____/_____/_____.

parallel

■ Write the entire word, saying it in syllables as you write: _____.

par*allel*

■ The parallel bars in the gymnasium are a pair of bars raised about five feet from the floor and *par*_____ to each other.

parallel

■ If two situations bear a marked likeness to each other, they can be called _____.

parallel

■ Extending in the same direction without meeting is the definition of the adjective _____.

parallel

■ The double l's in parallel are _____.

possess

■ The verb *possess* can be defined as to own, as in this sentence: The elderly woman cannot _____ very much property.

pos/sess

■ There are only two syllables in *possess:* pos/sess. The first syllable is _____.

pos/*sess*

■ The second syllable is pos/_____.

pos/sess

■ The two syllables of *possess* are _____/_____.

possess

■ Write the entire word, saying it in syllables as you write: _____.

possess

■ The boy's ambition was to _____ a knife of his own.

possess

■ Because the old man gave away much of the salary he earned, he could never _____ great wealth.

s

■ Remember the word *possess* has two double __'s.

m

■ The last word having a double consonant that we shall study is the verb *recommend*. The verb *recommend* has a double __.

recommend

■ To *recommend* means to praise, as in this sentence: The committee will _____ highly the work of the housing commission.

recommend

■ The verb *recommend* also means to offer or suggest, as in the following sentence: When you asked the plumber about the drainpipe, what did he _____?

rec/om/mend

■ The verb *recommend* has three syllables: rec/om/mend. The first syllable is _____.

rec/*om*/mend

■ The second syllable is rec/_____/mend.

rec/om/*mend*

■ The last syllable is rec/om/_____.

rec/om/mend

■ The three syllables are _____/_____/_____.

recommend

■ Write the entire word, saying it in syllables as you write: _____.

recommend

■ When Mr. Green was asked his opinion, he stated that he planned to _____ that a public referendum be held in the fall.

recommend

■ Because Lois Hastings does such fine work, it is easy to _____ that she be promoted.

recommend

■ When the employment counselor called about Mr. Harmon, I said I could _____ him highly.

recommend

■ To praise means to *rec*____.

recommend

■ To suggest also means to _____.

recommend

■ Don't forget the two *m*'s in *reco*____*end*.

possess

■ To own is to _____.

parallel

■ In placing two pictures on the wall, the artist wanted one *par*____*el* to the other.

recommend

■ I shall *rec*____*mend* that the wages be increased.

commence

■ We waited an hour for the festivities to _____ [begin].

necessary

■ Indispensable means *nec*____.

essential

■ Indispensable also means *es*____.

committee

■ Joe was asked to explain the recommendations to his _____ [body of persons studying a matter].

embarrass

■ When I rise to speak for the approval of the amendment, I hope that I will not *embar*____ my parents.

occasion

■ It was a very happy _____ [occurrence] for all.

immediately

■ To go to school without delay is to go _____.

opposite

■ Opposed or hostile means *op*____*site*.

accommodate

■ To oblige or favor is to *ac*____*date*.

accompany

■ To escort is to *ac*____*pany*.

appreciate

■ To be thankful for is to *ap*_____.

*ar*range

■ To put in order is to ____*range.*

arrive

■ When a group reach a certain place, they _____.

begin*ning*

■ The start of a play is the *begin*____.

a*p*prove

■ To sanction is to *a*____*rove.*

a*p*pear

■ When the actors come in sight on the stage, they *a*____*ear.*

accumulate

■ To amass or collect is to _____.

a*p*point

■ The commissioner will ____*point* a committee to study the highway problem.

c
one

■ The verb *accumulate* has a double __ and ____ m.

m

■ The verb *accommodate* has two *c*'s and two __'s.

p

■ The verbs *approve, appear,* and *appoint* have a double __.

r

■ The verbs *arrange* and *arrive* have a double __.

m

■ The words *committee, commence,* and *recommend* have a double __.

s

■ The adjectives *necessary* and *essential* have a double __.

c
one

■ The noun *occasion* has a double __ and _____ s.

para*ll*el

■ Remember that the double *l*'s in parallel are *para*____*el.*

two

■ There are _____ double *s*'s in *possess.*

Single Consonants

■ Some words are misspelled by putting in more consonants than those required. For example, the word *across* has only _____ *c*.

one

■ The word *across* has two syllables: a/cross. The first syllable is __.

a/cross

■ The second syllable is a/_____.

a/*cross*

■ The two syllables are __/_____.

a/cross

■ The preposition *across* means to or on the opposite side of, as in this sentence: If David goes to the other side of the lake, he will have to go _____ the lake.

across

■ In order to reach the village on the opposite side of the river, one has to row _____ the river.

across

■ To reach the store, you must go _____ the schoolyard and turn to the left.

across

■ To get to the other side of the stream, you must walk _____ the bridge.

across

■ There is only _____ *c* in *across*.

one

■ Like *across,* the word *around* has two syllables. These syllables are a/round, the first of which is __.

a/round

■ The second syllable is a/_____.

a/*round*

■ The two syllables of *around* are __/_____.

a/round

■ The preposition *around* means on all sides of, as in the following sentence: To keep trespassers away, the caretaker constructed a fence _____ the estate.

around

■ We motored _____ the lake.

around

around

■ It took the father and his two sons an hour to go _____ the farm.

a

■ *Across* and *around* have the same first syllable: __.

across

■ To get to the opposite side you go __*cross*.

around

■ The park board had to build a fence __*round* the tennis court.

imagine

■ The verb *imagine* means to form a mental image, as in this sentence: After hearing about the new buildings being constructed, we had to _____ what the city looked like.

imagine

■ The verb *imagine* can also mean to suppose, to think to be, as in this sentence: Because it was a closed meeting, we had to _____ what was going on.

im/ag/ine

■ The verb *imagine* has three syllables: im/ag/ine. The first syllable is _____.

im/*ag*/ine

■ The second syllable is im/_____/ine.

im/ag/*ine*

■ The third syllable is im/ag/_____.

im/ag/ine

■ The three syllables are _____/_____/_____.

imagine

■ Write the entire word, saying it in syllables as you write: _____.

imagine

■ When Bill told us he had good news, we could not _____ what it could be.

one

■ The verb *operate* has only _____ p.

operate

■ The verb *operate* means to work or to function, as in this sentence: The foreman was not sure that the machine would _____ properly.

op/er/ate

■ There are three syllables in *operate:* op/er/ate. The first syllable is _____.

op/*er*/ate

■ The second syllable is op/_____/ate.

op/er/*ate*

■ The third syllable is op/er/_____.

op/er/ate

■ The three syllables are _____/_____/_____.

operate

■ Write the entire word, saying it in syllables as you write: _____.

operate

■ The supervisor asked the new employee to _____ the mimeograph machine.

operate

■ The old multilith machine seems to _____ better than the new one.

one

■ Our last word in this group is *professor*. This noun has only _____ *f*.

professor

■ A *professor* is one who teaches in higher education, as in this sentence: On the first day of college classes, we were given our first assignments by the mathematics _____.

pro/fes/sor

■ The noun *professor* has three syllables: pro/fes/sor. The first syllable is _____.

pro/*fes*/sor

■ The second syllable is pro/_____/sor.

pro/fes/*sor*

■ The third syllable is pro/fes/_____.

pro/fes/sor

■ The three syllables are _____/_____/_____.

professor

■ Write the entire word, saying it in syllables as you write: _____.

professor

■ When Dick accepted the position at the university, he was given the rank of assistant _____.

professor

■ A college teacher who has been given academic rank is usually called a _____.

professor

■ Although some of my teachers are instructors, the one who conducts my English class is a *pro*_____.

operate

■ To work or to function means to _____.

imagine

■ When asked if I had heard the rumor, I replied, "I can only _____ [form a mental image] what he said."

around

■ The school children marked lines ___*round* the school.

across

■ Why do you have to go ___*cross* the bridge to get to the opposite side?

professor

■ After receiving a failure on the midsemester examination, Carol asked the *pro*_____*sor* for help.

operate

■ Neither machine will _____ [function] properly.

professor

■ Fill in the missing letter: *pro*___*essor*.

operate

■ Fill in the missing letter: *o*___*erate*.

imagine

■ Fill in the missing letter: *i*___*agine*.

across
around

■ Fill in the missing letters: *a*___*ross*, *a*___*ound*.

Silent Letters

■ Silent letters cause a certain amount of misspelling. For example, you are familiar with the word *answer*. The silent letter, or the letter for which there is no sound, would be the letter ___ in *answer*.

w

■ The silent letter in *answer* is ___.

w

answer

■ The noun *answer* means a reply, as in this sentence: When the instructor asked her a question, Joan quickly gave him an _____.

answer

■ The noun *answer* also means a solution to a problem, as in this sentence: The mathematics professor was surprised that I had the correct _____.

an/swer

■ Now let us take a look at the word *answer* and its syllables: an/swer. There are just two syllables, the first of which is _____/swer.

an/*swer*

■ The second syllable is an/_____.

an/swer

■ The two syllables are _____/_____.

answer

■ Write the entire word, saying it in syllables as you write: _____.

answer

■ My father liked the arithmetic books that he used years ago because he could always find the _____ in the back of the book.

answer

■ The question was so complicated that the speaker could not give a simple _____.

answer

■ Our parents have taught us to _____ promptly when called.

doubt

■ The word *doubt* means to be undecided, as in the following sentence: I _____ whether the machine will work.

doubt

■ If you question something, you *doubt* it, as in this sentence: I sincerely _____ his honesty.

b

■ The word *doubt* has only one syllable: doubt/. It also has a silent letter: dou___t.

doubt

■ The fact that I am undecided as to which person to believe puts me in _____.

doubt

■ Lucy is in _____ about which coat to buy.

doubt

■ Mr. Cunningham stated that he had never had any reason to _____ my brother's word.

b

■ Like the word *doubt,* the word *debt* has a silent ___.

one

■ The noun *debt* also has only _____ syllable: debt/.

debt

■ The noun *debt* can be defined as a state of owing, as in this sentence: Because he purchased a new house and a new car at the same time, George Simmons will be in _____ for a long time.

debt

■ The noun *debt* is also a thing owed, as in the following sentence: He must pay his _____ at the store before the manager will give him more credit.

debt

■ The state of owing is called _____.

debt

■ A thing owed is known as a _____.

is not

■ Another common and useful word containing a silent letter is *mortgage.* The *t* in *mortgage* [is, is not] pronounced.

mortgage

■ To *mortgage* a house is to subject it to claim or obligation, as in this sentence: In order to get the large loan I needed, I had to _____ my house.

mort/gage

■ The noun *mortgage* has two syllables: mort/gage. The first syllable is _____.

mort/*gage*

■ The second syllable is mort/_____.

■ Write the entire word, saying it in syllables as you write: _____.

mortgage

■ In the verb *mortgage* there is a silent __.

t

■ If you want to borrow a large sum of money, you may have to _____ your house.

mortgage

■ The word *guardian* has a silent letter right after the g. That letter is __.

u

■ One who guards or keeps safe or secure is called a g__ardian.

guardian

■ The noun *guardian* has three syllables: guard/i/an. The first syllable is the same as the verb _____.

guard/i/an

■ The second syllable is guard/__/an.

guard/i/an

■ The third syllable is guard/i/_____.

guard/i/an

■ The three syllables are _____/__/_____.

guard/i/an

■ Write the entire word, saying it in syllables as you write: _____.

guardian

■ The court finally appointed a _____ for the elderly man.

guardian

■ When the parents were killed in a car crash, the administrator of the estate requested that a _____ be appointed for the children.

guardian

■ Always spell *guardian* with a __ after the g.

u

■ Fill in the missing letter: *mor__gage*.

mortgage

■ Fill in the missing letter: *g__ardian*.

guardian

■ A thing owed is a _____.

debt

answer

■ A solution to a problem is an *ans___er*.

doubt

■ To question someone's integrity is to *dou___t* it.

guardian

■ One who guards is known as a _____.

answer

■ A reply is an _____.

mortgage

■ If Joe borrows a large sum of money, he will have to _____ his house as security.

doubt

■ To be undecided is to _____.

debt

■ Before the credit union would lend him any money, they told him he would have to pay his outstanding _____ [thing owed].

guardian

■ The court appointed a _____ [one who keeps safe] for my mother.

answer

■ There were only two students who could supply the correct _____ [solution] to the problem.

is not

■ Two important words in your vocabulary are *knowledge* and *psychology*. Pronounce both words. Each is written with a beginning letter that [is, is not] pronounced.

k

■ The noun *knowledge* begins with the silent consonant ___.

knowledge

■ The noun *knowledge* can be defined as learning, as in this sentence: If a student studies hard, he can accumulate a vast amount of _____.

knowledge

■ The noun *knowledge* can also be defined as practical skill gained by experience, as in this sentence: Although Mr. Dunn has never attended college, he has a considerable _____ about economics and government.

■ The noun *knowledge* has only two syllables: knowl/edge. The first is _____.

knowl/edge

■ The second syllable is knowl/_____.

knowl/*edge*

■ The two syllables are _____/_____.

knowl/edge

■ Write the entire word, saying it in syllables as you write: _____.

knowledge

■ A comprehensive examination usually tests a student's _____ of a subject in many aspects.

knowledge

■ Through diligent study of books on mechanics and experience in his uncle's shop, William has acquired a _____ of the automobile repair trade.

knowledge

■ Like the word *knowledge,* the noun *psychology* also begins with a _____ letter.

silent

■ Say the word *psychology.* The consonant *p* at the beginning of the word is _____ pronounced.

not

■ The noun *psychology* can be defined as the science of the mind, as in this sentence: Because Barbara is interested in the behavior of people, she has decided to major in _____ in college.

psychology

■ The noun *psychology* is divided into syllables in this manner: psy/chol/o/gy. The first syllable is _____.

psy/chol/o/gy

■ The second syllable is psy/_____/o/gy.

psy/*chol*/o/gy

■ The third syllable is psy/chol/___/gy.

psy/chol/*o*/gy

■ The last syllable is psy/chol/o/_____.

psy/chol/o/*gy*

■ The four syllables are _____/_____/___/_____.

psy/chol/o/gy

psychology

■ Write the entire word, saying it in syllables as you write: _____.

psychology

■ The science that deals with the mind is called _____.

psychology

■ It is important for an elementary teacher to be trained in child _____.

knowledge

■ An astronomer has considerable _____ [learning] of celestial bodies and their functions.

k

■ In pronouncing the noun *knowledge,* the first sound you utter is represented by the letter *n.* However, in writing this word, the first letter you write is __.

s p

■ Pronounce the word *psychology.* The first sound you utter is represented by the letter __. However, the first letter that you write in spelling this word is __.

psychology

■ The public school administrator is concentrating on the study of _____ [science of the mind] for his doctorate.

silent

■ Three words with a silent *gh* that give students much trouble are *although, ought,* and *through.* Pronounce each one carefully. Notice that the *gh* in each word is _____.

although

■ Say the word *although.* It rhymes with the word "go." The word with the silent *gh* that rhymes with "go" is _____.

al/though

■ *Although* has just two syllables, the first of which is ____/*though.*

al/*though*

■ The second syllable is al/____.

although

■ Write the entire word, saying it in syllables as you write: _____.

although

■ The word *although* is a conjunction meaning in spite of the fact that, as in this sentence: I shall go to the party _____ I do not care to dance.

although

■ The carpenter can still work a ten-hour day _____ he is seventy-five years old.

gh

■ The second word with the silent *gh* is *ought*. Remember that the verb *ought* has a silent _____.

ought

■ The verb *ought* rhymes with the word "taught." Say the word *ought* and now write the word that rhymes with "taught" _____.

ought

■ *Ought* is an auxiliary or helping verb which is usually followed by an infinitive: I _____ to go home.

ought

■ *Ought* can mean to be necessary, as in this sentence: To be able to live comfortably, a man _____ to make a good monthly salary.

ought

■ Although I did not want to leave the concert early, I _____ to catch the nine o'clock train for Milwaukee.

ou*ght*

■ Complete the spelling of the auxiliary verb that means to be necessary: *ou*_____.

al*though*

■ Complete the spelling of the conjunction that can be defined as in spite of the fact that: *al*_____.

Although
ought

■ Complete the following sentence by using the two words with a silent *gh* that you have just learned: _____ I trust the cashier, I _____ to check the receipts more carefully.

gh

■ The last word with a silent *gh* is *through*. Remember that this word ends in a silent _____.

■ The word *through* rhymes with "too." Say the word. Although it sounds like "too," it ends in a _____ gh.

silent

■ *Through* is a preposition which means in at one side and out the opposite side, as in this sentence: I pounded the nail _____ the piece of wood.

through

■ The preposition *through* also means from the beginning to the end, as in this sentence: He managed to make money _____ the years of the Great Depression.

through

■ I plan to be in Scotland _____ the month of September.

through

■ No matter how hard I tried, I could not press the tack _____ the cardboard.

through

■ The auxiliary verb which means to be necessary is _____.

ought

■ The science of the mind is called _____.

psychology

■ Harold has gained considerable _____ [learning] from his travels in foreign countries.

knowledge

■ The school of nursing agreed to consider Lucy's application _____ [in spite of the fact that] she was over the maximum age limit.

although

"ense" Difficulty

■ There are four useful words that end in *ense: defense, expense, license,* and *sen___e.*

sense

■ A common definition of the noun *sense* is sound reasoning, as in this sentence: When confronted with a very difficult problem to solve, the boys always show _____ in arriving at a solution.

sense

sen*se*	■ There is only one syllable: sense. The noun is spelled *sen*____.
s*ense*	■ Sound reasoning is called s____.
sense	■ The father feared for his son's life because he did not always show good _____ when faced with an emergency.
def*ense*	■ The second word ending in *ense* is *def*____.
defense	■ The noun *defense* can be defined as protection from attack, as in the following sentence: The nation must build a strong _____.
de/fense	■ The noun *defense* has two syllables: de/fense. The first syllable is ____.
de/*fense*	■ The second syllable is de/____.
de/fense	■ The two syllables are ____/____.
defense	■ Protection from attack means _____.
defense	■ *Defense* can also mean an argument used to support or justify one's action, as in this sentence: When asked about his violent behavior, the prisoner put up a good _____.
defense	■ The traitor publicly stated that he would never go to the _____ of his country.
exp*ense*	■ The third noun ending in *ense* is *exp*____.
expense	■ The noun *expense* can be defined as outlay or expenditure, as in this sentence: To send a boy or girl to college can be quite an _____.
ex/pense	■ The noun *expense* has two syllables: ex/pense. The first syllable is ____.

ex/*pense*	■ The second syllable is ex/_____.
ex/pense	■ The two syllables are _____/_____.
ense	■ Like *defense,* the noun *expense* also ends in _____.
expense	■ A complete wardrobe for school can amount to quite a large _____.
expense	■ An expenditure or outlay is called an _____.
ense	■ *License* also ends in *ense.* Although it can be spelled licence, the preferred spelling is en__e.
license	■ The noun *license* is a formal permission from authorities to do something, as in the following sentence: An operator of a cafe must have a _____.
license	■ The verb *license* means to permit, or authorize, as in this sentence: The city will _____ only ten people to run the concessions at the county fair.
li/cense	■ The word *license* has two syllables: li/cense. The first syllable is _____.
li/*cense*	■ The second syllable is li/_____.
li/cense	■ The two syllables are _____/_____.
license	■ To permit or authorize is to _____.
license	■ Formal permission from authorities to do something is known as a _____.
license	■ Mary applied for a driver's _____ last Thursday.
license	■ The fee for a marriage _____ has been raised two dollars.

■ Although the word *license* can be spelled *ence,* you should use the preferred spelling: *li_____.*

license

■ The noun that means outlay or expenditure is _____.

expense

■ The noun that can be defined as protection from attack is _____.

defense

■ Sound reasoning is called _____.

sense

■ To permit or to authorize means to _____.

license

Mispronunciation Difficulty

■ Some words are misspelled because they are not pronounced correctly. For example, the word *February* is sometimes pronounced "Febuary" and spelled without the first ___.

r

■ The noun *February* stands for the second month of the year, as in this sentence: The second month of the year is _____.

February

■ The noun *February* is divided into syllables like this: Feb/ru/ar/y. The first syllable is _____.

Feb/ru/ar/y

■ The second syllable contains two letters: Feb/_____/ ar/y.

Feb/*ru*/ar/y

■ The third syllable is Feb/ru/_____/y.

Feb/ru/*ar*/y

■ The last syllable is Feb/ru/ar/__.

Feb/ru/ar/*y*

■ The four syllables are _____/_____/_____/__.

Feb/ru/ar/y

■ Write the entire noun, saying it in syllables as you write: _____.

February

February ■ The second month in the year is called _____.

February ■ Valentine's Day always comes on the fourteenth of _____.

February ■ The only month in the year that has only twenty-eight days, except in Leap Year when it has twenty-nine, is _____.

February ■ In Leap Year the month of _____ has twenty-nine days instead of twenty-eight.

February ■ Don't forget to pronounce and write both the *r*'s in *Feb__ua__y.*

govern ■ Remember that the noun *government* consists of the root word *govern* and the suffix *ment,* and the root word ends in *gover__.*

government ■ *Government* is an established form of political administration, as in this sentence: New Hope has a city-manager type of _____.

gov/ern/ment ■ The noun *government* has three syllables: gov/ern/ment. The first syllable is _____.

gov/*ern*/ment ■ The second syllable is gov/_____/ment.

gov/ern/*ment* ■ The third syllable is gov/ern/_____.

gov/ern/ment ■ The three syllables are _____/_____/_____.

government ■ Write the entire word, saying it in syllables as you write: _____.

government ■ An established form of political administration is a _____.

government ■ All high officials of any _____ should be elected with great care.

government

■ Sam Smith has just received a position with the United States _____.

two

■ Because students often mispronounce the word *athlete,* they misspell it. Look at the word *ath/lete* and then pronounce it. The word has only _____ syllables.

athlete

■ The noun *athlete* can be defined as a person who is trained to contend in exercises that require physical endurance and agility, as in this sentence: John Daniel has been chosen as the finest _____ in the history of Elm Senior High School.

ath/lete

■ The noun *athlete* has two syllables, the first of which is ____/lete.

ath/*lete*

■ The second syllable is ath/_____.

athlete

■ Write the entire word, saying it in syllables as you write: _____.

athlete

■ Jerry's ambition is to be a famous _____ like his brother.

athlete

■ The sports writers are predicting that Bill Bascom will be a famous _____.

three

■ Now look at a similar word: *athletics,* and pronounce it. There are _____ syllables in this word.

ath/let/ics

■ The first syllable of ath/let/ics is ____.

ath/*let*/ics

■ The second syllable is ath/_____/ics.

ath/let/*ics*

■ The last syllable is ath/let/_____.

athletics

■ Write the entire word, saying it in syllables as you write: _____.

athletics

■ Athletics can be defined as the games and sports of athletes, as in this sentence: Our high school has a fine program of _____.

athletics

■ The games and sports of athletes are called _____.

athlete

■ A person who is trained to contend in physical exercises that require physical stamina and agility is an _____.

t

■ The noun *kindergarten* is mispronounced quite frequently, resulting in the misspelling of this word. If you remember that the noun comes from the German (meaning children's garden), and that garden in German is spelled gar__en, you will spell this noun correctly.

kindergar*t*en

■ A school for young children about the age of five is called a *kindergar__en*.

kin/der/gar/ten

■ The noun *kindergarten* has four syllables: kin/der/gar/ten. The first syllable is _____.

kin/*der*/gar/ten

■ The second syllable is kin/_____/gar/ten.

kin/der/*gar*/ten

■ The third syllable is kin/der/_____ten.

kin/der/gar/*ten*

■ The last syllable is kin/der/gar/_____.

kin/der/gar/ten

■ The four syllables are _____/_____/_____/_____.

kindergarten

■ Write the entire word, saying it in syllables as you write: _____.

kindergarten

■ One principal advantage of _____ is that children learn to get along with each other.

kindergarten

■ The five-year-old twins will enroll in _____ this fall.

kindergarten

■ Fill in the missing letter: *kindergar___en.*

t

■ Another word for which a *d* is sometimes wrongly written for a *t* is the noun *gratitude.* Remember to pronounce both *t*'s in gra___itude.

■ The noun *gratitude* can be defined as the state of being grateful, or thankfulness, as in this sentence: The girl expressed her _____ for the kindness shown gratitude by her neighbors.

grat/i/tude

■ The noun *gratitude* has three syllables: grat/i/tude. The first syllable is ___.

grat/*i*/tude

■ The second syllable is grat/___/tude.

grat/i/*tude*

■ The third syllable is grat/i/___.

grat/i/tude

■ The three syllables are ___/___/___.

gratitude

■ Write the entire word, saying it in syllables as you write: _____.

gratitude

■ More people would endear themselves to others if they expressed their _____ more often.

gratitude

■ The family expressed its _____ to the lifeguards for saving their son's life.

three

■ The last three words that we shall study in this chapter are frequently mispronounced and misspelled because they are not syllabified correctly. For example, *interest* has three syllables, not two. There are _____ syllables in the word *interest.*

in/ter/est

■ The word *interest* is divided into syllables like this: in/ter/est. The first syllable is ___.

in/*ter*/est

■ The second syllable is in/___/est.

in/ter/*est*

■ The third syllable is in/ter/_____.

in/ter/est

■ The three syllables are _____/_____/_____.

interest

■ Write the word, saying it in syllables as you write: _____.

interest

■ *Interest* can be used as a verb meaning to engage the attention of, as in the following sentence: Carol hopes to _____ her friends in doing volunteer work at the hospital.

interest

■ *Interest* can also be used as a noun meaning the excitement of feeling accompanying special attention to some object, as in this sentence: The speaker was able to hold the _____ of his listeners.

interest

■ Reading mystery stories is the only hobby that might _____ him.

interest

■ Because of my dislike for winter weather, I could never develop an _____ in ice skating.

disastrous

■ The next word we shall study is *disastrous,* which means producing or attended with disaster or misfortune, as in this sentence: The decision of the board had a _____ effect on the fund-raising campaign.

dis/as/trous

■ The adjective *disastrous* has only three syllables: dis/as/trous. The first syllable is _____.

dis/*as*/trous

■ The second syllable is dis/_____/trous.

dis/as/*trous*

■ The last syllable is dis/as/_____.

dis/as/trous

■ The three syllables are _____/_____/_____.

disastrous

■ Write the entire word, saying it in syllables as you write: _____.

■ The adjective which means producing or attended
with disaster or misfortune is _____.

disastrous

■ The trip to Europe proved to be very _____
for the Ericksons.

disastrous

■ The results of investing too much money in stocks
and bonds might be _____ [attended with disaster].

disastrous

■ Another word that is frequently misspelled because
it is mispronounced is *vacuum*. Remember that there are
_____ syllables in this word: vac/u/um.

three

■ The noun *vacuum* has three syllables: vac/u/um.
The first syllable is _____.

vac/u/um

■ The second syllable is vac/___/um.

vac/*u*/um

■ The last syllable is vac/u/_____.

vac/u/*um*

■ The three syllables are _____/___/_____.

vac/u/um

■ Write the entire word, saying it in syllables as you
write: _____.

vacuum

■ Remember there are two ___'s in *vacuum*.

u

■ As an adjective *vacuum* means operated by a device
producing a partial vacuum, as in this sentence: We just
purchased a brand new _____ cleaner.

vacuum

■ The noun *vacuum* means a gap or void, as in this
sentence: The father's death has left a _____ in
their lives.

vacuum

■ Mother went shopping for a _____ cleaner.

vacuum

■ Attended with disaster or misfortune is the definition
of the adjective _____.

disastrous

in/ter/est

■ Divide the word *interest* into syllables: _____.

u

■ There are two ___'s in *vacuum*.

February

■ The month that ordinarily has only twenty-eight days is called _____.

athlete

■ A person who takes part in games of endurance and wins high honors can be called a fine _____.

government

■ An established form of political administration is a _____.

kindergarten

■ A school for very young children is known as a _____.

vacuum

■ It is easier to do housework if you have a _____ cleaner.

disastrous

■ Attended with disaster or misfortune is the definition of the adjective _____.

interest

■ To engage the attention of is to *in*_____.

gratitude

■ The act of being grateful is called _____.

disastrous

■ The announcement of the railroad strike will have a _____*trous* effect on the nation's transportation.

vacuum

■ The newlyweds purchased a refrigerator, a dish washer, and a *vac*___*um* cleaner.

February

■ Don't forget the first *r* in *Feb*___*uary*.

athletics

■ Games and sports are called _____.

chapter 9

Suffixes

Do you know what happens to a word when you add a suffix like *ance* or *ly?* Do you know that the ending *ance* forms a noun, and that the suffix *ly* forms either an adjective or an adverb? If you know the *why* of anything, you will be able to understand the process involved.

Suffixes (the elements added to the end of words) cause spelling difficulty for two reasons. First, there are alternative spellings: *ance-ence, able-ible, ary-ery.* Secondly, the spelling of some basic words must be changed before adding suffixes beginning with a vowel.

The suffixes that cause the greatest confusion in spelling are included in this chapter: *ance-ence, able-ible, ary-ery, ous, ly, efy-ify,* and *ize-ise-yze.* In reading these variant spellings you have undoubtedly recognized those that cause you some or considerable difficulty. Study the generalizations carefully, learn to spell the words in the unit, and you will be well on your way toward becoming a better speller.

Test for Chapter 9

Fill in the appropriate endings as indicated in parts *A, B, C.*

A. ance-ence

 1. attend_____
 2. resist_____
 3. remembr_____
 4. prefer_____
 5. audi_____
 6. signific_____
 7. occurr_____
 8. appear_____
 9. import_____
 10. confer_____

 11. exist_____
 12. consci_____
 13. intellig_____
 14. acquaint_____
 15. brilli_____
 16. conveni_____
 17. independ_____
 18. guid_____
 19. ignor_____
 20. correspond_____

B. *able-ible*

1. laugh_____
2. terr_____
3. toler_____
4. permiss_____
5. advis_____
6. tax_____
7. sens_____
8. separ_____
9. reduc_____
10. elig_____

11. reli_____
12. respons_____
13. horr_____
14. read_____
15. comprehens_____
16. digest_____
17. leg_____
18. comfort_____
19. forc_____
20. destruct_____

C. *ary-ery*

1. libr_____
2. diction_____
3. cemet_____
4. vocabul_____
5. millin_____

6. annivers_____
7. gall_____
8. bound_____
9. custom_____
10. cream_____

Add the suffixes as indicated in *D* and *E* to the words listed in each part, and write the words in the spaces provided.

D. *ous*

1. peril _____
2. hazard _____
3. danger _____
4. pore _____
5. murder _____
6. adventure _____
7. slander _____
8. advantage _____
9. marvel _____
10. mountain _____

11. poison _____
12. grief _____
13. courage _____
14. humor _____
15. desire _____
16. outrage _____
17. trouble _____
18. riot _____
19. fame _____
20. mischief _____

E. *ly*

1. certain _____
2. physical _____
3. due _____
4. happy _____
5. formal _____
6. mental _____
7. verbal _____
8. basic _____
9. whole _____
10. month _____

11. foolish _____
12. usual _____
13. true _____
14. critical _____
15. accidental _____
16. public _____
17. drastic _____
18. frequent _____
19. neat _____
20. scarce _____

Fill in the appropriate endings as indicated in parts *F* and *G*.

F. efy-ify

1. stup_____		6. liqu_____
2. rect_____		7. fals_____
3. class_____		8. just_____
4. rar_____		9. test_____
5. rat_____		10. putr_____

G. ize, ise, yze

1. advert_____		11. item_____
2. exerc_____		12. adv_____
3. anal_____		13. franch_____
4. emphas_____		14. modern_____
5. superv_____		15. disgu_____
6. desp_____		16. real_____
7. critic_____		17. enterpr_____
8. paral_____		18. general_____
9. surpr_____		19. rev_____
10. recogn_____		20. central_____

Suffix Confusion

■ An element that is added to the *end* of a root word is known as a *suffix*. For example, elements like *ance, able, ous,* or *ly* can be added to the ends of words. Each is called a _____.

> suffix

■ An element that is added to the end of a word is called a _____*fix.*

> *suf*fix

■ An element which is added to the end of a word is a _____.

> suffix

■ Elements such as *ance, able, ous,* or *ly* are examples of _____*es.*

> *suffix*es

■ A suffix is an element that is added to the [beginning, end] of a word.

> end

■ Suffixes such as *ed* or *ing* are added to verbs to show the change in tense. By adding *ed* to the verb *wash* you form the past tense: My sister *wash_____* clothes yesterday.

> wash*ed*

washing

■ By adding the suffix *ing* to the verb *wash* you form the present participle: She is *wash*____ clothes now.

speaking

■ You can also form a noun by adding *ing* to a verb: I shall take a course in public *speak*____.

suffix

■ If you drop the *e* from the verb *continue* and add *ance,* you form the noun *continuance.* Because *ance* forms a noun, then the word *continuance* is a noun which is formed by adding the _____ *ance* to the verb *continue.*

poison

■ The suffix *ous* is an adjective suffix, meaning full of or abounding in the qualities of. For example, by adding the suffix *ous* to the noun *poison,* you form the adjective *poisonous,* meaning full of _____.

queenly

■ A suffix changes a word in some way. For example, adding *ly* to the noun *queen* makes that noun an adjective, as in this sentence: She is a very queenly person. The noun *person* is described by the adjective _____.

slowly

■ If you add *ly* to an adjective, you form an adverb. If you add the suffix *ly* to the adjective *slow,* you form the adverb _____.

suffix

■ You may change one part of speech to another (a noun into an adjective or an adjective into an adverb) by adding to the end of the word an element called a _____.

to the end of a word

■ A suffix is an element that is added _____.

ance and ence

assistance

■ The suffix *ance* forms a noun from other parts of speech. By adding the suffix *ance* to the verb *assist,* you form the noun _____.

noun

■ The suffix *ance* forms a [noun, verb].

existence

■ Sometimes the suffix is spelled *ence* instead of *ance* as in the noun *exist___nce*.

ance

■ The best way to learn how to spell words ending in *ance* or *ence* is to study them individually. The word *assistance* ends in _____.

*assist*ance

■ The noun *assistance* can be defined as the act of assisting. If a person is in the act of assisting another, he comes to his _____*ance*.

as/sist/ance

■ The noun *assistance* has three syllables: as/sist/ance. The first syllable is _____.

as/*sist*/ance

■ The second syllable is as/_____/ance.

as/sist/*ance*

■ The last syllable is the suffix _____.

assistance

■ *Assistance* means help or aid. The words help or aid have the same meaning as the noun _____.

assistance

■ The supervisor asked his employees to come to his _____.

assistance

■ The man could not work without the _____ of his daughter.

ance

■ The noun *resistance* also has the ___nce ending.

resist*ance*

■ The act of resisting is called *resist_____*.

re/sist/ance

■ *Resistance* has three syllables: _____/sist/ance.

re/*sist*/ance

■ The second syllable is re/_____/ance.

re/sist/*ance*

■ The last syllable is re/sist/_____.

resistance

■ When Marcia requested three weeks' vacation, her employer offered no _____.

resistance

■ When a person encounters some opposition to a proposal, he meets some _____.

resistance

■ Some opposing force could therefore be called _____.

resistance

■ The new highway plan was met with a great deal of _____ from some of the board members.

assistance

■ The act of assisting is called _____.

resistance

■ The act of resisting is called _____.

import*ance*

■ If a problem is important, you could say that it has the quality of being important. The noun which describes this quality of being important is *import*___.

ance

■ The noun *importance* ends in ___.

im/port/ance

■ *Importance* also has three syllables: im/port/ance. The first syllable is ___.

im/*port*/ance

■ The second syllable is im/___/ance.

im/port/*ance*

■ The last syllable is the suffix ___.

importance

■ The speaker emphasized the words of _____ in his speech.

importance

■ The issues were taken up in order of their _____.

main/te/nance

■ The noun *maintenance* also ends in *ance* and has three syllables: main/te/nance. The first syllable is ___.

main/*te*/nance

■ The second syllable is main/___/ance.

main/te/*nance*

■ The last syllable is main/te/___.

maintenance	■ Write the entire word, saying it in syllables as you write: _____.
maintenance	■ The act of maintaining or the state of being maintained is called _____.
maintenance	■ Our neighbor spends a lot of money on the _____ [upkeep] of her two homes.
maintenance	■ The state of being kept up or maintained is called _____.
ance	■ The noun *appearance* also ends in _____.
appear*ance*	■ If a person is in the act of appearing, he makes an *appear*_____.
ap/pear/ance	■ The noun *appearance* has three syllables: ap/pear/ance. The first syllable is _____.
ap/*pear*/ance	■ The second syllable is ap/_____/ance.
ap/pear/*ance*	■ The last syllable is ap/pear/_____.
appearance	■ Write the entire word, saying it in syllables as you write: _____.
appear*ance*	■ The actor did not put in an *appear*_____ at the evening show.
p	■ Remember that the noun *appearance* has a double __.
t	■ The noun *attendance* ends in *ance* and has a double __.
at/tend/ance	■ The noun *attendance* has three syllables: at/tend/ance. The first syllable is _____.
at/*tend*/ance	■ The second syllable is at/_____/ance.

at/tend/*ance*

■ The third syllable is at/tend/_____.

■ Write the entire word, saying it in syllables as you
write: _____.

attendance

■ The number of persons who are present on a certain
occasion is also called the _____.

attendance

■ The revival meeting claimed a large _____.

attendance

■ Joe received a gold star for perfect _____.

attendance

■ One requirement of the new club is _____ at
all the meetings.

attendance

■ The noun that can be defined as the act of performing
is _____ance.

*perform*ance

■ The act of performing is called _____.

performance

■ The noun *performance* has three syllables: per/form/
ance. The first syllable is _____.

per/form/ance

■ The second syllable is per/_____/ance.

per/*form*/ance

■ The third syllable is per/form/_____.

per/form/*ance*

■ Even though it was a school play, the actors gave a
fine _____.

performance

■ My sister had rehearsed her lines for months, but
she still gave a very bad _____.

performance

■ Now let us take the noun *acquaintance*. This noun
also ends in _____.

ance

■ *Acquaintance* is not difficult to spell if you do it by
syllables: ac/quaint/ance. The first syllable is _____.

ac/quaint/ance

ac/*quaint*/ance	■ The second syllable is ac/_____/ance.
ac/quaint/*ance*	■ The last syllable is ac/quaint/_____.
acquaintance	■ Write the entire word, saying it in syllables as you write: _____.
acquaint*ance*	■ Personal knowledge of a person or thing is called *acquaint*_____.
acquaintance	■ A person with whom you are acquainted is also known as an _____.
acquaintance	■ Mr. Jones is an _____ [person known slightly] of my father.
acquaintance	■ Because Jim does not know John well enough to call him a friend, he calls John an _____.
acquaintance	■ A person whom you know slightly could be called an _____.
ance	■ Another word that you should be able to spell is *brilliance. Brilliance* also ends in _____.
bril/liance	■ The noun *brilliance* has two syllables: _____/liance.
bril/*liance*	■ The second syllable is bril/_____.
brilliance	■ Write the entire word, saying it in syllables as you write: _____.
brilliance	■ The noun *brilliance* can be defined as brightness, as in this sentence: The diamonds had an exceptional _____.
brilliance	■ The noun *brilliance* can also be defined as intellectual acuteness, as in this sentence: The young boy was not aware of his own _____.

brilliance	■ I was dazzled by the _____ of the stars.
brilliance	■ Some precious stones have much more _____ than others.
three	■ The noun *remembrance* has only three syllables: re/mem/brance. When you pronounce *remembrance,* be sure to say only _____ syllables.
re/mem/brance	■ *Remembrance* is divided into syllables like this: re/mem/brance. The first syllable is _____.
re/*mem*/brance	■ The second syllable is re/_____/brance.
re/mem/*brance*	■ The last syllable is re/mem/_____.
remembrance	■ Write the entire word, saying it in syllables as you write: _____.
remembrance	■ The act of remembering is called _____.
remembrance	■ A little token or gift to remember one by can also be called a _____.
remembrance	■ Aunt Susan gave each of us a _____ before she went to Europe to live.
abundance	■ An *abundance* of an item or article is a great plenty or supply, as in this sentence: This year the farmers have an _____ of crops.
a/bun/dance	■ The noun *abundance* has three syllables: a/bun/dance. The first syllable is ____.
a/*bun*/dance	■ The second syllable is a/_____/dance.
a/bun/*dance*	■ The third syllable is a/bun/_____.

abundance

■ Write the entire word, saying it in syllables as you write: _____.

abundance

■ The owner of the Groveland orchards predicted he would have an _____ of apples this year.

ance

■ The noun *guidance* is another useful word that ends in _____.

guidance

■ The noun *guidance* is the act of guiding or advising, as in this sentence: Sandra Webster works in the field of _____, earning her living by advising people who are in trouble.

guid/ance

■ The noun *guidance* has two syllables: _____/ance.

guid/*ance*

■ The second syllable is guid/_____.

guidance

■ The principal told Tom's father that the boy needed better _____.

guidance

■ Some young people would not get into trouble if they had better _____.

ignorance

■ The noun *ignorance* can be defined as the state of being ignorant or uninformed, as in this sentence: A person who lacks knowledge of a particular fact is in _____.

ig/no/rance

■ There are three syllables in *ignorance:* _____/no/rance.

ig/*no*/rance

■ The second syllable is ig/_____/rance.

ig/no/*rance*

■ The last syllable is ig/no/_____.

ignorance

■ Write the entire word, saying it in syllables as you write: _____.

ignorance

■ The state of being ignorant is called _____.

ignorance

■ Lack of knowledge about one or more facts is called _____.

ignorance

■ At the tax meeting Mr. Lewis displayed his complete _____ about the subject.

ignorance

■ If one does not have sufficient knowledge of a subject, it is sometimes better for him to keep silent than to show his _____.

ance

■ Another word ending in _____ is *significance*.

significance

■ If something has importance it has *significance*. The noun importance means the same as the noun _____.

sig/nif/i/cance

■ There are four syllables in the noun *significance:* sig/nif/i/cance. The first syllable is _____.

sig/*nif*/i/cance

■ The second syllable is sig/_____/i/cance.

sig/nif/*i*/cance

■ The third syllable is sig/nif/___/cance.

sig/nif/i/*cance*

■ The last syllable is sig/nif/i/_____.

significance

■ Write the entire word, saying it in syllables as you write: _____.

sig*nificance*

■ The letter that Joseph wrote to his brother in Arizona had special *sig*_____.

significance

■ Recalling the manager's speech, I did not think it contained any special _____ [importance].

significance

■ The state of being significant is called _____.

a

■ Now let us turn our attention to some of the most common and useful nouns that end in *ence*. The suffix *ence* is another spelling of the suffix ___nce.

ence	■ The state or condition of existing is known as *existence*. This noun ends in _____.
ex/is/tence	■ The noun *existence* has three syllables: ex/is/tence. The first syllable is _____.
ex/*is*/tence	■ The second syllable is ex/_____/tence.
ex/is/*tence*	■ The last syllable is ex/is/_____.
existence	■ Write the entire word, saying it in syllables as you write: _____.
existence	■ The old grandfather credited his long _____ to moderation in his daily living.
existence	■ Chain stores have been in _____ for a number of years.
ence	■ Like *existence,* the noun *subsistence* ends in _____.
subsist*ence*	■ The act of subsisting, or livelihood, is the definition of the noun *subsist*_____.
sub/sist/ence	■ The noun *subsistence* has three syllables: sub/sist/ence. The first syllable is _____.
sub/*sist*/ence	■ The second syllable is sub/_____/ence.
sub/sist/*ence*	■ The third syllable is sub/sist/_____.
subsistence	■ Write the entire word, saying it in syllables as you write: _____.
subsistence	■ The officers were paid a _____ [act of subsisting] allowance in addition to the allowance for their quarters.

subsistence	■ The only way that she can provide for her _____ is to braid rag rugs.
*insist*ence	■ If a person *insists,* he takes a firm stand and does not waver from this stand. The act of insisting or taking this stand would be known as _____*ence.*
in/sist/ence	■ The noun *insistence* has three syllables: _____/sist/ ence.
in/*sist*/ence	■ The second syllable is in/_____/ence.
in/sist/*ence*	■ The last syllable is in/sist/_____.
insistence	■ Write the entire word, saying it in syllables as you write: _____.
insistence	■ Jack had decided to buy a red car, but his wife's _____ on a blue one forced him to change his mind.
insistence	■ Taking a firm stand on a point and holding to that stand is the definition of the noun _____.
ence	■ The noun *preference* has only *one r* in the second syllable and ends in _____.
pref/er/ence	■ There are three syllables in the noun *preference:* pref/er/ence. The first syllable is _____.
pref/*er*/ence	■ The second syllable is pref/_____/ence.
pref/er/*ence*	■ The last syllable is pref/er/_____.
preference	■ Write the entire word, saying it in syllables as you write: _____.
preference	■ To prefer is to like better or to place something in a higher position or estimation. The act of placing something in a high position would be called _____.

preference

■ The teacher asked if we had a _____ [better liking] for classical or jazz records.

preference

■ The placing of one article or item in a higher position or estimation is called _____.

ex/pe/ri/ence

■ The noun *experience* has four syllables: ex/pe/ri/ence. The first syllable is _____.

ex/*pe*/ri/ence

■ The second syllable is ex/_____/ri/ence.

ex/pe/*ri*/ence

■ The third syllable is ex/pe/_____/ence.

ex/pe/ri/*ence*

■ The last syllable is ex/pe/ri/_____.

experience

■ Write the entire word, saying it in syllables as you write: _____.

experience

■ On their way back from Yellowstone Park, my brother and his family had a frightening _____.

experience

■ Raymond had a very exciting _____ while traveling in Italy.

ence

■ Like the word *experience,* the noun *audience* ends in _____.

au/di/ence

■ The noun *audience* has three syllables: au/di/ence. The first syllable is _____.

au/*di*/ence

■ The second syllable is au/_____/ence.

au/di/*ence*

■ The last syllable is au/di/_____.

audience

■ Write the entire word, saying it in syllables as you write: _____.

audience

■ The opportunity of being heard is called an *audience,* as in this sentence: The prime minister was granted an _____.

audience

■ The spectators at a performance can also be called an _____.

audience

■ When the tenor finished his last aria, the _____ stood up and shouted "Bravo!"

con/ve/nience

■ The noun *convenience* is easy to spell if you take it by syllables: con/ve/nience. The first syllable is _____.

con/*ve*/nience

■ The second syllable is con/_____/nience.

con/ve/*nience*

■ The last syllable is con/ve/_____.

con/ve/nience

■ The three syllables are _____/_____/_____.

convenience

■ Write the entire word, saying it in syllables as you write: _____.

convenience

■ The eleven o'clock appointment is a great _____ [state of being convenient] to all of us.

convenience

■ Any device which adds to personal comfort can also be defined as a *convenience,* as in this sentence: An electric iron is certainly a _____ while traveling in distant cities.

convenience

■ Living near a shopping center is quite a _____ [state of being convenient].

in/de/pen/dence

■ The noun *independence* can be separated easily into four syllables: in/de/pen/dence. The first syllable is _____.

in/*de*/pen/dence

■ The second syllable is in/_____/pen/dence.

in/de/*pen*/dence

■ The third syllable is in/de/_____/dence.

in/de/pen/*dence*

■ The last syllable is in/de/pen/_____.

independence

■ Write the entire word, saying it in syllables as you write: _____.

independence	■ If one has freedom from control by others he has _____ .
independence	■ Jack wants to leave home to work in a distant city since he feels he needs his _____ .
ence	■ The noun *correspondence* also ends in _____ .
cor/re/spon/dence	■ *Correspondence* is divided easily into syllables as follows: cor/re/spon/dence. The first syllable is _____ .
cor/*re*/spon/dence	■ The second syllable is cor/_____/spon/dence.
cor/re/*spon*/dence	■ The third syllable is cor/re/_____/dence.
cor/re/spon/*dence*	■ The last syllable is cor/re/spon/_____ .
correspondence	■ Write the entire word, saying it in syllables as you write: _____ .
correspondence	■ Letters written by one person to another are known as _____ .
correspondence	■ When his uncle died, he left boxes and boxes of _____ [letters] between him and his friends in foreign countries.
correspondence	■ At the present time Mae is carrying on a _____ with a girl in France.
ence	■ Like the noun *correspondence,* the noun *competence* also ends in _____ .
competence	■ The noun *competence* means the quality of being competent, or able, as in this sentence: The foreman has demonstrated his _____ on many occasions.
com/pe/tence	■ The noun *competence* can be divided into syllables like this: com/pe/tence. The first syllable is _____ .

com/*pe*/tence	■ The second syllable is com/_____/tence.
com/pe/*tence*	■ The last syllable is com/pe/_____.
competence	■ Write the entire word, saying it in syllables as you write: _____.
competence	■ The quality of being competent is called _____.
competence	■ The personnel director assured Bill that he had sufficient _____ [quality of being competent] to hold the new job.
com*petence*	■ If *competence* is the state or quality of being competent or able, then the noun ability would have the same meaning as the noun *com*_____.
competence	■ Mary has demonstrated enough _____ in her work to be promoted to the next salary bracket.
independence	■ Freedom from control by others is the definition of the noun _____.
correspondence	■ Letters written between two people are called _____.
existence	■ The act of existing is called _____.
insistence	■ At John's _____ [act of insisting] I purchased a new car.
subsistence	■ The quality or state of subsisting is _____.
preference	■ A liking of one kind of pie over another is known as a _____.
experience	■ Living through an event or a series of events is known as an _____.

audience

■ An assembly of listeners or spectators is an _____.

convenience

■ An appliance that adds to personal comfort is a _____.

con/science

■ The noun *conscience* is easy to spell if you learn it by syllables: con/science. The first syllable is _____.

con/*science*

■ The last syllable is con/_____.

con/*science*

■ An easy way to remember the second syllable of the noun *conscience* is that it also spells *science*. The second syllable of *conscience* is _____.

conscience

■ Write the entire word, saying it in syllables as you write: _____.

conscience

■ The noun *conscience* can be defined as the sense of both the good and bad of one's own conduct, as in this sentence: He acted according to the dictates of his _____.

conscience

■ The politician was so dishonest that many people felt that he had no _____.

conscience

■ The sense to know good and bad of one's own conduct is called a _____.

consequence

■ The noun *consequence* can be defined as a natural or necessary result, as in this sentence: His disapproval of the bill will have a drastic _____.

con/se/quence

■ The noun *consequence* has three syllables: con/se/quence. The first syllable is _____.

con/*se*/quence

■ The second syllable is con/_____/quence.

con/se/*quence*

■ The last syllable is con/se/_____.

consequence

■ Write the entire word, saying it in syllables as you write: _____.

consequence

■ When Jim said that he was running away from school, I knew there would be a dire _____.

consequence

■ Marie wondered what the _____ [necessary result] of the appointment would be.

ence

■ The last word ending in *ence* that we shall study is *intelligence. Intelligence* also ends in _____.

intelligence

■ The noun *intelligence* can be defined as the power of understanding, as in this sentence: Some people do not use their _____ as much as they should.

in/tel/li/gence

■ The noun *intelligence* is divided into four syllables: in/tel/li/gence. The first syllable is _____.

in/*tel*/li/gence

■ The second syllable is in/_____/li/gence.

in/tel/*li*/gence

■ The third syllable is in/tel/_____/gence.

in/tel/li/*gence*

■ The last syllable is in/tel/li/_____.

intelligence

■ Write the entire word, saying it in syllables as you write: _____.

intelligence

■ The power of understanding is known as _____.

intelligence

■ The magazine article stated that the new director was a man of great _____.

independence

■ Many small countries that have been controlled by large powers are constantly seeking their _____ [freedom from control].

correspondence

■ The act of corresponding is known as _____.

competence

■ Ability is another word for _____.

conscience

■ The power to know the good and bad of one's own conduct is a _____.

consequence

■ A natural or necessary result is a _____.

intelligence

■ The power of understanding is called _____.

syllable or element
end
change, modify,
   alter

■ A suffix is a _____ that is added to the _____ of a root word to _____ it in some way.

able and ible

eat*able*

■ When the suffix *able* is added to another part of speech, such as a verb or noun, it makes that part of speech an adjective. For example, if you add *able* to the verb *eat,* you form the adjective *eat*____.

adjective

■ When you add the suffix *able* to a word, you form an [adjective, noun].

ible

■ The suffix *able* is sometimes spelled *ible.* There are two spellings: *able* and ____.

eatable

■ In adding the suffix *able* to the verb *eat,* you form the adjective _____.

readable

■ If you add the suffix *able* to the verb *read,* you form the adjective _____.

read

■ The adjective *eatable* can be defined as fit to be eaten. The adjective *readable* can be defined as capable of being _____.

*eat*en

■ The suffix *able* therefore implies a fitness or capacity. *Eatable* would be defined as fit to be ____*en.*

read

■ *Readable* would be defined as capable of being
_____.

eat*able*
read*able*

■ Many words take the *able* ending. You have already
seen two words that take this spelling: *eat*____ and
*read*____.

eatable

■ Although the fruit in the basket is very ripe, it is
_____ [fit to be eaten].

readable

■ Even though the print in the old Bible is not distinct,
it is still _____ [capable of being read].

laugh*able*

■ If a situation is capable of exciting laughter it can
be said to be *laugh*____.

able

■ To form the adjective *laughable* you add the suffix
____ to the verb *laugh*.

*tax*able

■ If an article or item is capable of being taxed it is
____*able*.

tax

■ You form the adjective *taxable* by adding the suffix
able to the root word ____.

able

■ The adjectives *laughable, eatable, readable,* and *taxable* all take the ____ ending.

able

■ The adjective *advisable* is formed from the verb
advise and the suffix *able*. Notice that the final *e* in advise
is dropped before adding the suffix ____.

drop

■ In adding the suffix *able* to a word like *advise,* which
ends in a final *e,* you [drop, keep] the *e*.

advisable

■ When you add the suffix *able* to the verb *advise,* you
form the adjective _____.

advisable

■ The adjective *advisable* means proper or fit to be
advised, as in this sentence: To continue the trip to
Rochester is the most _____ procedure.

ad/vis/a/ble	■ The adjective *advisable* has four syllables: ad/vis/a/ble. The first syllable is _____.
ad/*vis*/a/ble	■ The second syllable is ad/_____/a/ble.
ad/vis/*a*/ble	■ The third syllable is ad/vis/__/able.
ad/vis/a/*ble*	■ The last syllable is ad/vis/a/_____.
advisable	■ It is _____ to study your lessons daily.
advisable	■ Proper or fit to be advised is the definition of the adjective _____.
able	■ Like *advisable,* the adjective *admirable* ends in _____.
able	■ The adjective *admirable* is the combination of the verb *admire* and the suffix _____.
e	■ The verb *admire* ends in a final __.
drop	■ Before you add the suffix *able* to the verb *admire,* you [drop, keep] the final *e*.
ad/mi/ra/ble	■ The adjective *admirable* has four syllables: ad/mi/ra/ble. The first syllable is _____.
ad/*mi*/ra/ble	■ The second syllable is ad/_____/ra/ble.
ad/mi/*ra*/ble	■ The third syllable is ad/mi/_____/ble.
ad/mi/ra/*ble*	■ The last syllable is ad/mi/ra/_____.
admirable	■ Write the entire word, saying it in syllables as you write: _____.
admirable	■ The adjective *admirable* can be defined as being capable of exciting admiration or esteem, as in this sentence: The new schoolteacher has many _____ qualities.

admirable

■ Something that can be admired is _____.

admirable

■ The conduct of both candidates during the presidential campaign was _____.

reliable

■ The adjective *reliable* can be defined as fit to be relied on, or trustworthy, as in this sentence: The store-keeper needs a _____ boy to deliver groceries.

y

■ The adjective *reliable* is formed by adding the suffix *able* to the verb *rely*. The verb *rely* ends in __ preceded by the consonant *l*.

y i

■ Because the verb *rely* ends in *y* which is preceded by a consonant, you must change the *y* to *i* before adding a suffix beginning with a vowel, like *able*. When you form the adjective from *rely* and *able*, you change the __ in *rely* to __ and add *able*.

reliable

■ Capable of being relied on is the definition of the adjective _____.

re/li/a/ble

■ *Reliable* has four syllables: re/li/a/ble. The first syllable is _____.

re/*li*/a/ble

■ The second syllable is re/_____/a/ble.

re/li/*a*/ble

■ The third syllable is re/li/___/ble.

re/li/a/*ble*

■ The last syllable is re/li/a/_____.

reliable

■ Write the entire word, saying it in syllables as you write: _____.

reliable

■ Capable of being relied on, or trustworthy, is the definition of the adjective _____.

reliable

■ Bill was promoted to the job of manager because he was intelligent and _____.

able	■ The adjective *commendable* also takes the _____ ending.
a	■ If it is difficult to remember that *commendable* ends in *a*ble, think of the noun *commendation*. If a noun ends in *a*tion, the corresponding adjective will usually end in __ble.
*a*tion able	■ The noun *commendation* ends in __*tion*. The adjective *commendable* ends in __*ble*.
com/mend/a/ble	■ The adjective *commendable* has four syllables: com/mend/a/ble. The first syllable is _____.
com/*mend*/a/ble	■ The second syllable is com/_____/a/ble.
com/mend/*a*/ble	■ The third syllable is com/mend/__/ble.
com/mend/a/*ble*	■ The last syllable is com/mend/a/_____.
commendable	■ Write the entire word, saying it in syllables as you write: _____.
commendable	■ *Commendable* can be defined as worthy of being commended or praised, as in this sentence: June's speech was very _____.
commendable	■ If an action or deed is fit to be commended or praised, it is _____.
commendable	■ The ladies' auxiliary sponsors many _____ projects.
a	■ Now look at the noun *consideration*. It ends in __tion.
*a*ble	■ The noun *consideration* ends in *a*tion; the adjective *considerable* ends in __ble.

■ The adjective *considerable* can be defined as worthy of consideration, as in this sentence: Only two of the four proposals are _____.

considerable

■ The adjective *considerable* can also be defined as large in extent, as in this sentence: Mr. Hamilton has had _____ experience in the field of economics.

considerable

■ The adjective *considerable* has five syllables: con/sid/er/a/ble. The first syllable is _____.

con/sid/er/a/ble

■ The second syllable is con/_____/er/a/ble.

con/*sid*/er/a/ble

■ The third syllable is con/sid/_____/a/ble.

con/sid/*er*/a/ble

■ The fourth syllable is con/sid/er/__/ble.

con/sid/er/*a*/ble

■ The last syllable is con/sid/er/a/_____.

con/sid/er/a/*ble*

■ Write the entire adjective, saying it in syllables as you write: _____.

considerable

■ Capable or worthy of being considered is the definition of the adjective _____.

considerable

■ The adjective that means worthy of being considered can also mean large in extent. This adjective is _____.

considerable

■ The salesman's territory is quite _____.

considerable

■ My uncle owns a chain of grocery stores and is a man of _____ [large in extent] means.

considerable

■ Some adjectives take the spelling *ible* instead of *able*. For example, three common and useful words, *horrible,* *terrible,* and *sensible,* end in _____.

ible

■ The adjective *horrible* means tending to excite horror, or dreadful. The word dreadful means the same as *horr*_____.

horr*ible*

hor/ri/ble	■ The adjective *horrible* has three syllables: hor/ri/ble. The first syllable of this word is _____.
hor/*ri*/ble	■ The second syllable is hor/_____/ble.
hor/ri/*ble*	■ The last syllable is hor/ri/_____.
horrible	■ Write the entire word, saying it in syllables as you write: _____.
horrible	■ If something tends to excite horror, it is _____.
horrible	■ Dreadful is another word for the adjective _____.
horrible	■ In Forster's novel, *A Passage to India,* an English-woman has a _____ [dreadful] experience in a cave.
ible	■ Like *horrible,* the adjective *terrible* ends in __ble.
terrible	■ The adjective *terrible* means exciting terror or dread, as in this sentence: The soldiers related many _____ experiences.
ter/ri/ble	■ The adjective *terrible* has three syllables: ter/ri/ble. The first syllable is _____.
ter/*ri*/ble	■ The second syllable is ter/_____/ble.
ter/ri/*ble*	■ The last syllable is ter/ri/_____.
terrible	■ Write the entire word, saying it in syllables as you write: _____.
terrible	■ Exciting terror, awe, or dread is the definition of the adjective _____.
terrible	■ Monica was frightened by the _____ [exciting terror] screams in the attic.

sensible	■ The adjective *sensible* can be defined as having good or common sense, as in this sentence: Martha is a very _____ girl.
sen/si/ble	■ The adjective *sensible* has three syllables: sen/si/ble. The first syllable is ____.
sen/*si*/ble	■ The second syllable is sen/____/ble.
sen/si/*ble*	■ The last syllable is sen/si/____.
sensible	■ Write the entire word, saying it in syllables as you write: _____.
sensible	■ Characterized by good or common sense is the definition of the adjective _____.
sensible	■ The businessman attributed his success to his being frugal and _____ [having good sense].
sensible	■ In spite of all their fame and fortune, the Simpsons are very _____ [having good sense] people.
*i*ble	■ The adjective *responsible* ends in __ble.
ible	■ The words *horrible, terrible, sensible,* and *responsible* all end in ____.
responsible	■ The adjective *responsible* can be defined as answerable, or able to respond or answer for one's conduct. Fill in the adjective in this sentence: William will be _____ for the purchase of the tickets.
respons*ible*	■ If a parent is answerable for the conduct of his child, he is *respons*____ for it.
re/spon/si/ble	■ The adjective *responsible* has four syllables: re/spon/si/ble. The first syllable is ____.
re/*spon*/si/ble	■ The second syllable is re/____/si/ble.

re/spon/*si*/ble	■ The third syllable is re/spon/_____/ble.
re/spon/si/*ble*	■ The last syllable is re/spon/si/_____.
responsible	■ Write the entire word, saying it in syllables as you write: _____.
responsible	■ I told the committee that I, alone, was _____ for the selection of the books.
responsible	■ When Uncle Ben offered to take Joe and me to the movies, he told my mother that he would be _____ for us.
responsible	■ Able to respond or answer for one's conduct means to be _____.
horrible	■ Exciting horror is the definition of the adjective _____.
ter*rible*	■ Tending to excite terror or dread is the definition of the adjective ter_____.
sensible	■ Having good or common sense is the definition of the adjective _____.
perfecti*ble*	■ Usually, if a noun ends in *ion*, the corresponding adjective will end in *ible*. For example, the noun *perfection* ends in *ion*. To form the adjective you drop the *on* and substitute *ble*. The adjective is spelled *perfecti*_____.
perfect*ible*	■ The noun is *perfection;* the adjective is *perfect*_____.
perfectible	■ The adjective *perfectible* can be defined as capable of being made perfect, as in this sentence: Dr. Brown stated that the faulty formula was _____.
per/fect/i/ble	■ The adjective *perfectible* has four syllables: per/fect/i/ble. The first syllable is _____.

per/*fect*/i/ble

■ The second syllable is per/_____/i/ble.

per/fect/*i*/ble

■ The third syllable is per/fect/___/ble.

per/fect/i/*ble*

■ The last syllable is per/fect/i/_____.

perfectible

■ Capable of being made perfect is the definition of the adjective _____.

perfectible

■ The new gas engine did not work perfectly, but mechanical experts maintained it was _____.

destruct*ible*

■ Now take the noun *destruction*. It ends in *ion,* so the corresponding adjective ends like this: *destruct*_____.

destructible

■ The adjective *destructible* means capable of being destroyed, as in this sentence: It is difficult to build a house that is not _____.

de/struc/ti/ble

■ The adjective *destructible* has four syllables: de/struc/ti/ble. The first syllable is _____.

de/*struc*/ti/ble

■ The second syllable is de/_____/ti/ble.

de/struc/*ti*/ble

■ The third syllable is de/struc/_____/ble.

de/struc/ti/*ble*

■ The last syllable is de/struc/ti/_____.

destructible

■ Write the entire word, saying it in syllables as you write: _____.

destructible

■ The new post office is not supposed to be _____ [capable of being destroyed].

comprehensible

■ Now take the noun *comprehension*. You form the adjective by keeping the *i* and substituting *ble* for *on*. Write the adjective: _____.

comprehensible

■ The adjective *comprehensible* means capable of being comprehended or understood, as in this sentence: David's theory was entirely _____.

com/pre/hen/si/ble

■ Now take the adjective *comprehensible* by syllables: com/pre/hen/si/ble. The first syllable is _____.

com/*pre*/hen/si/ble

■ The second syllable is com/_____/hen/si/ble.

com/pre/*hen*/si/ble

■ The third syllable is com/pre/_____/si/ble.

com/pre/hen/*si*/ble

■ The fourth syllable is com/pre/hen/_____/ble.

com/pre/hen/si/*ble*

■ The last syllable is com/pre/hen/si/_____.

comprehensible

■ Write the entire word, saying it in syllables as you write: _____.

comprehensible

■ Capable of being comprehended or understood is the definition of the adjective _____.

comprehensible

■ Einstein's theories are not _____ [capable of being comprehended] to many adults.

perfectible

■ If the noun is *perfection,* the corresponding adjective is _____.

destructible

■ If the noun is *destruction,* the adjective is _____.

comprehensible

■ If the noun is *comprehension,* the adjective is _____.

tolerable

■ If the noun is toler*ation,* the adjective is _____.

separable

■ If the noun is separ*ation,* the adjective is _____.

accessible

■ Now look at the noun *accession.* It ends in *ion;* therefore the adjective is _____.

digestible

■ If the noun is *digestion,* the adjective is _____.

able

■ If a noun ends in *ation,* like *consolation,* then the adjective ends in _____.

ible

■ If a noun ends in *ion,* like *digestion,* then the adjective ends in _____.

soft

■ Let us take up the soft sound of *c* and *g.* Say the words *get* and *go.* This *g* has a hard sound. Now say the words *rage* and *engine.* These words have the _____ sound of *g.*

soft

■ Say the words *can* and *cup.* This is the *hard* sound of *c.* Now say the words *city* and *civil.* The *c* in *city* and *civil* is the _____ sound of *c.*

soft

■ The *ible* ending is added to a word containing the soft sound of *c* or *g* to keep the [soft, hard] sound of *c* or *g.*

ible

■ If a word contains the soft sound of *c* or *g,* you add [able, ible] to keep the soft sound of *c* or *g.*

soft

■ The *c* in *reduce* has the [soft, hard] sound of *c.*

ible

■ To form the adjective from the word *reduce,* you drop the *e* and add _____.

reducible

■ Form the adjective by adding *ible* to *reduce:* _____.

reducible

■ Capable of being reduced is the definition of the adjective _____.

re/duc/i/ble

■ The adjective *reducible* has four syllables: re/duc/i/ble. The first syllable is _____.

re/*duc*/i/ble

■ The second syllable is re/_____/i/ble.

re/duc/*i*/ble

■ The third syllable is re/duc/___/ble.

re/duc/i/*ble*

■ The last syllable is re/duc/i/_____.

reducible

■ Write the entire word, saying it in syllables as you write: _____.

reducible

■ Obesity is _____ [capable of being reduced] by proper diet.

reducible

■ The principal advantage of the new blower is that the pressure is _____ [capable of being reduced].

soft

■ If a person's handwriting can be read it is *legible*. Pronounce the word legible to yourself. The g in *legible* does not have the same sound as the g in *go*. Therefore, it has a [soft, hard] sound.

ible

■ Look again at the word *legible*. Because you must keep the soft sound of *g*, the ending is spelled _____.

leg/i/ble

■ The adjective *legible* has three syllables: leg/i/ble. The first syllable is _____.

leg/*i*/ble

■ The second syllable is leg/___/ble.

leg/i/*ble*

■ The last syllable is leg/i/_____.

legible

■ Write the entire word, saying it in syllables as you write: _____.

legible

■ Easy to read or capable of being read is the meaning of the adjective _____.

legible

■ The teacher criticized Maxine's handwriting because it was not very _____.

legible

■ The English instructor can read his students' themes much faster if the handwriting is _____.

ible	■ Like the adjective *legible,* the adjective *eligible* ends in ____.
el/i/gi/ble	■ The adjective *eligible* has four syllables: el/i/gi/ble. The first syllable is ____.
el/*i*/gi/ble	■ The second syllable is el/___/gi/ble.
el/i/*gi*/ble	■ The third syllable is el/i/_____/ble.
el/i/gi/*ble*	■ The last syllable is el/i/gi/____.
eligible	■ Write the entire word, saying it in syllables as you write: _____.
eli*gible*	■ If a person is qualified to be chosen for an office or a position, he is *eli*____.
eligible	■ Amos Brown was considered an _____ [qualified to be chosen] candidate for office.
eligible	■ Because of his grades in school, Stanley James was _____ for a scholarship.
soft	■ Like the adjective *reducible,* the adjective *forcible* has the [soft, hard] sound of *c.*
c	■ You use the *ible* ending for the word *forcible* because you must keep the soft sound of ___.
forc/i/ble	■ The adjective *forcible* has three syllables: forc/i/ble. The first syllable is ____.
forc/*i*/ble	■ The second syllable is forc/___/ble.
forc/i/*ble*	■ The last syllable is forc/i/____.
forcible	■ Write the entire word, saying it in syllables as you write: _____.

■ Characterized by force is the meaning of the adjective _____ .

forcible

■ The two men made a _____ [characterized by force] entry into the building.

forcible

■ The adjective that can be defined as capable of being reduced is _____ .

reducible

■ If your handwriting is easy to read, it is _____ .

legible

■ A man who is qualified to be chosen for office is considered to be _____ for that office.

eligible

■ The adjective that means characterized by force is _____ .

forcible

■ The ending *ible* is used when there is a *c* or *g* whose [soft, hard] sound must be retained.

soft

■ When a noun ends in *ion,* the corresponding adjective will end in [able, ible].

ible

■ When a noun ends in *ation,* the adjective will end in [able, ible].

able

■ Capable of being made perfect is the definition of the adjective _____ .

perfectible

■ Filled with horror is the definition of the adjective _____ .

horrible

■ If a piece of fruit can be eaten, it is _____ .

eatable

■ Of the twenty-five items that Jack sold, fifteen were *tax*_____ .

tax*able*

■ Having good or common sense is the definition of the adjective _____ .

sensible

respon*sible*

■ Answerable is another word for *respon*_____.

advis*able*

■ I doubt if this is an *advis*_____ solution.

reli*able*

■ Trustworthy is another word for *reli*_____.

considerable

■ There has been _____ [large in extent] difficulty at the plant.

commendable

■ If an action can be commended or praised, it is _____.

admirable

■ Worthy of admiration is the definition of the adjective _____.

terrible

■ The adjective that can be defined as capable of exciting terror is _____.

reducible

■ Obesity is _____ [capable of being reduced] by proper diet.

destructible

■ The adjective that can be defined as capable of being destroyed is _____.

The noun ends in *ion*; therefore the adjective ends in *ible*.

■ The adjective *comprehensible* ends in *ible*. State the generalization used.

The noun ends in *ation*; therefore the adjective ends in *able*.

■ The adjective *commendable* ends in *able*. State the generalization used.

The *ible* ending is used to preserve the soft sound of *g*.

■ The adjective *intelligible* ends in *ible*. State the generalization used.

ible

■ In order to preserve the soft sound of *c* or *g*, you add [able, ible] to form the adjective.

ary and ery

■ The two endings *ary* and *ery* are sometimes confused. The best way to learn the *ary-ery* endings are to master the words having these endings. We shall study some of the most common and useful words that end in *ary* and _____.

ery

■ More words end in *ary* than *ery*. An important *ary* noun is *dictionary*. The noun *dictionary* ends in _____.

ary

■ A reference book in which words are listed and defined in alphabetical order is known as a *diction*_____.

diction*ary*

■ The noun *dictionary* has four syllables: dic/tion/ar/y. The first syllable is _____.

***dic*/tion/ar/y**

■ The second syllable is dic/_____/ar/y.

dic/*tion*/ar/y

■ The third syllable is dic/tion/_____/y.

dic/tion/*ar*/y

■ The last syllable is dic/tion/ar/__.

dic/tion/ar/*y*

■ Write the entire word, saying it in syllables as you write: _____.

dictionary

■ Every student should learn how to use the _____.

dictionary

■ You will find the correct spelling and pronunciation of a word in the _____.

dictionary

■ Another useful noun ending in the suffix *ary* is the noun *vocabulary*. Like *dictionary*, this noun also ends in _____.

ary

■ The noun *vocabulary* can be defined as the sum of words used by an individual, as in this sentence: The young boy has a large _____.

vocabulary

■ The noun *vocabulary* has five syllables: vo/cab/u/lar/y. The first syllable is _____.

***vo*/cab/u/lar/y**

vo/*cab*/u/lar/y	■ The second syllable is vo/____/u/lar/y.
vo/cab/*u*/lar/y	■ The third syllable is vo/cab/__/lar/y.
vo/cab/u/*lar*/y	■ The fourth syllable is vo/cab/u/____/y.
vo/cab/u/lar/*y*	■ The last syllable is vo/cab/u/lar/__.
vo/cab/u/lar/y	■ The five syllables are ____/____/__/____/__.
vocabulary	■ Write the entire word, saying it in syllables as you write: _____.
vocabulary	■ You can read better and faster if you build up your _____ [words you use].
vocabulary	■ The words you use in speaking are known as your speaking _____.
vocabulary	■ The words you recognize and understand are considered your reading _____.
vocabulary	■ The words you understand and use in your writing are considered your writing _____.
ary	■ Now look at the word *boundary*. It too ends in _____.
boundary	■ A *boundary* is that which fixes a limit, as in this sentence: The salesman must become acquainted with the _____ of his territory.
bound/a/ry	■ The noun *boundary* has three syllables: bound/a/ry. The first syllable is _____.
bound/*a*/ry	■ The second syllable is bound/__/ry.
bound/a/*ry*	■ The last syllable is bound/a/_____.
bound/a/ry	■ The three syllables of *boundary* are _____/__/_____.

boundary

■ Write the entire word, saying it in syllables as you write: _____.

boundary

■ Guards are stationed on both sides of the _____.

boundary

■ Barbed wire marks the eastern _____ [limit] of the country.

dictionary

■ A reference book of words that are listed and defined alphabetically is a _____.

vocabulary

■ The sum total of words used by an individual is known as his _____.

boundary

■ That which bounds or fixes a limit is a _____.

diction*ary*

■ The noun *anniversary* ends in *ary*. It has the same ending as *diction*____.

anniversary

■ An *anniversary* is the annual return of a certain day or event, as in this sentence: My parents celebrate their wedding _____ every August first.

an/ni/ver/sa/ry

■ There are five syllables in *anniversary:* an/ni/ver/sa/ry. The first syllable is ____.

an/*ni*/ver/sa/ry

■ The second syllable is an/____/ver/sa/ry.

an/ni/*ver*/sa/ry

■ The third syllable is an/ni/____/sa/ry.

an/ni/ver/*sa*/ry

■ The fourth syllable is an/ni/ver/____/ry.

an/ni/ver/sa/*ry*

■ The last syllable is an/ni/ver/sa/____.

an/ni/ver/sa/ry

■ The five syllables are ____/____/____/____/____.

anniversary

■ Write the entire word, saying it in syllables as you write: _____.

anniversary

■ On the first of July I shall celebrate the first
_____ of my new job.

anniversary

■ Grandfather is looking forward to the party we are
planning for his fiftieth _____.

*custom*ary

■ The adjective *customary* ends in *ary* and means
agreeing with custom, or habitual. If a certain procedure
agrees with what is usually done it is considered ____*ary*.

*custom*ary

■ If the company picnic is usually held on the twelfth
of July, according to custom, you could say this was
_____*ary*.

cus/tom/ar/y

■ The adjective *customary* has four syllables: cus/tom/
ar/y. The first syllable is ____.

cus/*tom*/ar/y

■ The second syllable is cus/____/ar/y.

cus/tom/*ar*/y

■ The third syllable is cus/tom/____/y.

cus/tom/ar/*y*

■ The last syllable is cus/tom/ar/__.

customary

■ Write the entire word, saying it in syllables as you
write: _____.

customary

■ An adjective which means habitual, or agreeing with
custom is _____.

customary

■ Taking a short rest in the afternoon is _____
in some countries.

customary

■ The six o'clock closing hour is _____ for many
shops in the city.

ary

■ The last word ending in *ary* that we shall study is
library. This word ends in ____.

libr*ary*

■ A collection of books is commonly called a *libr*____.

li/brar/y	■ The noun *library* has three syllables: li/brar/y. The first syllable is _____.
li/*brar*/y	■ The second syllable is li/_____/y.
li/brar/*y*	■ The last syllable is li/brar/__.
li/brar/y	■ The three syllables are _____/_____/__.
library	■ Write the entire word, saying it in syllables as you write: _____.
library	■ The building where books, manuscripts, magazines, and the like are kept for reading is known as a _____.
library	■ Joe asked his sister if she wanted any books from the _____.
library	■ The millionaire donated a large sum of money for a new _____ in his home town.
anniversary	■ The annual return of a past event is called an _____.
customary	■ If a procedure is usual or agrees with custom, it is _____.
library	■ A building where books are kept for reading is a _____.
dictionary	■ Whenever you want the correct spelling and definition of a word, consult the _____ [reference word book].
vocabulary	■ The words you use in speaking and conversing are known as your speaking _____.
boundary	■ That which bounds or fixes a limit is a _____.
ery	■ There are four common words ending in *ery*. The first word is the noun *cemetery*. *Cemetery* ends in _____.

cem/e/ter/y	■ The noun *cemetery* has four syllables: cem/e/ter/y. The first syllable is _____.
cem/*e*/ter/y	■ The second syllable is cem/___/ter/y.
cem/e/*ter*/y	■ The third syllable is cem/e/_____/y.
cem/e/ter/*y*	■ The last syllable is cem/e/ter/___.
cem/e/ter/y	■ The four syllables are _____/___/_____/___.
cemetery	■ Write the entire word, saying it in syllables as you write: _____.
cemetery	■ Remember that three *e*'s are buried in c___m___t___ry.
cemetery	■ Usually a church in a small town will have its own _____ [burial place].
cemetery	■ Every Memorial Day my sister goes to the _____ and places a wreath on Father's grave.
cemetery	■ A burial place or ground is called a _____.
ery	■ Another common word that ends in *ery* is *creamery*. Remember that *creamery* ends in _____.
creamery	■ A *creamery* is a place where butter and cheese are made, as in this sentence: My grandparents make butter and cheese in their own _____.
creamery	■ A *creamery* is also a place where milk and cream are prepared for market, as in this sentence: My two cousins have good jobs at the local _____.
cream/er/y	■ The noun *creamery* has three syllables: cream/er/y. The first syllable is _____.
cream/*er*/y	■ The second syllable is cream/_____/y.

cream/er/*y*	■ The last syllable is cream/er/___.
cream/er/y	■ The three syllables are ___/___/___.
creamery	■ Write the entire word, saying it in syllables as you write: _____.
Creamery	■ Farmers from all the neighboring communities bring their milk to the O'Brien _____ [place where milk is prepared for market].
creamery	■ Our social studies class plans to tour the local _____ to see how milk is pasteurized.
creamery	■ A place where butter and cheese are made is called a _____.
creamery	■ An establishment where milk and butter are prepared for market is known as a _____.
ery	■ Like the noun *creamery*, the noun *gallery* also ends in ___.
gallery	■ A *gallery* can be a room for the exhibition of works of art, as shown in this sentence: Three of Jane's paintings are being exhibited at the _____.
gallery	■ The highest part of a theater in which spectators can sit is often called a *gallery*, as in this sentence: The only tickets that Jack could buy were for seats in the _____.
gal/ler/y	■ The noun *gallery* has three syllables: gal/ler/y. The first syllable is ___.
gal/*ler*/y	■ The second syllable is gal/___/y.
gal/ler/*y*	■ The last syllable is gal/ler/___.
gal/ler/y	■ The three syllables are ___/___/___.

gallery

■ Write the entire word, saying it in syllables as you write: _____.

gallery

■ A room or building in which paintings can be exhibited is known as a picture _____.

gallery

■ The cheapest seats for the theater are usually in the _____.

cemetery

■ A burial place or ground is a _____.

creamery

■ An establishment where butter and cheese are made is known as a _____.

gallery

■ The highest part of a theater in which spectators can sit is called the _____.

ery

■ The last common word we shall study in this group is *millinery,* which also ends in _____.

millinery

■ The noun *millinery* can be defined as the business of a milliner, a person who makes or trims ladies' hats, as in this sentence: My aunt has been in the _____ business for twenty-five years.

mil/li/ner/y

■ The noun *millinery* has four syllables: mil/li/ner/y. The first syllable is _____.

mil/*li*/ner/y

■ The second syllable is mil/_____/ner/y.

mil/li/*ner*/y

■ The third syllable is mil/li/_____/y.

mil/li/ner/*y*

■ The last syllable is mil/li/ner/__.

mil/li/ner/y

■ The four syllables are _____/_____/_____/__.

millinery

■ Write the entire word, saying it in syllables as you write: _____.

millinery	■ Every winter Mrs. Brown goes to New York to buy trimmings for use in her _____ business.
millinery	■ The business of making and trimming ladies' hats is known as the _____ business.
cemetery	■ There was a simple graveside service at the _____.
creamery	■ An establishment where milk and cheese are prepared for market is called a _____.
gallery	■ The highest part of a theater where spectators can sit is a _____.
dictionary	■ A reference book in which words are listed and defined in alphabetical order is a _____.
anniversary	■ We celebrate my parents' wedding _____ on May first.
library	■ A collection of books can be called a _____.
millinery	■ The business of a person who makes and trims ladies' hats is the _____ business.
vocabulary	■ The words which an individual uses is known as his _____.
customary	■ If something agrees with custom it is _____.
boundary	■ That which bounds or fixes a limit is a _____.
cream*ery*	■ A place where butter and cheese are made is a *cream*___.
li*brary*	■ There are over 5,000 books in our *li*___.
millin*ery*	■ A person who makes and trims ladies' hats is in the *millin*___ business.

vocabu*lary*

■ The reading vocabulary of many adults is usually larger than their writing *vocabu*_____.

custom*ary*

■ An eight o'clock dinner is the *custom*_____ procedure.

anniver*sary*

■ We do not know how to celebrate our *anniver*_____.

cem*etery*

■ A church in a small town usually has its own c___m___t___ry.

gall*ery*

■ A room in which paintings are exhibited can be called a picture *gall*_____.

bound*ary*

■ The river forms the *bound*_____ of the town.

library

■ Dr. Huntington left a million dollars to the city for an addition to the _____ [building for books].

ous

peril*ous*

■ The suffix *ous* forms an adjective from a noun. Take the word *peril*. By adding *ous* we can form the adjective *peril*_____.

peril

■ *Ous* is a suffix which forms an adjective from a noun. *Perilous* is an adjective formed from the noun _____.

ous

■ The adjective *perilous* is formed by adding the suffix _____ to the noun *peril*.

peril

■ The suffix *ous* means full of, abounding in. If a trip is *perilous,* it is full of _____.

humor

■ The adjective *humorous* can be defined as full of or abounding in _____.

ous

■ The adjective *humorous* is formed by adding the suffix _____ to the noun *humor*.

■ The suffix *ous* forms an [adjective, adverb] from a noun.

adjective

■ The adjective *perilous* is formed by adding _____ to the noun _____.

ous
peril

■ The adjective *humorous* is formed by adding the suffix _____ to the noun _____.

ous
humor

■ The suffix that can be defined as full of or abounding in is _____.

ous

■ The suffix *ous* forms [adjectives, nouns].

adjectives

■ Generally, the suffix *ous* can be added to a word without changing that word in any other way. When you add *ous* to the noun *peril* you [do, do not] change that word in any other way.

do not

■ To be full of peril is to be _____.

perilous

■ To be full of, or abounding in humor is to be _____.

humorous

■ If you add the suffix *ous* to the noun *danger,* you [do, do not] change the spelling of *danger* in any way.

do not

■ To be full of danger is to be _____.

dangerous

■ Joe Lansing was a flyer in World War II and went on many _____ [full of danger] missions.

dangerous

■ Combine the noun *marvel* and the suffix *ous* to form the adjective which means abounding in marvel or astonishment: _____.

marvelous

■ The adjective *marvelous* is the combination of the suffix *ous* and the noun _____.

marvel

marvelous

■ The view of the Taj Mahal was _____ [marvel + ous].

marvelous

■ My trip through the mountains was _____.

dangerous

■ The adjective defined as full of danger is _____.

humorous

■ A situation which could be filled with humor would be a _____ situation.

perilous

■ A mission filled with much peril could be called a _____ mission.

marvelous

■ The adjective meaning abounding in wonder and astonishment is _____.

slanderous

■ When a woman makes a statement that is filled with slander, she makes a _____ statement.

mountainous

■ Switzerland is famous for its mountains. Inasmuch as it has many mountains, we could say it is a _____ country.

consonant

■ The nouns *peril* and *danger* end in a [consonant, vowel].

consonant

■ The nouns *humor* and *marvel* also end in a [consonant, vowel].

do not

■ In adding the suffix *ous* to nouns like *peril, humor,* and *marvel,* which end in a consonant, you [do, do not] change the spelling of these nouns.

e

■ Now look at the noun *adventure.* It ends in the vowel __.

e

■ The noun *adventure* ends in a silent __.

ous

■ When you add the suffix *ous* to the noun *adventure,* which ends in a final *e,* you drop the *e* before adding the suffix _____.

■ When adding the suffix *ous* to a noun ending in a final *e,* you [drop, keep] the *e* before adding the suffix.

drop

■ The noun *adventure* ends in a final *e.* You [drop, keep] the *e* before adding the suffix *ous.*

drop

■ Form the adjective by adding *ous* to the noun *adventure:* _____.

adventurous

■ The adjective *adventurous* has four syllables: ad/ven/tur/ous. The first syllable is _____.

ad/ven/tur/ous

■ The second syllable is ad/_____/tur/ous.

ad/*ven*/tur/ous

■ The third syllable is ad/ven/_____/ous.

ad/ven/*tur*/ous

■ The last syllable is ad/ven/tur/_____.

ad/ven/tur/*ous*

■ Write the entire word, saying it in syllables as you write: _____.

adventurous

■ A mariner leads an _____ life on the sea.

adventurous

■ Jim's uncle was awarded a medal for his _____ acts.

adventurous

■ Like the noun *adventure,* the noun *desire* ends in __.

e

■ If you add the suffix *ous* to the noun *desire,* you will [keep, drop] the *e* before adding *ous.*

drop

■ To be filled with desire is to be _____.

desirous

■ John is too _____ [filled with desire] of his friend's wealth.

desirous

■ When you add the suffix *ous* to the nouns *adventure* and *desire,* you must [drop, keep] the *e* before adding the suffix.

drop

g

■ When a noun ending in a final *e* is preceded by **c** or **g**, you keep the *e* to preserve the *soft* pronunciation of the *c* or ___.

soft

■ If a word ends in *ce* or *ge*, the *e* must be retained to keep the [soft, hard] sound of the *c* or *g*.

is not

■ Look at the word *advantage* and pronounce it. The sound of the *g* in *advantage* is a *soft g*. It [is, is not] the same sound as the *g* in *get*.

is

■ The *g* in *get* is a *hard* sound of *g*. It [is, is not] the same sound as the *g* in *tag*.

soft

■ The *g* in *advantage* has a [soft, hard] sound.

keep

■ Before adding the suffix *ous* to a word ending in *ge*, you [drop, keep] the *e* to preserve the soft sound of *g*.

ad/van/tage

■ The noun *advantage* has three syllables: ___/van/tage.

ad/*van*/tage

■ The second syllable is ad/___/tage.

ad/van/*tage*

■ The third syllable is ad/van/___.

advantageous

■ Now add the suffix *ous* to *advantage* and write the entire adjective: _____.

advantageous

■ If a plan has many advantages it can be called _____.

advantageous

■ Because there is a possibility of Mary's getting a job in New York, it is _____ [filled with advantages] for her to go there soon.

does

■ Now look at the word *courage* and pronounce it. Like the noun *advantage,* it [does, does not] have the soft sound of *g*.

cour/age

■ The noun *courage* has two syllables: _____/age.

cour/*age*

■ The second syllable is cour/_____.

courage

■ Write the entire noun _____.

courageous

■ Form the adjective by adding *ous* to the noun *courage:* _____.

courageous

■ The early explorers were very _____ men.

perilous

■ The adjective which can be defined as full of peril is _____.

dangerous

■ A spy leads an extremely _____ [filled with danger] life.

humorous

■ When a person has a sense of humor, he is called _____.

hazardous

■ In the construction business there are many _____ [full of hazard] jobs.

adventurous

■ I envy my uncle because he has an _____ [full of adventure] nature.

advantageous

■ To be filled with advantages is to be _____.

marvelous

■ To be filled with marvel or astonishment is to be _____.

drop

■ Before adding the suffix *ous* to a word ending in a final *e,* you usually [drop, keep] the *e.*

keep

■ If a word ends in *ce* or *ge,* you [drop, keep] the *e* to retain the soft sound of the *c* or *g.*

outrageous

■ Form the adjective meaning full of outrage by combining the noun *outrage* and the suffix *ous:* _____.

■ Some plants are called _____ [poison + ous] as they cannot be eaten without causing death.

poisonous

■ If a word ends in *f*, like *grief*, you should change the *f* to *v* before adding the suffix *ous*. For example, grief changes to grie___ous.

v

■ The word *grief* ends in *f*. Before adding the suffix *ous* you change the ___ to ___.

f v

■ To be filled with grief is the meaning of the adjective _____ous.

*griev*ous

■ The death of her mother was a _____ [grief + ous] loss.

grievous

■ Like *grief*, the noun *mischief* ends in ___.

f

■ Like *grief*, the noun *mischief* ends in these last three letters: _____.

ief

■ To form the adjective meaning full of mischief, you must change the ___ to ___ and add _____.

f v
ous

■ To be full of mischief is to be *mis*_____*ous*.

mis*chiev*ous

■ To be full of or abounding in mischief is to be _____.

mischievous

■ The little girl is very _____ today.

mischievous

■ Bonnie was sent home from school because of her _____ conduct.

mischievous

■ When a word ends in *f*, change the *f* to *v* before adding the suffix _____.

ous

■ Full of grief is the definition of the adjective _____.

grievous

mischievous

■ To be full of mischief is to be _____.

is not

■ In adding the suffix *ous* to the noun *murder,* it [is, is not] necessary to change the spelling of the noun *murder.*

murderous

■ Form the adjective from the noun *murder* and the suffix *ous:* _____.

desirous

■ The adjective which means filled with desire is _____.

mischievous

■ If a child is full of mischief he is called _____.

slanderous

■ To be filled with slander is to be _____.

advantageous

■ Mr. Birmingham's plan is quite _____ [full of advantages] for his group of workers.

thunderous

■ When the principal players returned to the stage they were greeted with _____ [filled with thunder] applause.

courageous

■ A scientist should be a _____ [filled with courage] man.

ly

■ In general, you can add the suffix *ly* to an adjective, noun, or other part of speech without changing the root word in any way. For instance, if you wish to form the adjective *lovely,* you just add the suffix _____ to the noun *love.*

ly

■ Form an adjective by adding *ly* to the noun *love:* _____.

lovely

lovely

■ Mrs. Jamison is a _____ [love + ly] person.

ly	■ The adjective *monthly* is the combination of the noun *month* and the suffix _____.
monthly	■ Lucy's aunt attends _____ [month + ly] meetings of her club.
monthly	■ Mr. Jones assigned me the job of compiling the _____ [month + ly] reports.
frequent	■ The adverb *frequently* is formed by adding the suffix *ly* to the adjective _____.
fre/quent	■ The word *frequent* consists of two syllables: _____/quent.
fre/*quent*	■ The second syllable is fre/_____.
frequently	■ Mrs. Buckingham attends church services _____ [frequent + ly].
certainly	■ Form an adverb by adding the suffix *ly* to the adjective *certain:* _____.
cer/tain	■ The word *certain* has two syllables cer/tain, the first of which is _____.
cer/*tain*	■ The second syllable is cer/_____.
certain*ly*	■ The adverb is spelled *certain*_____.
certainly	■ When Mr. Dickinson expected full payment for his services, he was _____ [certain + ly] within his rights.
certainly	■ I will _____ [certain + ly] do what the doctor says.
ly	■ You can form an adverb from the adjective *scarce* by adding the suffix _____.

■ In general, you do not change the root word in any way when you add the suffix *ly*. Adding *ly* to the adjective *scarce* would form the adverb _____.

scarcely

■ Joan could _____ [scarce + ly] imagine that 500 people had crowded into the school auditorium.

scarcely

■ Many adjectives ending in *al* can be formed into adverbs by adding *ly*. Like the other words we have studied, these adjectives ending in *al* [do, do not] change in any way before the *ly* is added.

do not

■ Look at the adjective *mental*. The adverb can be formed by adding *ly:* _____.

mentally

■ The adjective *mental* has two syllables: ____/tal.

men/tal

■ The second syllable is men/____.

men/*tal*

■ In forming the adverb *mentally,* you add the suffix *ly* to the adjective _____.

mental

■ The examination showed that the man was _____ [mental + ly] capable of appearing as a witness.

mentally

■ The boys were judged both _____ [mental + ly] and physically fit for military service.

mentally

■ Like the adjective *mental,* the adjective *physical* ends in ____.

al

■ The word *physical* has three syllables: ____/i/cal.

phys/i/cal

■ The second syllable is phys/____/cal.

phys/*i*/cal

■ The last syllable is phys/i/____.

phys/i/*cal*

■ Combine *physical* and *ly:* _____.

physically

physically

■ Raymond is certain that he will be _____ [physical + ly] fit for the race.

physically
mentally

■ I feel fine _____ [physical + ly], but _____ [mental + ly] am very depressed.

us<i>ual</i>

■ The adjective *usual* ends in *al*. It means in the ordinary course of events—nothing strange or unexpected. An event that is not strange is *us____*.

usual

■ Ordinary means ____*ual*.

usual

■ An event which is ordinary is _____.

ly

■ To form an adverb from the adjective *usual* you add _____.

usually

■ I have my breakfast _____ [usual + ly] at seven o'clock.

usually

■ This procedure _____ [usual + ly] works out.

usually

■ On Sundays we _____ [usual + ly] sit in the park.

ly

■ The adjective *annual* also ends in *al*, and the adverb is formed by adding _____.

annual

■ The word *annual* pertains to a year, as in this sentence: The company publishes the magazine on an _____ basis.

an/nu/al

■ The adjective *annual* has three syllables: _____/nu/al.

an/<i>nu</i>/al

■ The second syllable is an/_____/al.

an/nu/<i>al</i>

■ The last syllable is an/nu/_____.

■ By adding the suffix *ly* to the adjective *annual,* you can form the adverb _____.

annually

■ The pilgrims travel _____ to the Holy Land.

annually

■ The contracts must be renewed _____.

annually

■ To form the adverb from the adjective *accidental* you add the suffix _____.

ly

■ The adjective *accidental* is divided into syllables like this: ac/ci/den/tal. The first syllable is _____.

ac/ci/den/tal

■ The second syllable is ac/_____/den/tal.

ac/*ci*/den/tal

■ The third syllable is ac/ci/_____/tal.

ac/ci/*den*/tal

■ The last syllable is ac/ci/den/_____.

ac/ci/den/*tal*

■ Form the adverb by combining *ly* and *accidental:* _____.

accidentally

■ The adverb *accidentally* means happening by chance, unexpectedly, as in this sentence: I found the missing book quite _____.

accidentally

■ He bumped my arm _____.

accidentally

■ On my way to the airport I saw my brother quite _____.

accidentally

■ If the adjective ends in *ic,* like *basic,* you usually add *ally* to form the adverb. The adverb formed from the adjective *basic* is basic_____.

basic*ally*

■ To form the adverb from an adjective ending in *ic,* you usually add _____.

ally

basically	■ The adjective *basic* ends in *ic*. The adverb is spelled _____.
basic	■ *Basic* means fundamental. A fundamental idea is therefore a _____ idea.
basic*ally*	■ The adverb *fundamentally* means *basic*_____.
basically	■ The issues are _____ [basic + ly] important to the entire community.
basically	■ The cause of the strike was _____ a matter of wage increases.
ally	■ To form the adverb from an adjective ending in *ic*, you add _____ to the adjective.
ic	■ Like the word *basic*, the adjective *automatic* ends in _____.
*auto*matic	■ The adjective *automatic* can be defined as mechanical. The word mechanical means the same as _____*matic*.
auto*matic*	■ To form the adverb from the adjective *automatic*, you add *ally* to the word *auto*_____.
automatic	■ Mechanical means the same as _____.
ally	■ Because *automatic* ends in *ic*, you add _____ to form the adverb.
auto*matically*	■ The boy went *auto*_____ [adverb] from one window to another.
automatically	■ Some refrigerators are _____ defrosted.
automatically	■ The toy trains move _____ through the tunnel and around the roundhouse.

■ Like *basic* and *automatic,* the adjective *drastic* forms its adverb by adding _____ .

ally

■ There are two syllables in *drastic:* _____/tic.

dras/tic

■ The second syllable is dras/_____ .

dras/*tic*

■ *Drastic* means extreme in effect or acting harshly, as in this sentence: They had to try _____ measures.

drastic

■ By adding *ally* to the adjective *drastic,* you form the adverb _____ .

drastically

■ The boy reacted _____ [harshly] to the news.

drastically

■ The *one* exception to the generalization about adjectives ending in *ic* is the adjective *public.* To form the adverb from the adjective *public,* you just add *ly:* _____ .

publicly

■ The adverb *publicly* is formed by adding _____ to the adjective *public.*

ly

■ The one exception to the generalization about adding *ally* to adjectives ending in *ic* is the word _____ .

public

■ The senator announced *public*_____ that he would not run for office.

public*ly*

■ The two candidates declared _____ [public + ly] that they disagreed on the tax issue.

publicly

■ The announcement was made _____ [in a public manner].

publicly

■ Generally, to form the adverb from an adjective, you add _____ .

ly

lovely	■ Form the adjective from the noun *love:* _____.
frequently	■ The boy's aunt goes _____ [frequent + ly] to the store.
certainly	■ I am _____ [certain + ly] aware of the consequences.
scarcely	■ Form the adverb from the adjective *scarce:* _____.
mentally	■ The doctors pronounced the boy physically and _____ [mental + ly] defective.
physically	■ Form the adverb from the adjective *physical:* _____.
annually	■ Our company takes the inventory _____ [annual + ly].
usually	■ The picnic is _____ [usual + ly] held on Monday.
accidentally	■ In looking for the missing book I _____ [accidental + ly] found a ten-dollar bill.
ally	■ When an adjective ends in *ic,* you add ____ to form the adverb.
public	■ The one exception to the *ic* generalization is the word _____.
basically	■ Form the adverb from the adjective *basic:* _____.
automatically	■ He moved each object _____ [automatic + ly].
drastically	■ Form the adverb from the adjective *drastic:* _____.
ly	■ To form the adverb from the adjective *public* you add ____.

■ To form the adverb by adding *ly* to an adjective which ends in *y* preceded by a consonant, change the ___ to ___ and add *ly*.

y i

■ Because *happy* ends in *y* preceded by the consonant *p*, you change the *y* to *i* and add *ly* to form the adverb: _____.

happily

■ Her father _____ [happy + ly] consented to drive Millie and her friends to the picnic grounds.

happily

■ Like *happy*, the adjective *hasty* ends in *y* preceded by a _____.

consonant

■ The stranger approached the farmer _____ [in a hasty manner].

hastily

■ After hearing about the floods in the northern part of the state, the Browns _____ [hasty + ly] put their belongings in a trailer and drove out of town.

hastily

■ If an adjective ends in *ic*, you add _____ to form the adverb.

ally

■ To form the adverb, you add _____ to the adjective *basic*.

ally

■ The one exception to adding *ally* to an adjective ending in *ic* is the word _____.

public

■ Form the adverb from the adjective *public*: _____.

publicly

■ To form the adverb from an adjective ending in *al*, like *mental*, just add _____.

ly

■ Yearly can be defined as *annual*_____.

annual*ly*

■ The man was _____ [critical + ly] ill for three weeks.

critically

longingly

■ The child looked _____ [longing +ly] at the dolls in the store window.

publicly

■ The congressman announced _____ [public + ly] that he favored a tax cut.

independently

■ The corner grocery is run _____ [independent + ly] by two local men.

neatly

■ Mrs. James was very _____ [neat + ly] dressed.

accidentally

■ The stranger bumped my arm _____ [accidental + ly].

formally

■ Susan's engagement was _____ [formal + ly] announced at the supper club dance.

ly

■ In general, just add _____ to an adjective to form the adverb.

i
ly

■ If an adjective ends in *y* preceded by a consonant, change the *y* to __ and add _____ to form the adverb.

ally

■ If an adjective ends in *ic*, add _____ to form the adverb.

public

■ The one exception to the *ic* generalization is the adjective _____.

ly

■ To form the adverb from the adjective *public*, just add _____.

really

■ Form the adverb from the adjective *real:* _____.

equally

■ Form the adverb from the adjective *equal:* _____.

verbally

■ Form the adverb from the adjective *verbal:* _____.

verbally

■ The orders from the foreman were given _____
[verbal + ly].

equally

■ The two issues are _____ [equal + ly] important.

fy

justi*fy*

■ *fy* is a verb suffix meaning to make, to form into,
and is preceded by *i* or *e*. For example, the verb to *justify*
means to prove or show to be just. To prove someone is
just is to *just*___.

rarefy

■ *fy* is a verb suffix meaning to make, to form into, and
is preceded by *i* or *e*. For example, the verb *rarefy* means
to make or become rare. To become rare is to _____.

e

■ The suffix *fy* is preceded by *i* or ___.

stup*efy*

■ Four common words that end in *efy* are *rarefy*,
putrefy, liquefy, and *stup*___.

efy

■ *Rarefy* ends in ___.

rarefy

■ *Rarefy* means to make or become rare, thin, or less
dense. To make rare is to _____.

rarefy

■ To make thin or less dense is to _____.

rarefy

■ The increasingly warm temperatures will *rar__fy*
the objects found on the expedition.

rarefy

■ *Putrefy, stupefy, liquefy,* and _____ end in *efy*.

putrefy

■ To *putrefy* means to decay or spoil. To decay means
to _____

pu/tre/fy

■ *Putrefy* has three syllables: ___/tre/fy.

pu/*tre*/fy	■ The second syllable is pu/_____/fy.
pu/tre/*fy*	■ The last syllable is pu/tre/_____.
putrefy	■ To spoil or decay is to _____.
putrefy	■ The plane crashed on an isolated mountain, and if the bodies of the passengers are not removed shortly, they will _____.
rarefy *putrefy*	■ Two words you have learned that end in *efy* are *r*_____ and *p*_____.
rarefy	■ To make rare is to _____.
putrefy	■ To decay or spoil is to _____.
rarefy putrefy	■ Four common verbs that end in *efy* are *stupefy, liquefy*, _____, and _____.
stupefy	■ To *stupefy* means to make stupid or dull. To make stupid means to _____.
efy	■ The verb *stupefy* ends in _____.
stu/pe/fy	■ *Stupefy* has three syllables: _____/pe/fy.
stu/*pe*/fy	■ The second syllable is stu/_____/fy.
stu/pe/*fy*	■ The last syllable is stu/pe/_____.
stupefy	■ To make stupid or dull is to _____.
stupefy	■ The constant brainwashing will _____ the prisoner so that he cannot testify.
rarefy *putrefy* *stupefy*	■ Three of the four common words ending in *efy* are *rar*_____, *pu*_____, and *stu*_____.

liquefy	■ To *liquefy* means to reduce to a liquid state. To reduce to a liquid state is to _____.
li/que/fy	■ The verb *liquefy* has three syllables: _____/que/fy.
li/*que*/fy	■ The second syllable is li/_____/fy.
li/que/*fy*	■ The last syllable is li/que/_____.
liquefy	■ To reduce to a liquid state means to _____.
liquefy	■ If you reduce a gas to a liquid state you _____ it.
liquefy	■ Extreme heat will _____ [reduce to liquid] iron and other metals.
efy	■ These four common words, *rarefy, putrefy, stupefy,* and *liquefy,* end in _____.
rarefy	■ One verb ending in *efy* means to make rare. That verb is _____.
putrefy	■ Another verb ending in *efy* means to decay or spoil. That verb is _____.
stupefy	■ The verb that means to make dull or stupid is _____.
liquefy	■ To reduce to a liquid state is to _____.
test*i*fy	■ Most verbs ending in *fy* are preceded by *i,* as in *test__fy.*
testify	■ To *testify* means to make a solemn declaration to establish a fact, as in this sentence: The witness will _____ in court.
tes/ti/fy	■ The verb *testify* has three syllables: _____/ti/fy.

tes/*ti*/fy

■ The second syllable is tes/____/fy.

tes/ti/*fy*

■ The last syllable is tes/ti/____.

testify

■ To make a solemn declaration to establish a fact is the meaning of the verb _____.

testify

■ The wife cannot _____ against her husband.

testify

■ Three witnesses will _____ against the bank robber.

rect*ify*

■ Just as the verb *testify* ends in *ify*, so does the verb *rect*____.

rectify

■ To *rectify* means to make or set right, as in this sentence: It is difficult to _____ the wrong.

rec/ti/fy

■ The verb *rectify* has three syllables: rec/ti/fy. The first syllable is ____.

rec/*ti*/fy

■ The second syllable is rec/____/fy.

rec/ti/*fy*

■ The last syllable is rec/ti/____.

rectify

■ To make or set right is to _____.

rectify

■ Sam said that he would _____ all his mistakes.

rectify

■ It is very difficult to _____ some blunders.

ify

■ The verbs *testify* and *rectify* both end in ____.

falsify

■ The verb *falsify* means to make false, as in this sentence: The bookkeeper was urged to _____ his records.

ify

■ Like *rectify*, the verb *falsify* ends in ____.

fal/si/fy

■ The verb *falsify* has three syllables: _____/si/fy.

fal/*si*/fy

■ The second syllable is fal/_____/fy.

fal/si/*fy*

■ The last syllable is fal/si/_____.

falsify

■ To make false is to _____.

falsify

■ To avoid letting his employer discover the cash shortages, Jim will _____ his accounts.

falsify

■ By changing one column of figures, Myrtle will _____ the accounting ledger.

testify

■ To make a solemn declaration to establish a fact is the definition of the verb _____.

rectify

■ To make or set right is to _____.

falsify

■ To make false is the definition of the verb _____.

rarefy

■ To make rare is to _____.

stupefy

■ To make stupid or dull is to _____.

liquefy

■ To reduce to a liquid state is to _____.

putrefy

■ To decay or spoil is to _____.

class*ify*

■ To group into classes is to *class*_____.

just*ify*

■ To prove or show to be just is to *just*_____.

rat*ify*

■ To approve formally, as a treaty or proclamation, is to *rat*_____.

classify

■ If you form into classes you _____.

justify	■ To prove to be just is to _____.
i	■ The verb *ratify*, like *justify* and *classify*, ends in __fy.
ratify	■ To approve formally, as a treaty or proclamation, is to _____.
rarefy putrefy stupefy liquefy (in any order)	■ Four common verbs ending in *efy* are _____, _____, _____, and _____.
i	■ Most verbs ending in the verb suffix *fy* are preceded by the vowel __.
e	■ In words like *rarefy* and *stupefy*, the suffix *fy* is preceded by __.

ize, ise, and yze

ise	■ The ending of some verbs is pronounced *iz* (a long *i* sound followed by the *z* sound). This ending can be spelled in three ways: *ize, ise,* or *yze.* The verb *advertise* is an example of a verb ending in ___.
ise	■ Some verbs have an ending that is pronounced with a long *i* sound followed by a *z* sound: *iz.* Such verbs can be spelled *ize, yze,* or ___.
ize	■ The ending of a verb that is pronounced *iz* can be spelled in one of three ways: *ise,* ___, or *yze.*
yze	■ The *iz* pronounced ending of a verb may be spelled *ise, ize,* or ___.
analyze paralyze	■ Two verbs that are spelled with the *yze* ending are *analyze* and *paralyze.* The *yze* ending pertains to the two words _____ and _____.

analyze

■ To *analyze* means to separate a whole into its parts and examine the parts carefully. If you examine a problem carefully, you _____ it.

an/a/lyze

■ The verb *analyze* has three syllables: an/a/lyze. The first syllable is _____.

an/*a*/lyze

■ The second syllable is an/__/lyze.

an/a/*lyze*

■ The last syllable is an/a/_____.

analyze

■ Write the entire word, saying it in syllables as you write: _____.

analyze

■ To separate a whole into its parts and examine these parts carefully is the definition of the verb _____.

analyze

■ To reach a definite solution to the problem, it will be necessary to _____ the entire problem.

yze

■ Like the verb *analyze,* the verb *paralyze* ends in _____.

paralyze

■ To *paralyze* means to affect with paralysis, as in this sentence: A severe attack of polio could _____ a person.

paralyze

■ To *paralyze* also means to unnerve or to render ineffective, as in this sentence: The effect of the car crash threatened to _____ me for a long time.

par/a/lyze

■ The verb *paralyze* has three syllables: par/a/lyze. The first syllable is _____.

par/*a*/lyze

■ The second syllable is par/__/lyze.

par/a/*lyze*

■ The last syllable is par/a/_____.

paralyze

■ To render ineffective is to _____.

paralyze

■ To unnerve means to _____.

paralyze

■ To affect or strike with paralysis is to _____.

p*aralyze*
analyze

■ Two verbs whose ending is pronounced *iz* and spelled *yze* are p_____ and a_____.

paralyze

■ Some forms of polio will usually _____ whomever they strike.

analyze

■ To separate a whole into its parts and examine the parts carefully is the definition of the verb _____.

paralyze

■ The doctor is afraid that the disease will _____ the child.

analyze

■ For the next assignment the instructor told us to _____ two economic theories.

paralyze
analyze
(in any order)

■ Two verbs that end in *yze* are _____ and _____.

ise

■ There are no hard and fast generalizations to follow for the spellings *ize* or *ise*. Therefore, it will be best to learn some of those verbs that end in *ize* and some that end in ___.

arise

■ To get up or to ascend means to *arise*. To ascend means to _____.

se

■ *Arise* is one verb that ends in i___.

arise

■ To get up is to _____.

arise

■ To ascend also means to _____.

arise

■ The student asked for an alarm clock so that he could _____ early the next morning.

arise	■ I prefer to _____ when the sun comes up.
ise	■ Like the verb *arise,* the verb *advertise* ends in ____.
advertise	■ The verb to *advertise* means to give public attention to something: Many firms _____ their products on television and radio.
ad/ver/tise	■ There are three syllables in *advertise:* ____/ver/tise.
ad/*ver*/tise	■ The second syllable is ad/____/tise.
ad/ver/*tise*	■ The last syllable is ad/ver/____.
advertise	■ To give public attention to something is the definition of the verb _____.
advertise	■ The verb *advertise* also means to make conspicuous, or call attention to, as in this sentence: She tried to _____ her many charms.
advertise	■ To make conspicuous is to _____.
ise	■ The verbs *arise* and *advertise* end in ____.
advertise	■ The newspapers urge the department stores to _____ their special sales.
ise	■ The ending of the noun *demise* is also pronounced *iz* and is spelled ____.
dem*ise*	■ If you read about the *death* of a royal person, you read about his *dem*____.
demise	■ The noun that means death is _____.
demise	■ The headlines announced the _____ [death] of the king.

demise	■ The death of a king is often spoken of as his _____.
ise	■ The word *exercise,* which can be used as a verb or a noun, is another word that ends in _____.
ex/er/cise	■ There are three syllables in *exercise:* ex/er/cise. The first syllable is _____.
ex/*er*/cise	■ The second syllable is ex/_____/cise.
ex/er/*cise*	■ The third syllable is ex/er/_____.
exercise	■ Write the entire word, saying it in syllables as you write: _____.
exercise	■ A particular study of fingering to be practiced over and over again could be called an _____.
exercise	■ To wield authority or influence over someone is to *exercise* that authority, as in this sentence: I intend to _____ my authority over him to see that the measure will not be vetoed.
exercise	■ He practiced the five-finger _____ for an hour.
exercise	■ Practice on a particular problem can be called an _____.
ise	■ Like the verb *exercise,* the verb *revise* ends in _____.
revise	■ To *revise* means to correct, as in this sentence: If a student has been told to correct and improve his themes, he has been told to _____ them.
revise	■ A writer usually has to _____ his manuscripts.
revise	■ To correct and improve means to _____.
revise	■ Many instructors teach their students how to _____ their themes.

revise

■ To look over a manuscript for correction means to
_____ it.

revise

■ I expect to _____ my paper several times.

ise

■ Just as the words *demise, exercise,* and *revise* end in
ise, so does the word *supervise. Supervise* is a verb ending
in _____.

supervise

■ To *supervise* means to oversee for correction. In other
words, if Miss Jones's job is to oversee seven employees,
her job is to _____ them.

su/per/vise

■ The verb *supervise* has three syllables: _____/per/vise.

su/*per*/vise

■ The second syllable is su/_____/vise.

su/per/*vise*

■ The last syllable is su/per/_____.

supervise

■ To oversee for correction is the definition of the
verb _____.

supervise

■ Mr. Haney asked me if I would like to _____
the girls in the typing pool.

supervise

■ Jane requested a transfer to another department
because she did not want to _____ the other girls
in the office.

advise

■ Because of Tom's stubbornness it is difficult to
_____ [counsel] him what to do.

demise

■ Queen Elizabeth II of England succeeded her father
George VI upon his _____.

exercise

■ The present governmental administration is recom-
mending a program of physical _____.

revise

■ The publishers suggested that I _____ [correct
and improve] one chapter.

supervise

■ To oversee for correction is the definition of the verb
_____.

analyze

■ To separate the whole into its parts and examine
the parts carefully is the meaning of the verb _____.

paralyze

■ To render ineffective is to _____.

analyze
paralyze
(in any order)

■ There are two words that end in *yze:* _____,
_____.

enterprise

■ · The undertaking of a plan or project is called an
enterprise, as in this sentence: When Joe embarked on
his new project, he began his _____.

en/ter/prise

■ *Enterprise* has three syllables: _____/ter/prise.

en/*ter*/prise

■ The second syllable is en/_____/prise.

en/ter/*prise*

■ The last syllable is en/ter/_____.

enterprise

■ An undertaking of a project can be called an
_____.

enterprise

■ As soon as he gets enough money, Richard will begin
his new _____.

enterprise

■ If one undertakes an important or daring project, he
is undertaking an _____.

ise

■ The noun *merchandise* also ends in _____.

mer/chan/dise

■ *Merchandise* has three syllables: mer/chan/dise. The
first syllable is _____.

mer/*chan*/dise

■ The second syllable is mer/_____/dise.

mer/chan/*dise*

■ The last syllable is mer/chan/_____.

■ The goods in a store are commonly known as
_____.

merchandise

■ Burton's Dress Shop has a lot of fine _____.

merchandise

■ Carol has an opportunity to supervise the buying of
all the _____ in the dress department.

merchandise

■ The noun *disguise* signifies anything which tends to
change a person's true identity. A mask can be called a
_____.

disguise

■ The word *disguise* has two syllables: _____/guise.

dis/guise

■ The last syllable is dis/_____.

dis/*guise*

■ Apparel which helps to conceal a person's true appearance or character is a _____.

disguise

■ The word *disguise* used as a verb means to hide the
true nature or character of someone. In other words, a
mask is used to _____ the person's facial features.

disguise

■ At the ball everyone must wear a mask to _____
himself.

disguise

■ After he escaped from prison, the convict dyed his
hair in order to _____ himself.

disguise

■ To *surmise* is to imagine or to guess, without much
evidence to back up the guess. If one has little proof of
what is going on, he can only _____ what is happening. ·

surmise

■ The two syllables of *surmise* are _____/mise.

sur/mise

■ The second syllable is sur/_____.

sur/*mise*

■ To guess what is going on is to _____.

surmise

■ Because Helen did not tell about the nature of the meeting, Harlan had to _____ what would happen at the conference.

surmise

■ When Nancy left home without a word, her mother was forced to _____ her reasons for leaving.

surmise

■ The word *surmise* used as a noun would signify a guess based on little or no evidence, as in this sentence: He was not afraid to voice his _____.

surmise

■ A *franchise* is a particular privilege to do something which a person might not otherwise be legally able to do: Some cab drivers operate under a _____.

franchise

■ *Franchise* consists of two syllables: fran/chise. The first syllable is _____.

fran/chise

■ The second syllable is fran/_____.

fran/*chise*

■ If an individual wanted to operate a certain business which he would be unable to do legally in ordinary circumstances, he could be granted a _____.

franchise

■ A particular privilege to do something otherwise not legally permissible is a _____.

franchise

■ To drive a cab for the Checkerboard Cab Company a man must have capital to buy a _____.

franchise

■ In the early part of this chapter we said that there are no hard and fast generalizations about the use of *ise* and *ize*. You have just learned many words that end in *ise*. Now let us look at some words that end in _____.

ize

■ The verb *emphasize* means to stress, or insist upon the importance of an object. To stress means to _____.

emphasize

■ *Emphasize* has three syllables: _____/pha/size.

em/pha/size

■ The second syllable is em/_____/size.

em/*pha*/size

em/pha/*size*	■ The last syllable is em/pha/_____.
emphasize	■ To stress is to _____.
emphasize	■ To insist upon the importance of an object is to _____ it.
emphasize	■ In reading poetry one must _____ words and phrases.
emphasize	■ The debating team will _____ both sides of the question.
ize	■ The verb *realize,* which means to make real, ends in _____.
re/al/ize	■ There are three syllables in *realize:* _____/al/ize.
re/*al*/ize	■ The second syllable is re/_____/ize.
re/al/*ize*	■ The last syllable is re/al/_____.
realize	■ To make real is to _____.
realize	■ To conceive or see something as real is to _____.
realize	■ As soon as he stepped outside the door, he began to _____ his danger.
realize	■ His one dream was to _____ the printing project.
recognize	■ The verb *recognize* means to know again. If you see a person you have already met, you will undoubtedly _____ him.
rec/og/nize	■ *Recognize* has three syllables: _____/og/nize.
rec/*og*/nize	■ The second syllable is rec/_____/nize.

rec/og/*nize*	■ The last syllable is rec/og/_____.
recognize	■ To know again is to _____.
recognize	■ To *recognize* also means to admit having knowledge of something: I, too, _____ that fact.
recognize	■ When the banker passed by without saying hello, I knew that he had failed to _____ me.
realize	■ Mary failed to _____ [see as real] the harm she was bringing to her family.
emphasize	■ If you stress a particular point or fact, you will _____ it.
criticize	■ The verb *criticize* means to judge the merits of something, as in this sentence: The instructor will _____ all the term papers.
crit/i/cize	■ *Criticize* has three syllables: crit/i/cize. The first syllable is _____.
crit/*i*/cize	■ The second syllable is crit/___/cize.
crit/i/*cize*	■ The third syllable is crit/i/_____.
criticize	■ To judge the merits of something is to _____.
criticize	■ To express criticism of a work of art is to _____ it.
criticize	■ Mr. Donaldson's job as a critic is to _____ the musical performances in the program.
criticize	■ The student body did not think it was right for the history teacher to _____ [judge merits] the class play.

criticize

■ Only after an objective analysis of my own work was I able to _____ [judge merits] someone else's efforts as a writer.

criticize

■ To express criticism is to _____.

emphasize

■ To stress one point more than another is to _____ that point.

realize

■ To make real or see as real is to _____.

recognize

■ To know again is to _____.

criticize

■ To judge as a critic is to _____.

franchise

■ A particular privilege to do something which a person might not otherwise be legally able to do is called a _____.

surmise

■ To imagine or guess without having much evidence on which to base a guess is to _____.

enterprise

■ The undertaking of a project is an _____.

merchandise

■ The wares or goods in a store are known as _____.

supervise

■ When Frank told me about the new job, I asked him how many people he would have to _____ [over-see].

disguise

■ A mask is used as a _____.

revise

■ My instructor told me that I would have to _____ [correct] the plot of my short story.

criticize

■ To express criticism is to _____.

recognize	■ I do not intend to _____ [know again] her when I see her.
demise	■ The Duke of Windsor became king upon the _____ [death] of his father George V.
exercise	■ The doctors say that everyone should get plenty of physical _____.
advertise	■ The slogan "It pays to _____" means that you get more results when you call public attention to an article or item.
advise	■ I do not know what to _____ [counsel] Ruby to do when she finishes school.
fran*chise*	■ Joe needs a lot of money to buy the *fran*_____.
emphasize	■ To stress a point is to _____ it.
item*ize*	■ Using your knowledge of the *verbs* that end in *ize,* work out the ending of this word: If I should put down quite a few items in a list, then I would *item*_____ them.
central*ize*	■ If the company decided to bring all the sub-offices under a central head, then it could be said that the company decided to *central*_____ its operations.
dramat*ize*	■ The faculty agreed that the senior class could *dramat*_____ the novel.
general*ize*	■ To make general or to reduce to a general law is to *general*_____.
modern*ize*	■ Mr. Jones felt that he would have to *modern*_____ his old house.
familiarize	■ To become familiar with a situation is to *familiar*_____ yourself with it.

chapter 10

ceed, cede, sede

The endings *ceed, cede,* and *sede* are confusing and perplexing because they sound exactly the same. However, there are very definite generalizations to guide you in the spelling of words with these endings.

Master these generalizations and you will never wonder how to spell *proceed, supersede, precede, succeed,* and other words with the *ceed, cede,* and *sede* endings.

Test for Chapter 10

Fill in the blanks with the appropriate ending: ceed, cede, or sede:

1. To replace is to super_____.
2. To go beyond in limit is to ex_____.
3. To advance is to pro_____.
4. To go back is to re_____.
5. To go before in position, rank or importance is to pre_____.
6. To be successful means to suc_____.
7. To withdraw formally from an organization, especially from a political or religious group, is to se_____.
8. To yield consent or agree is to ac_____.
9. To yield or to grant, as a privilege, is the definition of the word con_____.
10. To act between parties to settle differences means to inter_____.

■ Words ending in the syllable which is pronounced *sēd* (with a long *e*) can be spelled *sede, ceed,* or *cede.* The three spellings of the last syllable of a word that is pronounced sēd are _____, _____, and _____.

sede
ceed
cede

■ There is only one word that ends in *sede: supersede.* The only word that ends in *sede* is _____sede.

*super*sede

■ *Supersede* is the only word that ends in _____.

sede

■ *Supersede* means to replace, as in this sentence: One edition will _____ another.

supersede

■ To replace means to super_____.

super*sede*

■ The only word that ends in *sede* is _____.

supersede

■ When the Army publishes a regulation to replace an earlier one, it can be said that the last regulation will _____ the first.

supersede

■ Look carefully at the following words: *exceed, proceed,* and *succeed.* These verbs are the only words that end in _____.

ceed

■ *Exceed, proceed,* and _____ceed end in *ceed.*

*succ*eed

■ *Proceed, succeed,* and _____ceed end in *ceed.*

*ex*ceed

■ *Exceed, succeed,* and _____ceed are the three words that end in *ceed.*

*pro*ceed

■ To *exceed* means to go beyond in quantity or extent. The word *exceed,* which means to go beyond, ends in _____.

ceed

■ If a person drives above the speed limit, he will _____ceed the limit.

*ex*ceed

exceed

■ When Mary drives her father's car, she will be careful not to _____ the speed limit.

exceed

■ To go beyond the quantity or limit is to _____.

*ex*ceed

■ There are three words that end in *ceed: succeed, proceed,* and ___*ceed.*

succeed

■ To *succeed* means to be successful, as in this sentence: The principal feels that Julie will _____ in college.

suc*ceed*

■ If you are determined to get ahead, you will probably *suc*___.

succeed

■ To be successful means to _____.

succeed

■ The motto of the graduating class is "The surest way not to fail is to determine to _____ [be successful]."

proceed

■ The three words that end in *ceed* are *exceed, succeed,* and _____.

proceed

■ To *proceed* means to advance. To advance means the same as _____.

pro*ceed*

■ When the road is cleared, the parade will *pro*___ up the street.

proceed

■ To advance means to _____.

proceed
exceed
succeed
(in any order)

■ Three words that end in *ceed* are _____, _____, _____.

supersede

■ Only one word ends in *sede:* _____.

supersede

■ To replace is to _____.

exceed
succeed
proceed
(in any order)

■ Three words ending in *ceed* are _____, _____, _____.

proceed

■ When you finish reading the directions, you may _____ to Part I of the test.

exceed

■ The amount of money spent on food and decorations will greatly _____ the amount donated by the businessmen of the community.

succeed

■ Always remember the motto, "If you don't _____ at first, try, try again."

cede

■ If only one word ends in *sede,* and only three words end in *ceed,* then the rest of the words in this group will end in *cede.* The word *precede* is a good example of a word ending in ____.

precede

■ The verb *precede* means to go before in position, importance, or rank, as in this sentence: The president will _____ the vice-president in rank.

precede

■ If Mary and Barbara are standing in front of John in the ticket line, it can be said that they _____ him in line.

precede

■ If Tuesday and Wednesday come before Thursday, they _____ Thursday.

precede

■ In the tournament parade, the Minnesota float will _____ [go before] the one from Missouri.

is not

■ The word *recede* [is, is not] included in the four words that end in either *sede* or *ceed.*

recede

■ The verb *recede* means to go back, as in this sentence: The water will _____ by tomorrow.

re*cede*

■ If an army plans to withdraw or go back, it will *re*____.

■ To go back means to _____.

recede

■ To go before in position, importance, or rank is to _____.

precede

■ Look carefully at the following words: *accede, secede,* and *concede.* These are examples of words that end in _____.

cede

■ Because the words *accede, concede,* and *secede* do not end in either *sede* or *ceed,* they must end in _____.

cede

■ To *accede* means to agree or to yield consent. To agree or to yield consent means the same as the word _____.

accede

■ To yield consent means to _____*cede.*

*ac*cede

■ The members of the minority party will eventually *ac*_____ to the wishes of the party.

ac*cede*

■ John and his brother will _____ to the demands of their parents.

accede

■ Another example of a word ending in *cede* is *secede.* The ending of this word is spelled the same as *ac*_____.

ac*cede*

■ To *secede* means to withdraw formally from an organization, especially from a political or religious group. If a state were to withdraw from the union of states, it would _____.

secede

■ To withdraw formally from an organization is to _____.

secede

■ At one time in the history of the United States, several states threatened to _____ from the Union.

secede

■ To *concede* means to yield or to grant as a privilege. To yield or grant as a privilege is to _____.

concede

concede

■ To grant as a privilege is the meaning of the word *con*____.

concede

■ The senator stated that he would _____ the point to his opponent in the debate.

supersede

■ One word ends in *sede:* _____.

exceed
proceed
succeed
(in any order)

■ The three words that end in *ceed* are _____, _____, _____.

cede

■ If there is only one word that ends in *sede* and only three words that end in *ceed*, then all other words ending in the syllable which is pronounced *sēd* are spelled ____.

proceed

■ The teacher told the students that it was time to _____ [advance] with the meeting.

precede

■ Mr. Ames suggested that the singing of the National Anthem should _____ [go before] the band concert.

accede

■ Joe urged his brother to _____ [agree] to the wishes of their parents.

exceed

■ According to the latest inventory, the number of pencils on hand will greatly _____ [go beyond] the number of pens.

supersede

■ As the age of automation continues, new methods of production and management will gradually _____ [replace] the old.

secede

■ At one time many prominent politicians and statesmen feared that the state of Virginia would _____ [formally withdraw] from the Union.

succeed

■ If you wish to accomplish a great deal, you must work hard and you will probably _____ [be successful].

recede

■ The weather bureau predicted that the river would reach its crest within three hours and then would start to _____ [go back].

concede

■ To yield or to grant as a privilege is the definition of the word _____.

cede

■ If the last syllable of a word which is pronounced *sēd* is *not* one of these words, *supersede, exceed, proceed,* and *succeed,* then the ending is spelled _____.

ante*cede*

■ There is a word ending in the syllable pronounced *sēd,* which means to precede in time and place. The first two syllables of this word are the Latin word *ante,* meaning before. According to the generalizations you have just learned, the ending of this word would be *ante_____.*

ante*cede*

■ To precede in time and place means to *ante_____.*

*ante*cede

■ A word which means to precede in time and place is _____*cede.*

antecede

■ The First World War must _____ [precede in time] the Second World War in history.

inter*cede*

■ There is another word ending in the pronounced syllable *sēd,* which means to mediate, or to act between parties to settle differences. The first two syllables of this word are the Latin word *inter,* meaning between or among. Using the generalizations you have just learned, spell this word: *inter_____.*

*inter*cede

■ To act between parties to settle differences means to _____*cede.*

intercede

■ If a person should decide to move in between two people involved in a serious disagreement, he would _____.

intercede

■ The teachers asked the superintendent to _____ [act between parties] in their dispute for higher wages.

Review

■ The verb *precede* is spelled with the *cede* ending. State the generalization used.

One word is spelled with sede (supersede), and three with ceed (exceed, proceed, and succeed). All others are spelled with cede.

succeed

■ To be successful is to _____.

recede

■ To go back is the definition of the verb _____.

Three words end in ceed: proceed, exceed, and succeed.

■ The verb *proceed* is spelled with the *ceed* ending. State the generalization used.

accede

■ To agree or to yield consent is to _____.

secede

■ To withdraw formally from an organization, especially from a political or religious group, is to _____.

proceed

■ To advance is to _____.

concede

■ To yield or grant as a privilege is to _____.

antecede

■ To precede in time or place is to _____.

intercede

■ To act between parties to settle differences is to _____.

One word is spelled with sede: supersede.

■ The verb *supersede* is spelled with the *sede* ending. State the generalization used.

proceed
succeed
exceed

■ The three words that end in *ceed* are _____, _____, _____.

cede

■ If a word does not end in *sede* or *ceed*, then it will end in _____.

chapter 11

Prefixes

Meaning plays an important part in reading, spelling, and writing. In spelling, some errors can be charged to the inability to recognize the difference between the various prefixes, such as *per* and *pre, de* and *dis. If* one knows that *de* means down and *dis* means away or not, he will probably not misspell the common word *describe.*

This chapter on prefixes (elements added to the beginning of words) concentrates on five of these elements, *per, pre, pro, de,* and *dis,* since they cause the greatest amount of confusion.

To help you with the meaning of many other prefixes, here is a handy guide for reference:

Prefix	*Meaning*	*Illustrative word*	*Meaning*
ab	away	abduct	to steal *away*
ante	before	ante-bellum	*before* the war
anti	against	anti-liberal	*against* the liberal
circum	around	circumvent	to go *around*
ex	out of, away	example	a sample, that which is *out of* a larger quantity
in	in, into	incase	to enclose *in* or as *in* a case
	not	intolerable	*not* tolerable
inter	among	interjacent	lying *among* or between
non	not	nonsense	that which has *no* sense

Prefix	Meaning	*Illustrative word*	Meaning
re	again	refresh	to become fresh *again*
	back	refrain	to hold *back*
se	aside, apart	seclude	to shut up *apart*, to isolate
sub	under	subway	an *under*ground passage
super	over, above	superhuman	*above* the human, divine
trans	across	transcontinental	*across* the continent

Test for Chapter 11

Fill in the missing prefix (*per, pre, pro, de,* or *dis*). Be sure to check the meaning of the word given in the right-hand column.

1. I have learned to _____spise my brother.   feel contempt for

2. The committee decided that the ladies would _____cede the men in the receiving line.   go before

3. It usually takes us a long time to _____pare for a family reunion.   get ready

4. Joan will try to _____scribe her European trip as quickly as possible.   tell in words

5. Smallpox is a contagious _____ease.   ill condition of the body

6. The doctor will _____scribe a new medicine for the patient.   give directions

7. Which color do you _____fer: red or green?   like better

8. He hoped to _____suade me to accompany him to the theater.   induce

9. The instructor told us to _____ceed with the demonstration.   go ahead

10. Farmers are predicting that this is a good year to _____duce crops.   bring forth

11. The store has a large ____play of merchandise.

    articles
    spread out

12. Fire will again ____stroy many buildings this year.

    ruin

13. I shall need assistance to ____cide which course of action to take.

    come to a
    conclusion

14. He hesitated at the closed door, not wanting to ____turb the author.

    interrupt

15. How long will it take you to ____pose of your books?

    get rid

16. Hot weather makes one ____spire freely.

    sweat

17. This magazine article does not ____tain to the main subject of our discussion.

    have reference

18. Susan will be ____moted to a better job next month.

    advance

19. The council is planning to ____pose a new solution to the housing problem.

    to offer for
    consideration

20. Children always like to ____form when company comes.

    act

---

beginning

■ A *prefix* is one or more letters or syllables added to the beginning of a root word to modify its meaning. A prefix is always added to the [beginning, end] of a word.

prefix

■ One or more letters or syllables added to the beginning of a root word is a *pre____*.

prefix

■ A syllable which is combined with the beginning of a root word to modify its meaning is known as a _____.

prefix

■ There are many prefixes in the English language, but we shall study only a few of those that create the most confusion in spelling. Look at the word *dissatisfy*. The first syllable *dis* is called a _____.

prefix

■ Look again at the word *dissatisfy*. The syllable at the beginning of the word, *dis,* changes the meaning of the word *satisfy* and is called a _____.

Prefix dis

■ The prefix *dis* means *apart,* or *not.* The word *dissatisfied* would therefore mean _____ satisfied.

not

■ The prefix *dis* means apart or _____.

not

■ The prefix *dis* can mean *apart,* as in this sentence: In biology I had to _____*member* a frog.

*dis*member

■ The prefix *dis* can also mean *not,* as in this sentence: I was _____*satisfied* with the results of the election.

*dis*satisfied

■ The prefix *dis* means _____ or _____.

apart
not

■ The verb *dislike* consists of the prefix _____ and the verb *like.*

dis

■ If you dislike a person, you do _____ like him.

not

■ Because my uncle has been so hateful and cruel, I _____*like* him intensely.

*dis*like

■ What I _____*like* the most is the fact that I am a part of this infamous plot.

*dis*like

■ If you do not like a person you _____ him.

dislike

■ In the word *dislike* the prefix *dis* means _____.

not

■ Now look at the word *disease.* This word consists of the word *ease,* meaning comfort, freedom from pain, and the prefix _____.

dis

■ The noun *ease* means comfort or freedom from pain. By adding the prefix *dis* you change the meaning of the word. In other words, you do _____ have comfort or freedom from pain.

not

disease

■ A *disease* is an ailment or a condition which impairs one's health, as in this sentence: The board of health is afraid that the _____ will become an epidemic.

dis/ease

■ The noun *disease* has two syllables: dis/ease. The first syllable is ___.

dis/*ease*

■ The second syllable is dis/___.

disease

■ Write the entire word, saying it in syllables as you write: _____.

disease

■ An ailment can be called a _____.

disease

■ A condition which impairs the health of the body is known as a _____.

discover

■ The verb to *discover* means to find out something, as in this sentence: It took me an entire week to _____ what everyone else knew.

discover

■ The prefix *dis* in the verb *discover* signifies a reversal of action. To *cover* means to hide or conceal; to _____ means to bring something out into the open.

dis/cov/er

■ The verb *discover* has three syllables: dis/cov/er. The first syllable is the prefix ___.

dis/*cov*/er

■ The second syllable is dis/___/er.

dis/cov/*er*

■ The last syllable is dis/cov/___.

discover

■ Write the entire word, saying it in syllables as you write: _____.

discover

■ When Christopher Columbus started on his famous voyage, he did not think he would _____ a new land.

discover

■ The two scientists hope to _____ art objects made by South American Indians.

■ The verb *display* means to show, to spread out, as in this sentence: The appliance store has a fine _____ of radios and television sets.

display

*dis*play

■ To show or spread out is to ____*play*.

■ The first syllable of the verb *display* is the prefix ____.

dis/play

dis/*play*

■ The second syllable is dis/____.

display

■ To show or spread out is to _____.

display

■ I intended to _____ all my pictures of Europe.

display

■ The photographs, paintings, letters from prominent people, and newspaper clippings made an interesting _____ at the fair.

disturb

■ The verb *disturb* means to agitate or throw into a state of confusion, as in this sentence: We knew that the noise of the rioters would _____ him.

disturb

■ The verb *disturb* can also mean to interrupt, as in this sentence: I did not knock on his door because I did not want to _____ him.

dis/turb

■ The first syllable of *disturb* is the prefix ____.

dis/*turb*

■ The second syllable is dis/____.

disturb

■ The constant drumming of his fingertips on the table would surely _____ the patient.

disturb

■ To agitate or throw into a state of confusion is the definition of the verb _____.

■ The arrival of the highway patrolman was enough to _____ [throw into confusion] the entire household.

disturb

■ To interrupt also means to _____.

disturb

■ He requested that no one _____ him until dinner time.

disturb

Prefix de

■ The prefix *de* means *down*. If you describe a picture, you write it _____ in words.

down

■ The verb *describe* begins with the prefix ____.

de/scribe

■ The second syllable is de/____.

de/*scribe*

■ My art teacher asked me to _____ the vase on the table.

describe

■ To tell about or write down in words is to _____.

describe

■ Our next assignment is to _____ a scene from a motion picture.

describe

■ The word that signifies the describing of an object or scene is *description*. This noun, of course, begins with the prefix ____.

de

■ The act of describing a picture is called a ____*scrip-tion*.

*de*scription

■ The noun *description* has three syllables: de/scrip/tion. The first syllable is ____.

de/scrip/tion

■ The second syllable is de/____/tion.

de/*scrip*/tion

■ The final syllable is de/scrip/____.

de/scrip/*tion*

■ Write the entire word, saying it in syllables as you write: _____.

description

■ Although it is easy for me to write a factual account of an event, it is difficult for me to write _____ [act of describing].

description

■ The verb *describe* and the noun *description* both begin with the prefix _____.

de

■ The professor gave a first-hand _____ of the riots.

description

■ The verb *despair* has as its first syllable the prefix _____.

de

■ The verb to *despair* means to be hopeless or to give up hope. Literally, you put hope *away* or *down*. To give up hope is to _____.

despair

■ The verb *despair* has two syllables: _____/spair.

de/spair

■ The second syllable is de/_____.

de/*spair*

■ The father of the little boy is filled with grief and _____ [loss of hope].

despair

■ The searchers tried to reassure me, but I knew I could feel nothing but absolute _____.

despair

■ The word *despise* also begins with the prefix _____.

de

■ To *despise* means to feel contempt for someone, as in this sentence: I have learned to _____ my brother.

despise

■ The first syllable of the verb *despise* is _____.

de/spise

■ The second syllable is de/_____.

de/*spise*

despise

■ To feel contempt for someone is to _____ him.

despise

■ Senator Fowler stated that he could easily _____ all dishonest businessmen.

despise

■ The tactics of some politicians makes one _____ them.

de

■ If you build *down*, you *destroy*. The verb *destroy* also begins with the prefix _____.

destroy

■ To *destroy* means to ruin, to put out of existence, as in this sentence: A severe earthquake will _____ well-constructed buildings.

de/stroy

■ The verb *destroy* has two syllables: _____/stroy.

de/*stroy*

■ The second syllable is de/_____.

destroy

■ The fire threatened to _____ three apartment buildings in the block.

destroy

■ The boy said that he would _____ all the baby's toys.

destroy

■ It has been impossible to find a chemical that will _____ all the weeds.

despise

■ To feel contempt for is to _____.

destroy

■ To ruin is to _____.

de

■ The verb *decide* also begins with the prefix _____.

decide

■ The verb to *decide* can be defined as to come to a decision, or literally to cut *off* all doubt and debate, as in this sentence: I must _____ which job I shall accept by Friday noon.

de/cide

■ The verb *decide* has two syllables: _____/cide.

de/*cide*

■ The second syllable is de/_____.

decide

■ The employment office asked me to _____ whether I would take the typing position.

decide

■ My mother always helps me _____ on a new coat.

off

■ The prefix *de* means down or off. The verb *decide* means to cut _____ doubt.

down

■ The prefix *de* means off or _____.

de

■ The meaning of down in the verb *destroy* is shown by _____.

down

■ If you *describe* something you write _____ or tell about it in words.

down

■ If you *despair* you put hope away or _____.

dis

■ The meaning of not in the verb *disapprove* is shown by _____.

not

■ If you *dislike* someone you do _____ like him.

dis

■ The meaning of apart in the verb *display* is shown by _____.

disturb

■ To agitate or to interrupt means to _____.

discover

■ To find out something is to _____.

disease

■ A condition which impairs the health of the body is a _____.

decide

■ To come to a decision is to _____.

despair

■ To give up hope is to _____.

describe

■ The chairman of the history department asked whether I would _____ [put into words] my trip to South America.

despise

■ After working with my cousin for over a year and watching him cheat many of his customers, I have learned to _____ [feel contempt for] him.

destroy

■ A tornado can _____ [ruin] many homes and buildings in a few minutes.

description

■ Reverend Jones gave a very vivid _____ [act of describing] of his journey to Africa.

Prefix pre

■ The next prefixes we shall study are *pre, per,* and *pro.* It is easy to confuse these prefixes and write *pre* for *per* unless you know what they mean. For example, the prefix *pre* means *before:* If you precede a person in line,

before

you stand in front of or _____ him.

before

■ The prefix *pre* means _____.

before

■ The verb *precede* means to go before in rank or dignity, to be or go in front of or before. The first syllable of *precede* means _____.

before

■ The verb *precede* means to go _____.

precede

■ Because Mrs. Lowe has been elected president of the club, she will _____ Mrs. Dunn in the receiving line.

precede

■ To go before or in front of is the definition of the verb _____.

pre

■ Like the verb *precede,* the verb *prefer* has the prefix
_____ as its first syllable.

prefer

■ The verb *prefer* means to set above or before in favor,
as in this sentence: I _____ the color red.

pre/fer

■ The first syllable of *prefer* is _____/fer.

pre/*fer*

■ The second syllable is pre/_____.

prefer

■ If you like one coat better than another, you
_____ that coat to the other.

prefer

■ To place a person or object in higher favor, liking,
or estimation is to _____ that person or object.

prefer

■ In writing correspondence, my employer seems to
_____ the block-style method of address.

prescribe

■ To *prescribe* can be defined as to dictate, or to lay
down directions. For example, a doctor will _____
a medicine before the patient takes it.

before

■ The verb *prescribe* contains the prefix which means
_____.

pre/scribe

■ The first syllable of *prescribe* is the prefix _____.

pre/*scribe*

■ The second syllable is pre/_____.

prescribe

■ To lay down or give directions is to _____.

prescribe

■ When my father had a severe reaction to the new
drug, the physician said that he would _____ another medicine.

prescribe

■ The only remedy I can _____ for Joe is a complete change from the printing business.

precede

■ To go before is to _____.

Prefix per

■ The prefix *per* means through or by; the prefix *pre* means _____.

before

■ The prefix *per* means *through,* as in the verb *perspire,* which can be defined as excreting a fluid _____ the pores of the skin.

through

■ To *perspire* means to sweat. The verb sweat has the same meaning as the verb _____.

perspire

■ The first syllable of the verb *perspire* is the prefix _____.

per/spire

■ The second syllable is per/_____.

per/*spire*

■ To sweat means to _____.

perspire

■ When a person does physical labor, he will _____ quite freely.

perspire

■ The first syllable of the verb *perspire* is the prefix *per* which means _____.

through

■ To sweat or excrete a fluid through the pores of the skin is to _____.

perspire

■ A few games of tennis on a warm day will make me _____ a great deal.

perspire

■ Another word having the prefix *per* is the **noun** *permission*. The noun *permission* can be defined as the act of permitting or consent. Remembering the meaning of *per,* you would allow or permit something to go _____.

through

■ The noun *permission* is divided into syllables like this: per/mis/sion. The first syllable is _____.

per/mis/sion

■ The second syllable is per/_____/sion.

per/*mis*/sion

per/mis/*sion*	■ The last syllable is per/mis/_____.
permission	■ The instructor gave his students _____ to use the dictionary during the final examination.
permission	■ To visit a patient who is critically ill, a person must have _____ from the doctor or nurse.
per	■ Like the verb *perspire,* the verb *perform* contains the prefix _____.
per	■ If you perform an act or deed, you carry it *through* to completion. The word *through* is shown by the prefix _____.
per/form	■ The verb *perform* has two syllables: per/form. The first syllable is _____.
per/*form*	■ The second syllable is per/_____.
perform	■ Because of his broken arm, the scoutmaster will not be able to _____ all his regular duties.
perform	■ If you do or carry an act or deed through to its completion, you will _____ that act or deed.
perform	■ From all the advance publicity notices, we can expect the aerialists to _____ their act in a very exciting and daring manner.
per	■ The verb *persuade* also begins with the prefix _____.
persuade	■ To *persuade* can be defined as to induce one to believe or do something, as in this sentence: We shall try to _____ William Beck to cast his vote with the liberals.
*per*suade	■ If you advise a person all the way *through* so that he will believe or do something, you will _____*suade* him.

per/suade	■ The first syllable of *persuade* is the prefix _____.
per/*suade*	■ The second syllable is per/_____.
persuade	■ To induce a person to do something is to _____ him.
persuade	■ It took Bob several hours to _____ his brother to accompany him on the trip.
persuade	■ The harder I tried to _____ him to change his mind, the more obstinate he became.
per	■ Like the verb *persuade,* the verb *pertain* contains the prefix _____.
pertain	■ To *pertain* means to belong to, as in this sentence: The instructor performs duties that _____ to the teaching profession.
pertain	■ To *pertain* also means to have reference to, as in this sentence: The document does not _____ to politics.
per/tain	■ The verb *pertain* has two syllables: per/tain. The first syllable is _____.
per/*tain*	■ The second syllable is per/_____.
pertain	■ After reading the outline for the term paper, the teacher said that he did not believe the material would _____ to the principal causes of the war.
pertain	■ Learning to use the dictionary does _____ to the subjects of reading and spelling.
pertain	■ The manager cautioned the employees that grievances must _____ to the fringe benefits.
pertain	■ To have reference to is the meaning of the verb _____.

before

■ The prefix *pre* means _____.

through

■ The prefix *per* means _____.

perspire

■ To sweat is to _____.

permission

■ The noun *consent* means the same as the noun _____.

perform

■ To carry an act or deed through to its completion is to _____ it.

persuade

■ To induce someone to do or believe something is to _____ him.

prefer

■ Of the two kinds of pie, I _____ the chocolate cream.

prescribe

■ The nurse asked the doctor to _____ a sleeping pill for the patient.

precede

■ Because the presidency is a higher office, it will ___cede the office of the vice-presidency.

per

■ The meaning of through is shown in the verb *perforate* by ___.

pre

■ The meaning of before in the verb *prevent* is shown by ___.

Prefix pro

forward

■ The prefix *pro* means forward. Look at the verb *propose,* which means to offer for consideration, or literally to place _____.

propose

■ The verb *propose* means to offer for consideration, as in this sentence: The secretary offered to _____ a new pension plan for the employees.

pro/pose	■ The verb *propose* has two syllables: ____/pose.
pro/*pose*	■ The second syllable is pro/____.
propose	■ Inasmuch as the present procedure works very well, I do not intend to _____ a new system.
forward	■ The first syllable of *propose* means _____.
produce	■ The verb *produce* means to bring out or forward, as in this sentence: The prosecutor promised to _____ a new witness at the trial.
pro/duce	■ The verb *produce* has two syllables: pro/duce. The first syllable is ____.
pro/*duce*	■ The second syllable is pro/____.
produce	■ Farmers work hard to _____ good crops.
produce	■ To bring out or forward is to _____.
produce	■ The community theaters of the country _____ [bring out] many new stars.
promote	■ The verb *promote* can be defined as advance, or literally to move forward. For example, take this sentence: It will take three years for the company to _____ my father to the position of district manager.
pro/mote	■ The first syllable of *promote* is the prefix ____.
pro/*mote*	■ The second syllable is pro/____.
promote	■ Even though I missed a month of school, the teachers decided they would _____ me to the next grade.
promote	■ Mr. Huntington agreed to _____ Mary to the position of assistant librarian.

■ The noun which means the act of promoting is *pro-motion,* as shown in this sentence: All the pupils merited _____ to the seventh grade.

promotion

■ The noun *promotion* has three syllables: pro/mo/tion. The first syllable is _____.

pro/mo/tion

■ The second syllable is pro/_____/tion.

pro/*mo*/tion

■ The third syllable is pro/mo/_____.

pro/mo/*tion*

■ The act of promoting is called _____.

promotion

■ An advance to a higher rank or position is known as a _____.

promotion

■ John Hamilton quit school because he was not on the _____ list.

promotion

■ The verb *proceed* means to move or go forward, as in this sentence: He told me to _____ with the test.

proceed

■ The first syllable of the verb *proceed* is the prefix _____.

pro/ceed

■ The second syllable is pro/_____.

pro/*ceed*

■ After a ten-minute rest, we were told to _____ with the discussion.

proceed

■ Although the scientist was uncertain of the outcome, he told his assistants to _____ with the experiment.

proceed

■ Before I had finished my rebuttal of the first point, I was ordered to _____ to the next point.

proceed

■ The noun that can be defined as the manner or method of proceeding is *procedure,* as in this sentence: Our firm is trying out a new _____ to handle the out-of-town accounts.

procedure

■ Whereas the verb proc*ee*d has a double *e* in the second syllable, the noun procedure has only _____.

one

■ The noun *procedure* has three syllables: pro/ce/dure. The first syllable is _____.

pro/ce/dure

■ The second syllable is pro/____/dure.

pro/*ce*/dure

■ The last syllable is pro/ce/____.

pro/ce/*dure*

■ The manner or method of proceeding is _____.

procedure

■ The high schools need a different _____ to speed up registration of new students.

procedure

■ An initiation ceremony of a sorority or fraternity usually follows an established _____.

procedure

■ The act of promoting is _____.

promotion

■ To go or move forward is to _____.

proceed

■ The manner or method of proceeding is called _____.

procedure

■ The meaning of forward in the verb *propose* is shown by _____.

pro

Review

■ The prefix *pre* means _____.

before

■ Homer and Sue are standing in line in front of Jack. Homer and Sue therefore _____ Jack in line.

precede

■ The prefix *de* means [not, down].

down

■ If you tell about or write down in words an experience you have had, you _____ it.

describe

through

■ The prefix *per* means _____.

perspire

■ In hot weather a person will _____ freely.

not

■ The prefix *dis* means [not, down].

dislike

■ If you do not like a person you _____ him.

forward

■ The prefix *pro* means _____.

produce

■ The farmer predicted that this would not be a good year to _____ [bring out] crops.

disease

■ A condition that may impair the health of the body is a _____.

description

■ Even though I can write expository material, I cannot write a good piece of _____ [act of describing].

discover

■ The neighbors were amazed to _____ [find out] that we did not own a television set.

despair

■ When the searchers failed to find the missing boy, the father began to _____ [give up hope].

prefer

■ Although I like the color red, I _____ [like better] blue.

dis

■ The prefix that means apart or not is _____.

perform

■ To do or carry an act or deed through to its completion is to _____ it.

destroy

■ To ruin a structure is to _____ it.

pre

■ The prefix that means before is _____.

proceed

■ The proctor told us to _____ [go forward] to the next page of the test.

despise

■ To feel contempt for someone is to _____ him.

pro

■ The prefix that means forward is _____.

decide

■ To remove all doubt and wavering about a problem is to _____ [come to a decision] about it.

persuade

■ To induce an individual to do or believe something is to _____ him.

de

■ The prefix that means down or off is _____.

procedure

■ The manner or method of proceeding is called a _____.

per

■ The prefix that means through is _____.

prefix

■ An element that is added to the beginning of a root word is called a _____.

syllable or element
beginning
meaning

■ A prefix is a _____ that is combined with the _____ of a root word to modify its _____.

chapter 12

Hyphen

You may wonder what the hyphen has to do with correct spelling. The hyphen is used to form many compound words, primarily compound nouns and adjectives, and it is important to know when to connect the parts of a compound noun or adjective with a hyphen.

There are three ways of writing a compound word: in *solid* form, in *separate* word form, and in *hyphenated* form. The chapter on the hyphen does not, in fact cannot, tell you when to write a compound word in solid or separate word form, as there are no generalizations to fit each case. For the most part, usage determines how quickly a new compound word or expression changes from the separate word or hyphenated form into the solid form. Suffice it to say that you must consult the dictionary when in doubt.

Some compound words are always written in solid form. A few of these are illustrated below:

airman	salesman
background	semicolon
inasmuch	shorthand
nevertheless	together

Some compound words are always written in separate word form:

all right	en route
each other	no one

Many compound words and expressions are hyphenated:

aide-de-camp	man-of-war
brother-in-law	mother-in-law
father-in-law	sister-in-law
jack-o'-lantern	son-in-law

Many more compound words and expressions are hyphenated, and by studying this chapter on the hyphen, you will have a better idea when to place hyphens between two or more distinct words to form a compound word.

Test for Chapter 12

Combine the words in the right-hand column into compound words, using the *hyphenated, separate,* or *solid* word form.

1. It is _____ to go today.   all right

2. The old-time medicine peddler specialized in selling a _____.   cure all

3. Jim and his father will attend the _____ banquet next Tuesday.   father son

4. The professor will leave Monday for a _____ vacation.   much needed

5. The elderly actor was recognized by his colleagues in the theater as a _____.   has been

6. The raft was sighted floating in the _____.   mid Atlantic

7. I do not wish to become a _____ in my mother's drapery business.   co owner

8. The child was instructed to go _____ to play.   down stairs

9. Too much _____ is not good for any person.   self pity

10. The winner of the beauty contest was a _____ blonde.   brown eyed

11. The prosecutor stated that he wanted to _____ the evidence.   re examine

12. Joe Brown found two _____ pieces in his back yard.   fifty cent

13. He had the appearance of an _____ man.   able bodied

14. An American who is a citizen of the United States but of English origin or descent can be called an _____.   Anglo American

15. The sculptor decided that it would be necessary to _____ the mold.   re form

16. Because of the fallen roof, the firemen could not _____ the blazing building.   re enter

17. The Asian flu epidemic has claimed its _____ victim.   twenty ninth

18. My cousin Sam Boss is an _____ in the Air Force.   air man

19. When the employee reported for work, he
filled out a questionnaire on his experience
and educational _____.   back ground

20. The author was a _____ writer and was
very proud of this fact.   self taught

---

compound

■ When two or more distinct words are joined together to form another word or expression, this new word is called a *compound* word. The word *baseball* consists of two words *base* and *ball* and is called a [single, compound] word.

compound

■ When two or more distinct words are joined together to form another word, like *lighthouse,* this new word is called a [single, compound] word.

compound

■ The words *lighthouse* and *baseball* are called [single, compound] words.

text
book

■ The word *textbook* consists of two distinct words: _____ and _____.

compound

■ Therefore, the word *textbook* can be called a _____ word.

solid

■ Compound words are sometimes written in *solid* form. Look at the word *baseball.* Although the word consists of two words, *base* and *ball,* these two parts are written together, in solid form. The word *lighthouse* is also written in _____ form.

are not

■ When a compound word, like *lighthouse,* is written in solid form, the parts of the word, *light* and *house,* [are, are not] separated in any way.

solid

■ The distinct words *text* and *book* which make up the compound word *textbook* are written in _____ form.

solid

■ The compound words *baseball, lighthouse,* and *textbook* are all written in _____ form.

■ Compound words are also written in *hyphenated* form. This means that the distinct words are connected by one or more hyphens to form another word or expression. Look at the word *runner-up*. The two parts, *runner* and *up*, form a compound word and are connected by a _____.

hyphen

■ Look at the word *jack-in-the-box*. Here you have four words joined together to form a different word. These four words are connected by _____.

hyphens

■ A *hyphen* is a punctuation mark (-) sometimes used to connect parts of a [single, compound] word or expression.

compound

■ The punctuation mark used to connect parts of a compound word or expression is called a _____.

hyphen

■ If a compound word is not written in solid form but is connected in some way, then you would probably use one or more _____ to connect the parts.

hyphens

■ If the parts of a compound word are written together, the word is written in _____ form.

solid

■ If the parts of a compound word are connected by one or more hyphens, the word is written in _____ *ated* form.

*hyphen*ated

■ The punctuation mark (-) which is used to connect parts of a compound word or expression is called the _____.

hyphen

■ Words can be combined to form a new noun. Look at the words *runner* and *up*. If you combine them and form a new word, *runner-up*, you make a [single, compound] word.

compound

■ In a contest the competitor who finishes next to the winner is usually called a _____ [runner + up].

runner-up

■ The meeting of the two brothers at the family picnic was the cause of the _____ [flare + up].

flare-up

■ To form a compound noun from the words *mother, in,* and *law,* place _____ between the words.

hyphens

■ My husband's mother is my _____ [mother + in + law].

mother-in-law

■ With all the experiments in space being conducted today, we constantly hear the word _____ [count + down].

count-down

■ One who passes by is called a _____ [passer + by].

passer-by

■ The compound words *runner-up, flare-up,* and *mother-in-law* are all connected with one or more _____.

hyphens

■ My aunt said that Uncle Charlie had always been a _____ [do + nothing].

do-nothing

■ Many of the old-time medicine peddlers sold their products as a _____ [cure + all].

cure-all

■ The two words *text* and *book* are written in solid form. Write this compound word: _____.

textbook

■ Now let us look at some instances where hyphens are used to form compound words used as adjectives. If you combine a noun like *fire* and a participle like *fighting* to modify a noun like *equipment* you would use a _____ to connect *fire* and *fighting*.

hyphen

■ Look at the phrase *fire-fighting equipment.* When you use the compound adjective *fire-fighting* to describe the noun *equipment,* you *modify* or *limit* the noun to a certain type of equipment. The compound word used to modify equipment is _____.

fire-fighting

one

■ Notice that in the phrase, *fire-fighting equipment,* the hyphenated words *fire-fighting* form _____ word.

hyphen

■ When you combine the words *fire* and *fighting* to form a compound adjective to describe a noun, you would connect them with a _____.

do

■ If you combine the words *blue* and *eyed* to describe the noun *girl,* you [do, do not] use the hyphen to combine *blue* and *eyed*.

is

■ In the sentence, The judges chose the green-eyed blonde as winner of the contest, the hyphen [is, is not] correctly used.

adjective

■ In the sentence, The politician promoted a city-wide campaign, the compound word *city-wide* is a compound [noun, adjective].

washing

■ In this sentence, The newlyweds were known by their tattletale-gray washing, the hyphen is correctly placed because the words *tattletale* and *gray* are combined to modify the noun _____.

lighthouse

■ Combine the two words *light* and *house* into a compound word: _____.

do

■ If you combine the words *gold* and *colored* to describe the noun *drapes,* you [do, do not] use the hyphen to form the compound adjective.

one

■ Look at the phrase *gold-colored drapes*. The two words *gold* and *colored* are combined into _____ word.

gold-colored

■ Look again at the phrase *gold-colored drapes*. There are not two adjectives describing the drapes: gold drapes and colored drapes. There is just one adjective: _____.

■ Short adverbs like *best, far, ill, long, much,* and *well* can be combined with other parts of speech to form compound adjectives. When a short adverb and another part of speech are combined to form a compound adjective, they are connected by a _____.

hyphen

■ In the sentence, The teachers selected the best-liked student to reign as King of Elmwood, the compound adjective consists of the words _____ and _____.

best
liked

■ In the phrase, a *far-fetched story,* the words *far* and *fetched* are used as an adjective to modify the noun _____.

story

■ In the sentence, The Queen of England rules over a far-flung empire, the hyphen [is, is not] correctly placed.

is

■ Read the following sentence: The ill-fated disaster was never forgotten by the residents of Shropshire. The hyphen [is, is not] correctly placed.

is

■ Look at the following phrases containing compound adjectives: *far-flung empire, ill-fated disaster, best-liked student.* Although there are two words preceding each noun, there is only _____ adjective describing each noun.

one

■ If you speak of a long-needed rest, you would place a hyphen between *long* and *needed* because these two words form a compound [noun, adjective].

adjective

■ Combine the adverb *long* and the participle *playing* into a compound adjective to modify the noun *records.*

long-playing

■ *Much* is an adverb which can be combined with another part of speech to be used as a compound adjective, as in this phrase, a _____ [much + needed] rest.

much-needed

■ When you combine the adverb *well* and the participle *meaning* in the phrase, a well-meaning person, you [would, would not] place a hyphen between *well* and *meaning.*

would

well-groomed

■ Combine the adverb *well* and the word *groomed* to modify the noun *man,* as in the following phrase: a _____ man.

banquet

■ Two nouns can be combined to form a compound adjective. In the phrase, a father-son banquet, the words *father* and *son* are hyphenated because they are used as one word to describe the noun _____.

father-son

■ Because his father was out of town, Jim asked his uncle to attend the _____ [father + son] dinner.

mother-daughter

■ The new department store specializes in _____ [mother + daughter] outfits.

hyphen

■ The punctuation mark which is used to connect parts of a compound word or expression is called a _____.

blue-eyed girl

■ Combine the noun *blue* and the participle *eyed* to modify the noun *girl* and write the entire phrase: _____.

city-wide campaign

■ Combine the noun *city* and the adjective *wide* to modify the noun *campaign* and write the entire phrase: _____.

far-reaching

■ Combine the adverb *far* and the participle *reaching* in the phrase, a _____ effect.

ill-tempered

■ The new president was an _____ [ill + tempered] man.

long-suffering

■ The grocer's wife was certainly a _____ [long + suffering] woman.

much-needed

■ The doctor was ordered to take a _____ [much + needed] rest.

well-founded

■ The attorney took the case because he felt that it was a _____ [well + founded] charge.

brother-sister

■ Jim and Jane presented a _____ [brother + sister] act.

■ Usually the hyphenated compound adjective comes before the noun it modifies, as in *a far-fetched story*. In the sentence, "The story is far fetched," the two words are not used as a compound word but as two words (far = adverb, fetched = adjective), and they follow the verb. In this case these two words [would, would not] be hyphenated.

would not

■ The empire of the Queen of England is _____ [far flung, far-flung].

far flung

■ The new president is very _____ [ill tempered, ill-tempered].

ill tempered

■ Verbs can also be used with other parts of speech to form a compound word or expression. For example, the verbs *hit* and *run* can be used to form a compound expression, as in the phrase, a _____-and-_____ driver.

hit
run

■ The verbs *hit* and *run* can be combined with *and* to form a compound expression *hit-and-run*. To connect these three words into a compound expression to modify a noun you would use two _____.

hyphens

■ The police searched the city for the _____ [hit + and + run] driver.

hit-and-run

■ The verb forms *would* and *be* can be combined into a compound word. Write the correct combination in the phrase, a _____ actor.

would-be

■ Mrs. Dixon had no time for the _____ [would + be] politician.

would-be

■ The statesman adopted a _____ [wait + and + see] policy.

wait-and-see

has-been

■ In the theater the elderly actor was known as a _____ [has + been].

bull's-eye

■ Although I tried three times I could not hit the _____ [bull's + eye].

merry-go-round

■ The children asked to ride on the _____ [merry + go + round].

full-fledged

■ Dennis has completed his training at the university and is now a _____ [full + fledged] accountant.

able-bodied

■ We could not understand why Jack Ames could not get a job because he was an _____ [able + bodied] man.

airman

■ John Dix is now serving in the Air Force and is called an _____ [airman, air man].

door-to-door

■ When I worked for the Miller Sales Company I had to make many _____ [door + to + door] calls.

able bodied

■ My uncle is strong and _____ [able-bodied, able bodied].

together

■ We shall go to the party _____ [together, to-gether].

would-be

■ I have no time for that _____ [would be, would-be] musician.

long needed

■ The author has _____ [long-needed, long needed] a vacation in the country.

well known

■ F. Scott Fitzgerald is _____ [well known, well-known] for his short stories and novels.

do

■ Remember when two different aspects are united into *one* person or thing, you must hyphenate the compound word. Secretary-treasurer is one word, with *one* function, so you [do, do not] connect the two distinct words *secretary* and *treasurer* with a hyphen.

secretary-treasurer	■ Jane's brother was promoted to the position of _____ [secretary + treasurer].
city-state	■ The electioneers wanted to make it a _____ [combine *city* and *state* in one function] affair.
secretary-treasurer	■ I was appointed _____ [secretary + treasurer] of the firm.
hyphen	■ Numerals and fractions are connected by hyphens. Compound numerals from twenty-one through ninety-nine are connected by a _____.
sixty-three	■ Combine *sixty* and *three* to form the compound numeral.
twenty-two	■ My brother is _____ [twenty + two] years old today.
ninety-three	■ The numerals *ninety* and *three* can be combined into the compound numeral _____.
thirty-fourth	■ Numerals and fractions used as compound adjectives are hyphenated, as in this sentence: Joey was the _____ [thirty + fourth] person to enter the fair grounds.
seventy-fifth	■ Congress passed its _____ [seventy + fifth] bill this week.
thirty-three	■ The meeting was attended by _____ [thirty + three] club members.
do	■ A numeral like *seven* and a noun like *point* can be combined to form an adjective. In the phrase, a seven-point plan, you [do, do not] use the hyphen to connect *seven* and *point*.
fifty-cent	■ The manager was selling _____ [fifty + cent] tickets.

■ The movie theater was crowded with many _____ [eleven + year] olds.

eleven-year

■ The recipe called for one and _____ [one + half] cups of butter.

one-half

■ The airplane crashed into the side of the mountain, killing _____ [forty + four] people.

forty-four

■ When two adjectives expressing nationality are combined into a compound adjective, use the hyphen to form the compound adjective. For instance, look at the compound adjective *Franco-Russian*. It consists of two adjectives of nationality, *Franco* and _____.

Russian

■ Use a hyphen to connect two adjectives expressing nationality into a _____ adjective.

compound

■ I have just finished studying about the _____ [Franco + Russian] War.

Franco-Russian

■ There seems to be a change in the _____ [Chino + Japanese] relations.

Chino-Japanese

■ The professor is an authority on the _____ [Anglo + Saxon] language.

Anglo-Saxon

■ When the *first* part of a compound is *self*, the compound word is hyphenated. For instance, the compound noun *self-sacrifice* is hyphenated because the first part consists of the word _____.

self

■ The clergyman stressed the quality of _____ [self + sacrifice].

self-sacrifice

■ My father was overcome with _____ [self + pity].

self-pity

■ Many a businessman will brag about his being a _____ [self + made] man.

self-made

■ The inventor thought the engine should have a
_____ [self + starter].

self-starter

■ Uncle Ben will be _____ [seventy + seven]
years old on September first.

seventy-seven

■ Mr. Jones interviewed _____ [thirty + five]
men for the job.

thirty-five

■ The topic for my term paper was based on interna-
tional relations, with particular emphasis on _____
[Franco + American] relations.

Franco-American

■ When I asked him his nationality, he replied "I am
_____ [Scotch + Irish]."

Scotch-Irish

■ Tonight I am filled with _____ [self + pity].

self-pity

■ Aunt Mary has had a long life of _____ [self +
sacrifice].

self-sacrifice

■ He always bragged that he was a _____ [self +
made] man.

self-made

■ What this machine needs is a _____ [self +
starter].

self-starter

■ When a prefix is added to a word beginning with a
capital letter to form a compound word, you use a hyphen
to combine the two words. For example, *mid-Atlantic*
is hyphenated because *Atlantic* begins with a capital __.

A

■ If the second part of a compound word begins with a
capital letter, use a _____ to combine the compound word.

hyphen

■ The compound word *mid-Atlantic* is hyphenated because the second part begins with a [capital, small] *a*.

capital

■ The compound word *pro-British* is hyphenated because the word *British* begins with a [capital, small] *b*.

capital

anti-Russian

■ Combine the prefix *anti* and the noun *Russian* into a compound word: _____.

■ When a prefix ends in the *same* vowel that begins the next word of the compound word, use a hyphen to combine the two words. For instance, the prefix *co* ends with the vowel *o*, just as the word *owner* _____ with the vowel *o*.

begins

■ In the compound word *co-owner*, the same vowel ends the prefix *co* and begins the next word _____.

owner

■ My mother and I are _____ [co + owners] of the business.

co-owners

■ She refused to be a _____ [co + owner].

co-owner

■ The prefix *pre* ends with the vowel *e*. The word *election* begins with the same vowel __.

e

■ In writing the compound word *pre-election*, you connect the two distinct words with a hyphen because *pre* ends and *election* _____ with the vowel *e*.

begins

■ The campaign speeches were filled with _____ [pre + election] promises.

pre-election

■ When the prefix *re*, which means *again*, is added to a verb beginning with the vowel *e*, a hyphen is usually used to separate the prefix and the verb. If you add *re* to *enter*, you would write the word _____.

re-enter

■ I did not want to _____ [re + enter] the building.

re-enter

■ If you add the prefix *re* to the verb *emerge*, you [would, would not] use the hyphen to combine the prefix and verb.

would

■ As I looked up at the sky, the sun began to _____ [re + emerge] from behind the clouds.

re-emerge

■ The attorney started to _____ [re + examine] the witness.

re-examine

■ The prefix *re* and the verb *emerge* are connected by a hyphen because the prefix ends with the vowel *e* and the verb begins with the vowel __.

e

Review

■ Various parts of speech can be combined to form a noun, and usually such compound nouns are hyphenated. The words *runner* and *up* are combined to form the noun _____.

runner-up

■ When the boys finished the shack, it was no more than a _____ [lean + to].

lean-to

■ I asked my _____ [brother + in + law] to come over.

brother-in-law

■ Joe regrets his emotional outburst; _____ [never the less, nevertheless] he is not sorry for what he said.

nevertheless

■ It was five o'clock when the _____ [count + down] started.

count-down

■ Uncle Ben is a _____ [good + for + nothing].

good-for-nothing

■ Various parts of speech can be combined to form compound adjectives to modify nouns. Such a compound adjective is usually connected by a _____.

hyphen

■ Grandfather stated emphatically that he would never go to a _____ [drive + in] theater.

drive-in

■ Read the following sentence: The drama critics agreed that it was a first-rate performance. The two words *first* and *rate* are hyphenated because they are combined to form _____ word which is called a _____ adjective.

one
compound

The two words are not used as a compound word to modify a noun. Also, they do follow the verb.

■ In this sentence, The performance was *first rate,* the italicized words are not hyphenated. State the generalization.

mid-Pacific

■ The raft floated for three hours in the _____ [mid + Pacific].

three-acre

■ James Shannon has just bought a _____ [three + acre] lot.

low priced

■ His new car is _____ [low-priced, low priced].

mild-tempered

■ The principal was known as a _____ [mild + tempered] man.

thirty-ninth

■ On the second day after the train crash, the _____ [thirty + ninth] victim died.

seven-day

■ The physician put Jim on a _____ [seven + day] reducing diet.

salesman

■ Jim's father is a _____ [sales man, salesman].

two-story

■ We are looking for a _____ [two + story] house to buy.

Compound words are hyphenated if the first part is *self.*

■ Read this sentence: Bill gave the appearance of a *self-possessed* person. State the generalization used in hyphenating this compound adjective.

anti-British

■ The new prime minister is extremely _____ [anti + British].

Two words expressing one function are hyphenated into one word.

■ Read this sentence: Everyone in the company acted in at least one play, even the *actor-manager.* State the generalization used to hyphenate the italicized word.

en route

■ Josie is _____ [en-route, en route) to California.

self-preservation

■ This is indeed an age for _____ [self + preservation].

pro-American

■ It is quite evident that the new king is _____ [pro + American].

self-confidence

■ To be successful one should possess _____ [self + confidence].

ready-made

■ Although the shop employs a custom tailor, it specializes in _____ [ready + made] garments.

well fed

■ The puppy was certainly _____ [well fed, well-fed].

Answers to Tests

Chapter 1: Syllables

A.
1. plătter
2. nīght
3. kĭtchen
4. mŏp
5. cūte
6. rōde
7. rŭsty
8. cĕntury
9. Lătin
10. cŭt

B.
1. re/ward
2. sil/ly
3. car/pen/ter
4. dil/i/gent
5. for/got/ten
6. ap/pear/ance
7. tri/ple
8. nec/es/sar/y
9. per/form/ance
10. ge/ol/o/gy
11. man/u/fac/ture
12. dic/tion/ar/y
13. ac/com/mo/date
14. sep/a/rate
15. in/flu/ence
16. syl/la/ble
17. par/a/ble
18. a/chieve/ment
19. un/doubt/ed/ly
20. trib/u/la/tion

Chapter 2: Doubling the Final Consonant

1. skimming
2. controlled
3. rebellion
4. swimming
5. omitted
6. transferring
7. preference
8. chagrined
9. galloping
10. designer
11. trapper
12. rebelling
13. equipped
14. planner
15. hopping
16. occurred
17. excelled
18. allotting
19. hoping
20. concealed
21. gossipy
22. pinning
23. recurrence
24. benefiting
25. conference

Chapter 3: Final e

A.
1. desiring
2. coming
3. singeing
4. pursuing
5. writing
6. dining
7. surprising
8. hoeing
9. receiving
10. losing
11. dyeing
12. using
13. arguing
14. achieving
15. praising
16. advising
17. purchasing
18. loving
19. judging
20. canoeing

B. 1. lovable
2. receivable
3. advisable
4. pleasurable

5. imaginable
6. serviceable
7. manageable
8. achievable

9. amusable
10. noticeable

C. 1. wholly
2. useless
3. fierceness
4. truly
5. argument

6. commencement
7. useful
8. graceful
9. remoteness
10. advertisement

11. duly
12. ageless
13. management
14. judgment
15. achievement

Chapter 4: Final y

1. chimneys
2. annoying
3. surveys
4. denying
5. pitiful
6. busily
7. destroyed

8. tragedies
9. accompanied
10. cemeteries
11. cozily
12. merciful
13. studying
14. societies

15. portrayal
16. annoyance
17. beautiful
18. copied
19. enemies
20. trolleys

Chapter 5: Plurals

1. addenda
2. princesses
3. penalties
4. tariffs
5. displays
6. vetoes
7. sopranos
8. prefixes
9. attorneys
10. witnesses

11. handkerchiefs
12. mosquitoes
13. allies
14. Negroes
15. data
16. wives
17. alleys
18. contraltos
19. pulleys
20. ambushes

21. knives
22. speeches
23. tragedies
24. cemeteries
25. armies
26. taxes
27. potatoes
28. plaintiffs
29. diaries
30. brushes

31. griefs
32. photos
33. suffixes
34. heroes
35. crises
36. churches
37. analyses
38. academies
39. parentheses
40. thieves

Chapter 6: ie-ei

1. ie
2. ie
3. ei
4. ei
5. ie
6. ei
7. ei

8. ei
9. ei
10. ei
11. ei
12. ie
13. ie
14. ie

15. ei
16. ie
17. ei
18. ei
19. ei
20. ei
21. ei

22. ie
23. ei
24. ei
25. ie ei

Chapter 7: Homonyms and Confused Words

1. there	15. capitol	29. ally
2. coarse	16. isle	30. except
3. stationery	17. already	31. affect
4. to	18. counsel	32. advice
5. two	19. their	33. personnel
6. You're	20. It's	34. weather
7. all ready	21. moral	35. lose
8. compliment	22. Breathe	36. breath
9. council	23. advise	37. excess
10. Whose	24. accept	38. quiet
11. its	25. latter	39. personal
12. aisle	26. quite	40. effect
13. principle	27. Whether	
14. dessert	28. loose	

Chapter 8: Demons

1. arate	16. i	31. ur	46. er
2. a	17. i	32. ur	47. ruary
3. perature	18. ilege	33. ap	48. let
4. lain	19. itate	34. preci	49. i
5. a	20. rifice	35. ar	50. tr
6. ilar	21. inite	36. rr	51. u
7. dar	22. iar	37. ning	52. w
8. e	23. iar	38. mence	53. b
9. emy	24. apology	39. rass	54. t
10. e	25. orate	40. sen ess	55. se
11. e	26. ur	41. medi	56. ense
12. etable	27. cumu	42. ll	57. b
13. manent	28. pear	43. po	58. se
14. cere	29. ur	44. ss	59. ense
15. i i	30. commo	45. mend	60. uard

Chapter 9: Suffixes

A.

1. ance	6. ance	11. ence	16. ence
2. ance	7. ence	12. ence	17. ence
3. ance	8. ance	13. ence	18. ance
4. ence	9. ance	14. ance	19. ance
5. ence	10. ence	15. ance	20. ence

B. 1. able   6. able   11. able   16. ible

B. 1. able	6. able	11. able	16. ible
2. ible	7. ible	12. ible	17. ible
3. able	8. able	13. ible	18. able
4. ible	9. ible	14. able	19. ible
5. able	10. ible	15. ible	20. ible

C. 1. ary	5. ery	8. ary
2. ary	6. ary	9. ary
3. ery	7. ery	10. ery
4. ary		

D. 1. perilous	8. advantageous	15. desirous
2. hazardous	9. marvelous	16. outrageous
3. dangerous	10. mountainous	17. troublous
4. porous	11. poisonous	18. riotous
5. murderous	12. grievous	19. famous
6. adventurous	13. courageous	20. mischievous
7. slanderous	14. humorous	

E. 1. certainly	8. basically	15. accidentally
2. physically	9. wholly	16. publicly
3. duly	10. monthly	17. drastically
4. happily	11. foolishly	18. frequently
5. formally	12. usually	19. neatly
6. mentally	13. truly	20. scarcely
7. verbally	14. critically	

F. 1. efy	5. ify	8. ify
2. ify	6. efy	9. ify
3. ify	7. ify	10. efy
4. efy		

G. 1. ise	6. ise	11. ize	16. ize
2. ise	7. ize	12. ise	17. ise
3. yze	8. yze	13. ise	18. ize
4. ize	9. ise	14. ize	19. ise
5. ise	10. ize	15. ise	20. ize

Chapter 10: ceed, cede, sede

1. sede	5. cede	8. cede
2. ceed	6. ceed	9. cede
3. ceed	7. cede	10. cede
4. cede		

Chapter 11: Prefixes

1. de	6. pre	11. dis	16. per
2. pre	7. pre	12. de	17. per
3. pre	8. per	13. de	18. pro
4. de	9. pro	14. dis	19. pro
5. dis	10. pro	15. dis	20. per

Chapter 12: Hyphen

1. all right	8. downstairs	15. re-form
2. cure-all	9. self-pity	16. re-enter
3. father-son	10. brown-eyed	17. twenty-ninth
4. much-needed	11. re-examine	18. airman
5. has-been	12. fifty-cent	19. background
6. mid-Atlantic	13. able-bodied	20. self-taught
7. co-owner	14. Anglo-American	

Index

a, difficulty in demons, 171–178
  long sound of, 10–11
    written as *ei,* 122–124
  short sound of, 13–14
  vowel, 10
able, words ending in, 259–264
Abundance, 248–249
Accede, 323
Accent, definition of, 23
  primary, 23
  review, 27–28
  secondary, 24
  shift in, 59–60
  symbols for, 23–25
Accept-except, 158
Access-excess, 159
Accidentally, 295
Accommodate, 199–200
Accompany, 200–201
Accumulate, 201
Acquaintance, 246–247
Across, 216
Admirable, 261–262
Advantageous, 288
Adventurous, 286–287
Advertise, 309
Advice-advise, 154–155
Advisable, 260–261
Affect-effect, 159–160
Aisle-isle, 136
All ready-already, 136–137
Alley-ally, 156–157
Although, 225–226
Analyze, 306–307
ance, words ending in, 242–250
Anniversary, 277–278
Annually, 294–295
Answer, 219–220
Antecede, 325
Apology, 195
Appear, 201–202
Appearance, 245

Appoint, 202–203
Appreciate, 203–204
Approve, 203
Around, 216–217
Arrange, 204–205
Arrive, 205
ary, words ending in, 275–279
Assistance, 242–243
Athlete, 232
Athletics, 232–233
Attendance, 245–246
Audience, 253–254
Automatically, 296

Basically, 296
Beginning, 206
Benefit, 180
Boundary, 276–277
Breath-breathe, 157–158
Brilliance, 247–248
Business, 187–188

c, hard sound of, 75, 270
  soft sound of, 75–76, 270, 272, 288
Calendar, 177
Canvas-canvass, 137
Capable, 172–173
Capital-capitol, 137–139
cede, ceed, sede endings, 319–326
  generalization, for *cede,* 322–326
    for *ceed,* 320–321
    for *sede,* 320
  review, 326
  test, 319
  (*See also* individual word entries)
Cemetery, 279–280
Certainly, 292
Chocolate, 193–194
cient, words ending in, 124–125
Coarse-course, 139

Commence, 206–207
Commendable, 263
Committee, 207
Competence, 255–256
Complement-compliment, 139–140
Compound words, definition of, 351
  hyphenated form, 349, 352
  re in, 362–363
  separate form, 349
  solid form, 349, 351
  use of hyphen in, 352–363
  (*See also* Hyphen)
Comprehensible, 268–269
Concede, 323–324
Confident, 187
Confused words, 154–167
  review, 165–167
  (*See also* individual word entries)
Conscience, 257
Consequence, 257–258
Considerable, 263–264
Consonants, double, in demons, 199–215
  final, doubling before suffix, 44–56
    not doubling before suffix, 56–60
  number of, 10
  single, in demons, 216–219
  in syllabication, 19–23, 28–33
  (*See also* Syllables)
Consul, 142
Convenience, 254
Correspondence, 255
Council-counsel, 140–142
Courageous, 288–289
Course-coarse, 139
Creamery, 280–281
Criticize, 316–317
Customary, 278

de, meaning of, 333
  words beginning with, 333–337
Debt, 221
Decide, 335–336
Defense, 228
Definite, 190
Demise, 310
Demons, 169–237
  a difficulty, 171–178
  double consonants, 199–215
  e difficulty, 179–185
  ense difficulty, 227–230
  i difficulty, 185–193
  mispronunciation, 230–237
  o-u difficulty, 193–199
  silent letters, 219–227

Demons, single consonants, 216–219
  test, 169–171
  (*See also* individual word entries)
Describe, 333
Description, 333–334
Desert-dessert, 142–143
Desirous, 287
Despair, 334
Despise, 334–335
Destructible, 268
Device-devise, 155–156
Dictionary, 275
dis, meaning of, 330
  words beginning with, 330–333
Disastrous, 235–236
Disease, 330–331
Disguise, 313
Divide, 185–186
Double consonants (*see* Demons)
Doubling final consonant (*see* Final consonant)
Doubt, 220–221
Drastically, 297

e, difficulty in demons, 179–185
  final, before suffix, 63–80
    (*See also* Final *e*)
  long sound of, 10–11
    written as *ie,* 120–122
  short sound of, 15
  vowel, 10
Effect-affect, 159–160
ei-ie (*see* ie-ei)
Elaborate, 194
Eligible, 272
Embarrass, 207–208
Emphasize, 314–315
ence, words ending in, 59–60, 242–243, 250–259
Enemy, 179–180
Enjoy, 179
ense in demons, 227–230
Enterprise, 312
ery, words ending in, 279–284
Essential, 208
Evident, 186–187
Exceed, 320–321
Except-accept, 158
Excess-access, 159
Exercise, 310
Existence, 251
Expense, 228–229
Experience, 253

Falsify, 304–305
Familiar, 190–191
February, 230–231
Final consonant, doubling before suffix, 43–62
  review, 60–62
  test, 43
  words, of one syllable, 44–48
    of two or more syllables, 48–60
      ending, in single vowel and consonant with accented last syllable, 48–56
        in single vowel and consonant without accented last syllable or in more than one vowel and consonant, 56–59
      exception, 56
      shift in accent, 59–60
Final *e,* 63–80
  definition of, 64
  generalizations, 64–78
    dropping before suffix, 64–72, 76–78
      in *argument* and *judgment,* 77–78
    basic generalization, 64–72
      in *truly, duly, wholly,* 76–77
    keeping before suffix, 72–76
      in *dye* and *singe,* 73–74
      in words, ending in *oe,* 72–73
      with soft *c* or *g,* 74–76
  review, 78–80
  test, 63–64
Final *y,* 81–93
  generalizations, 82–90
    preceded by consonant, 86–88
      with suffix *ing,* 87
    preceded by vowel, 82–86
      with suffix *ly,* 89–90
    third person singular verb form, 89
  review, 91–93
  test, 81–82
  (*See also* Plurals)
Forcible, 272–273
Franchise, 314
fy, function of, 301
  words, ending in *efy,* 301–303
    ending in *ify,* 303–306

g, hard sound of, 74–75, 270, 288
  soft sound of, 74–75, 270–271, 288
Gallery, 281–282
Government, 231–232
Grammar, 175–176
Gratitude, 234

Grievous, 290
Guardian, 222
Guidance, 249

h, semivowel, 10
Hard sound, of *c,* 74–75, 270
  of *g,* 74–75, 270, 288
Heard-herd, 135
Hesitate, 188–189
Homonyms, 133–154
  definition of, 135
  review, 151–154
  test, 133–134
  (*See also* individual word entries)
Horrible, 264–265
Hyphen, 349–365
  definition of compound words, 351
  forms of compound words, 351–352
  review, 363–365
  test, 350–351
  use of hyphen in compound words, 352–363
    in adjectives, 353–360
      of nationality, 359
    in nouns and expressions, 352–353
    in numerals and fractions, 359–360
    with one capitalized word, 361–362
    with *re,* 362–363
    same vowel in parts of compound, 362–363
    with *self,* 360–361
    with words of one function, 358–359
  (*See also* Compound words)

i, difficulty in demons, 185–193
  long sound of, 11–12
  short sound of, 13–14
  vowel, 10
ible, words ending in, 259, 264–274
ie-ei, 119–132
  exceptions, 127–129
  generalizations, 120–125
    sound, of long *a,* 122–124
      of long *e,* 120–122
      of *sh*(*cient*), 124–125
  review (chapter), 130–132
  review (partial), 125–126
  test, 119–120
Ignorance, 249–250
Imagine, 217
Immediately, 208–209
Importance, 244

Independence, 254
ing, with words ending in *y,* 87
Insistence, 252
Intelligence, 258
Intercede, 325
Interest, 234–235
ise, words ending in, 308–314
Isle-aisle, 136
It's-its, 150–151
ize, words ending in, 314–318

Kindergarten, 233–234
Knowledge, 223–225

Later-latter, 160–161
Legible, 271
Library, 278–279
License, 229–230
Liquefy, 303
Long sound of vowels, 10–13
Loose-lose, 161–162
ly, function of, 291–292
    with words, ending in *al,* 293–295
        ending in *ic,* 295–297
            exception to, 297
        ending in *y,* 89–90, 299–300

Maintenance, 244–245
Mentally, 293–294
Merchandise, 312–313
Millinery, 282–283
Mischievous, 290–291
Mispronunciation in demons, 230–237
Moral-morale, 162–163
Mortgage, 221–222

Necessary, 209–210
Nouns, plural of, 95–118
    (*See also* Plurals)

o, difficulty in demons, 193–195
    long sound of, 11–13
    short sound of, 15–16
    vowel, 10
    words ending in, 103–107
    (*See also* Plurals)
Occasion, 210
oe, words ending in, 72–73
    (*See also* Final *e*)

Operate, 217–218
Opposite, 211
Ought, 226
ous, words ending in, 284–291

Parallel, 211–212
Paralyze, 307–308
Peculiar, 191–192
per, meaning of, 339
    words beginning with, 339–342
Perfectible, 267–268
Perform, 340
Permanent, 183
Personal-personnel, 163–164
Perspire, 339
Persuade, 340–341
Pertain, 341
Physically, 293–294
Pleasant, 174
Plurals, definition of, 96
    general formation of, 96–97
    of Latin nouns, 112–116
    of nouns ending in *ch, sh, s, x, z,* 97–100
        ending in *f, fe, ff,* 109–112
        ending in *o,* 103–107
            musical in nature, 106–107
            preceded, by consonant, 104–106
                by vowel, 103
        ending in *y,* 82–85, 87, 100–103
    review (chapter), 116–118
    review (partial), 107–109
    test, 95
Possess, 212–213
pre, meaning of, 337
    words beginning with, 337–338
Precede, 322–323, 337
Prefer, 338
Preference, 59–60, 252–253
Prefixes, 327–347
    de, meaning of, 333
        words beginning with, 333–337
    definition of, 329
    dis, meaning of, 329
        words beginning with, 329–333
    per, meaning of, 339
        words beginning with, 339–342
    pre, meaning of, 337
        words beginning with, 337–338
    pro, meaning of, 342
        words beginning with, 342–345
    reference guide, 327–328
    review, 345–347

Prefixes, test, 328–329
  (*See also* individual word entries)
Prescribe, 338
Primary accent, definition of, 23
  symbol for, 23–25
Principal-principle, 143–144
Privilege, 188
pro, meaning of, 342
  words beginning with, 342–345
Procedure, 344–345
Proceed, 320–321, 344
Professor, 218–219
Propose, 342–343
Psychology, 224–225
Publicly, 297
Purchase, 196
Purpose, 196–197
Pursue, 195–196
Putrefy, 301–302

Quiet-quite, 164

r, semivowel, 10
Rarefy, 301
re in compound words, 362–363
Realize, 315
Recede, 322–323
Recognize, 315–316
Recommend, 213–214
Rectify, 304
Reducible, 270–271
Reliable, 262
Remembrance, 248
Repetition, 181
Resistance, 243–244
Responsible, 266–267
Revise, 310–311

Sacrifice, 189–190
Secede, 323
Secondary accent, definition of, 23–24
  symbol for, 24–25
Secretary, 182–183
sede ending (*see cede, ceed, sede* endings)
Semivowels, definition of, 10
Sense, 227–228
Sensible, 266
Separate, 171–172
Separate form of compound words, 349
sh sound (*see ie-ei,* generalizations)
Short sound of vowels, 13–17

Significance, 250
Silent *e,* 64
Silent letters in demons, 219–227
Similar, 176–177
Sincerely, 183–184
Single consonant in demons, 216–219
Singular, definition of, 96
Soft sound, of *c,* 75–76, 270–272, 288
  of *g,* 74–75, 270–271, 288
Solid form of compound words, 349, 351
Stationary-stationery, 144–145
Stress (*see* Accent)
Stupefy, 302
Subsistence, 251–252
Succeed, 320–321
Suffixes, *able-ible,* 259–274
  ance-ence, 242–259
  ary-ery, 275–284
  definition of, 241–242
  fy, 301–306
  ise-ize-yze, 306–318
  ly, 89–90, 291–301
  ous, 284–291
  test, 239–241
  (*See also* individual word entries)
Supersede, 320
Supervise, 311
Surmise, 313–314
Surprise, 197–198
Syllables, 9–42
  definition of, 18–19
  generalizations, 19–23, 28–34
    one consonant between two vowels,
      28–33
    with long accented first vowel, 28–30
    with short accented first vowel, 30–
      33
    two consonants between two vowels,
      19–23
    words ending in *le,* 33–34
  review and practice, 34–42
  test, 9
Symbols, for accent, 23–25
  for vowels, 25–26

Temperature, 173–174
Terrible, 265
Testify, 303–304
Their-there-they're, 145–147
Third person singular verb form of words
  ending in *y,* 89
Through, 226–227
To-too-two, 147–149

u, difficulty in demons, 195–198
  long sound of, 11–13
  short sound of, 16
  vowel, 10
Usually, 294

Vacuum, 236
Vegetable, 181–182
Verb form, third person singular of words
    ending in *y*, 89
Villain, 174–175
Vocabulary, 275–276
Vowels, long sound of, 10–13, 17–18, 26–27
  number of, 10
  short sound of, 13–18, 26–27

Vowels, in syllabication, 18–23, 28–33
    (*See also* Syllables)
  symbols for, 25–26

w, semivowel, 10
Weather-whether, 165
Who's-whose, 149–150

y, final (*see* Final *y*)
  plural of nouns ending in, 100–103
  semivowel, 10, 20–21
You're-your, 151
yze, words ending in, 306–308